PARTICIPATORY RESEARCH
WITH
CHILDREN AND YOUNG PEOPLE

SAGE has been part of the global academic community since 1965, supporting high quality research and learning that transforms society and our understanding of individuals, groups, and cultures. SAGE is the independent, innovative, natural home for authors, editors and societies who share our commitment and passion for the social sciences.

Find out more at: **www.sagepublications.com**

Connect, Debate, Engage on Methodspace

- **Connect with other researchers and discuss your research interests**
- **Keep up with announcements in the field, for example calls for papers and jobs**
- **Discover and review resources**
- **Engage with featured content such as key articles, podcasts and videos**
- **Find out about relevant conferences and events**

Methodspace
Connecting the Research Community

www.methodspace.com

brought to you by

$SAGE

PARTICIPATORY RESEARCH WITH CHILDREN AND YOUNG PEOPLE

SUSAN GROUNDWATER-SMITH
SUE DOCKETT
DOROTHY BOTTRELL

$SAGE

⊛SAGE

Los Angeles | London | New Delhi
Singapore | Washington DC

SAGE Publications Ltd
1 Oliver's Yard
55 City Road
London EC1Y 1SP

SAGE Publications Inc.
2455 Teller Road
Thousand Oaks, California 91320

SAGE Publications India Pvt Ltd
B 1/I 1 Mohan Cooperative Industrial Area
Mathura Road
New Delhi 110 044

SAGE Publications Asia-Pacific Pte Ltd
3 Church Street
#10-04 Samsung Hub
Singapore 049483

Editor: Katie Metzler
Production editor: Victoria Nicholas
Copyeditor: Andy Baxter
Proofreader: Derek Markham
Indexer: David Rudeforth
Marketing manager: Dilhara Attygalle
Cover design: Shaun Mercier
Typeset by: C&M Digitals (P) Ltd, Chennai, India
Printed in Great Britain by CPI Group (UK) Ltd,
Croydon, CR0 4YY

© Susan Groundwater-Smith, Sue Dockett and Dorothy Bottrell 2015

Apart from any fair dealing for the purposes of research or private study, or criticism or review, as permitted under the Copyright, Designs and Patents Act, 1988, this publication may be reproduced, stored or transmitted in any form, or by any means, only with the prior permission in writing of the publishers, or in the case of reprographic reproduction, in accordance with the terms of licences issued by the Copyright Licensing Agency. Enquiries concerning reproduction outside those terms should be sent to the publishers.

Library of Congress Control Number: 2014940554

British Library Cataloguing in Publication data

A catalogue record for this book is available from the British Library

ISBN 978-1-4462-7286-2
ISBN 978-1-4462-7287-9 (pbk)

At SAGE we take sustainability seriously. Most of our products are printed in the UK using FSC papers and boards. When we print overseas we ensure sustainable papers are used as measured by the Egmont grading system. We undertake an annual audit to monitor our sustainability.

CONTENTS

List of Figures vi
About the Authors vii
Acknowledgements viii

1 Introduction: Arguing the case for participatory research with children and young people 1

2 Developing new methodological understandings of social research with children and young people 19

3 Ethical questions in relation to participatory research with children and young people 37

4 Designing a project with children and young people: investigating the 'researchable question' 55

5 A political ecology of access and cooperation 75

6 Innovative methods 101

7 Issues of impact and sustainability in the context of participatory design and construction 139

8 Publication and dissemination 159

9 Action and participation 181

Index 198

LIST OF FIGURES

2.1	More of this type of learning please	29
2.2	Not so good for me	30
2.3	Still learning	30
3.1	Indicating dissent	46
4.1	Playing the game	60
4.2	Looking at crocodiles	64
4.3	Reporting the transport survey	65
4.4	Sorting recyclables from non-recyclables	66
6.1	Drawing in the sand	105
6.2	The Reflections task	106
6.3	Photographing the local environment	108
6.4	Teacher's recording of the data contributed by school children who were planning a visit to the nearby pre-school class to share what they knew about school	108
6.5	BMX track	109
6.6	Anzac memorial	109
6.7	Jim's map	114
6.8	Constructing an 'ideal' school	116
6.9	Conversations during play	118
6.10	This child's recollections of starting school were recorded in written form	123
6.11	One child's starting school journal	125
7.1	The ladder of participation	145
9.1	Posters with key messages from children and young people	193
9.2	Council report to children and young people	194

ABOUT THE AUTHORS

Susan Groundwater-Smith is Honorary Professor, Faculty of Education and Social Work, The University of Sydney and Visiting Professor, Wilf Malcolm Institute of Educational Research, University of Waikato. She has had an extensive career in teacher education, especially in relation to teachers-as-researchers, see Groundwater-Smith, S., Mitchell, J., Mockler, N., Ponte, P. & Ronnerman, K. (2013) *Facilitating Practitioner Research*. London: Routledge. She is the convener of the Coalition of Knowledge Building Schools, a Special Interest Group in the Faculty of Education and Social work. This group has functioned for over ten years and includes schools and cultural institutions. It has a continuing commitment to consulting children and young people and, where possible, including them as active researchers. This work has drawn the attention of researchers in Australia, the Netherlands and the United Kingdom.

Sue Dockett is Professor, Early Childhood Education, Charles Sturt University, Australia. Sue's background is in early childhood and tertiary education. Over many years, Sue has engaged in research with children and young people, particularly in the years before school and the early years of school. Much of this research has focused on children's experiences and expectations, as well as those of families, educators and communities at times of transition. She is co-author of *Transition to school: Perceptions, expectations and experiences* (with Bob Perry), co-editor of *Transitions to school – International research, policy and practice* (with Bob Perry and Anne Petriwskyj) and *Varied perspectives on play and learning: Theory and research on early years education* (with Bob Perry and Ole Fredrik Lillemyr).

Dorothy Bottrell is a Senior Lecturer in Social Pedagogy, in the College of Education, Victoria University Melbourne and Honorary Senior Lecturer in the Faculty of Education and Social Work, University of Sydney. Her background is in secondary teaching, juvenile justice, youth and community work and TAFE teaching in community services. She has extensive experience working with marginalised young people and has led or contributed to participatory projects with young people and community organisations, including murals, girls' film-making, establishing a young parents' group, community-based education for early school-leavers and community development forums with children, young people, Aboriginal families and an older women's group. Her research has focused on the resilience of marginalised young people, including theoretical and qualitative empirical work that centres young people's accounts of school, community and service systems. She is currently researching the interrelationship of resilience and responsibility, using political ecology and social justice frameworks; and is associate researcher with Kitty te Riele and Vicky Plows (Victoria Institute) on alternative education programs. Dorothy is co-author of *A political ecology of youth and crime;* and co-editor of *Schools, communities and social inclusion;* and *Communities and change.*

ACKNOWLEDGEMENTS

We would like to acknowledge the many children and young people that we have encountered in our varied research and program adventures, as well as during the preparation of this book for their generous agreements to have their various photos and artefacts included as a means of illustrating the text and bringing it to life.

ONE

INTRODUCTION: ARGUING THE CASE FOR PARTICIPATORY RESEARCH WITH CHILDREN AND YOUNG PEOPLE

This book is directed to those who have an interest in researching *with* children and young people and is designed to be of practical assistance to students, practitioners and researchers in the fields of early childhood education, school education, community-based services and community development. Our aim is to bridge these fields through the discussion of theory, practice, approaches and issues in participatory research involving children and young people. Drawing on the very broad international literature, many exemplars of the varied forms of participatory work and a close discussion of case studies, we wish to highlight some of the common (and some not so common) problematics.

In developing and writing the book, we have drawn on our own experience as researchers, educators and collaborators with children and young people – and their teachers, families, youth workers, a range of other professionals and our research teams. Our early discussions about what constitutes research and participation frequently focused on the specificities of *children's* and *young people's* interests and the varied cultural contexts of working with children and young people. In part this reflects our different experiences of working with children and young people.

Susan's work with children and young people has principally been in schools, both primary and secondary, where they as students, have had opportunities to contribute to the corporate intelligence of individual schools and investigate the ways in which they operate. As well, she has facilitated audience research in cultural institutions (CIs) where young people have had a voice in the planning and evaluation of exhibitions over a number of years. This work in both schools and CIs has been shared through a constellation of practice, known as the Coalition of Knowledge Building Schools (Mockler and Groundwater-Smith (2011), and has thus contributed not only to individual institutions but also to collective professional knowledge and increased student agency. She has encouraged participation to move beyond students being seen as data sources to conditions where they have designed, enacted and interpreted inquiries and been honoured as an authentic critical voice.

Sue's research is grounded in early childhood education. It has focused on young children's perceptions, expectations and experiences, and the many and varied ways in which they may choose to share these with others. Both as an early childhood educator and as a researcher, Sue's work aims to promote views of young children as competent and capable and to consider the obligations of adults to acknowledge and respect these strengths. Projects that have sought young children's input about their experiences of community, museums and of their transition to school, have highlighted the potential for positive change that derives from actively listening to children. They have also provided a wide range of evidence to support the view that young children make important contributions to the environments in which they exist and that, in supportive circumstances, they are usually willing to do so.

Dorothy's research with young people has focused on voice and listening to young people's accounts of their experience of education, local communities and youth justice. But she also brings a practitioner perspective to engaging with the situated challenges and dilemmas we explore, based on participatory projects undertaken as teacher and youth worker. These projects did not involve formalised research yet always involved informal research as part of young people's learning, planning, organising and showing their accomplishments. The projects included public art murals, film making, music, sports events and community forums, some initiated and led by young people, others arranged in response to young people's requests, with open participation and often involving individuals and groups dipping in and out of the projects.

Our different experiences and perspectives have been a rich terrain for focusing on the problematics of research with children and young people. They have generated a dynamic of inquiry that has been full of if's and but's regarding *who* participates in research, how and why. In certain respects there are significant differences between researching with children and researching with older young people. Yet more often we found in our own work and the literature complementary perspectives on the research problematics. The most significant differences relate to the contexts of the children and young people, and we have found that there is much to be gained for our understanding of participatory processes by engaging with divergent projects, groups and purposes to think through the research issues. The synergy of theory and practice has been the pivot of our process. We understand this synergy to be located not only in the theory and practice of research but in the synergy of researcher-practitioner ways of seeing, doing and knowing, and in their intersections with children and young people's diverse ways of seeing, doing and knowing, and their right to participate in shaping our research, theory and practice.

This introductory chapter makes the case for the participation of children and young people in the context of the Convention on the Rights of the Child (1990) and the provisions made for actualising these rights. It will discuss the nature of participatory research and its evolution in several jurisdictions, and the ways in which young people and children have been traditionally positioned.

It addresses:

- The Rights of the Child.
- Actualising the rights of the child.
- Children, young people and participatory research.
- Positioning children and young people with regard to participatory research.
- Supporting participatory research with children and young people.

The Rights of the Child – a precursor to participatory research

> If I could make one change to support children and young people, it would be for kids' views to be taken seriously and treated with respect. (Calvert, 2008: 2)

> 'Kids aren't as naïve as you think. I think the reason that people don't listen to kids is that they're kids.' (Quoted from a young person at the conclusion to Cossar et al., 2011: 84)

> Children do not have an official or defined role to play in mainstream politics and policy making. It is easy, therefore, for decision makers to overlook including children in these processes. And, if children are invited to 'sit at the table' their voices are rarely truly heard. (Australian Human Rights Commissioner, 2010)

In our consideration of participatory research with 'children and young people' we need to first reflect upon the breadth of that phrase and whom it incorporates. After all, working with a three-year-old child in the context of her sharing her play experiences in pre-school is a very different experience from negotiating with a seventeen-year-old about the ways in which he has been dealt with by a juvenile justice facility. Yet, on the face of it they are both children within the ambit of the United Nations Convention on the Rights of the Child (Convention on the Rights of the Child, 1990). For this reason we shall begin this chapter by looking closely at this critical convention before moving on to better elucidate what we mean by participatory research and the ways in which it is undertaken.

Children, as human beings, are said to possess the same rights as all people. This assertion is recognised by The United Nations Convention on the Rights of the Child (1990). The Convention sets out a broad range of rights in addition to the universal human rights shared by everyone. Children are defined under Article 1 of the Convention as including 'every human being below the age of eighteen years'. The Convention is comprehensive and entitles children to a broad range of rights including, *inter alia*, the rights:

- to express views in all decisions that affect them and the opportunity to be heard in any court or administrative proceedings;
- to freedom of expression and the right to seek, receive and impart information of all kinds;
- to have their best interests treated as a primary consideration in all actions concerning them, including decisions related to their care and protection;
- to free education available on the basis of their capacity; and
- to enjoy the highest attainable standard of health and an adequate standard of living.

In particular, Article 12 states that every child has the right to say what they think in all matters affecting them, and to have their views taken seriously.

While the Convention discusses 'childhood' as embodying birth to eighteen years of age, the term is often taken to mean the young. In our discussion of participatory research with children and young people we have chosen to be inclusive of all of those years but also to attend to the needs of particular groups of children and young people, drawing attention to both early childhood and late adolescence at either end of the spectrum. At times, there is a tendency to omit these groups from discussions about the Convention, with assumptions that young children have neither the experience nor the maturity to assert rights, and that those who are 'almost adults' are treated more as adults than children. We support neither of these assumptions.

The Committee on Rights of the Child in its General Comment 7 (2005) draws particular attention to the need to discuss the broader implications of the Convention with respect to younger children, emphasising that they too are rights holders and are to be afforded opportunities to enact those rights.

Through this general comment, the Committee wishes to encourage recognition that young children are holders of all rights enshrined in the Convention and that early childhood is a critical period for the realisation of these rights. The Committee's working definition of 'early childhood' is all young children: at birth and throughout infancy; during the pre-school years; as well as during the transition to school.

The Committee encourages State parties to construct a positive agenda for rights in early childhood. A shift away from traditional beliefs that regard early childhood mainly as a period for the socialisation of the immature human being towards mature adult status is required. The Convention requires that children, including the very youngest children, be respected as persons in their own right. Young children should be recognised as active members of families, communities and societies, with their own concerns, interests and points of view. For the exercise of their rights, young children have particular requirements for physical nurturance, emotional care and sensitive guidance, as well as for time and space for social play, exploration and learning. These requirements can best be planned for within a framework of laws, policies and programmes for early childhood, including a plan for implementation and independent monitoring, for example through the appointment of a children's rights commissioner, and through assessments of the impact of laws and policies regarding children on the role of independent human rights institutions (Committee on Rights of the Child, General Comment 7, 2005).

Similarly, but in a different vein, it is important to recognise that young people on the cusp of adulthood will have specific needs in relation to their developmental status. Here we are mindful that we are not writing solely of cognitive development, as important as that may be, but also of social and cultural status. Suffice it to point out here that there are some inherent difficulties in seeing development as a series of invariant stages that can limit what is important and possible when considering the rights of the child and young person.

Thus the Convention recognises that children have existing as well as developing competencies, membership of particular groups and contexts, and agency. At the same time, it recognises that children and young people also have particular needs and vulnerabilities that require special protection beyond the rights to which adults are entitled. Further, it establishes four principles to guide the interpretation of the Convention and assist countries in implementing their obligations, these being: i) non-discrimination; ii) that the best interests of the child must be a primary consideration in all decisions concerning children; iii) the right to survival; and iv) the development of and respect for the views of the child. Thus these rights outline the minimum standards necessary to ensure the well-being of children – including the right to an adequate standard of living, the right to health care, the right to education, the right to family life, the right to protection from violence and the right to participate in one's culture.

In this way the Convention does not grade children's rights according to developmental age or stage. Nor does it define competence in line with age-related skills or development. Rather, the Convention accords the same rights to all children and young people and emphasises the obligations of adults to create contexts in which these rights can be enacted. Such a view promotes recognition that competencies are evolving, rather than fixed, and will vary according to context and experience (Mason and Urquhart, 2001). The focus on experience, rather than age, is important as it moves 'away from the narrow focus of socialisation and child development (the study of what children become) to a sociology which attempts to take children seriously as they experience their lives in the here and now as children' (Morrow and Richards, 1996: 92).

Provisions for actualising the Rights of the Child

Various countries have introduced agencies and appointments that work to meet the rights of their children and young people. The front-runner in these provisions has been Norway which appointed an Ombudsman for Children in 1981, prefiguring the United Nations Convention. The Ombudsman is independent and investigates complaints from individual children, monitors and analyses legislation and policy, and undertakes a range of public education activities. The Norwegian Ombudsman for Children is currently focusing on the incorporation of the Convention on the Rights of the Child into all areas of society, strengthening the security net for vulnerable children and increasing the quantity and quality of children's participation as active citizens. The Norwegian model is one of active engagement by young people: children write letters or email the

Ombudsman for Children for advice or to express their opinion about a certain matter, and may even call the Ombudsman's office or use the children's hotline on the Ombudsman's homepage, 'Straight Talk' (Barneombudet, 2006).

England, Ireland, Scotland and Wales have responded more recently and all have introduced 'Children's Commissioners', the most common provision made in the English-speaking world. Cossar et al. (2011: 6) write of the duties of the Children's Commissioner in England thus:

> The Children's Commissioner has a duty to promote the views and interests of all children in England, in particular those whose voices are least likely to be heard, to the people who make decisions about their lives. She also has a duty to speak on behalf of all children in the UK on non-devolved issues which include immigration, for the whole of the UK, and youth justice, for England and Wales. One of the Children's Commissioner's key functions is encouraging organisations that provide services for children always to operate from the child's perspective.
>
> Under the Children Act 2004 the Children's Commissioner is required both to publish what she finds from talking and listening to children and young people, and to draw national policymakers' and agencies' attention to the particular circumstances of a child or small group of children which should inform both policy and practice.

The UK commissions have paid serious attention to issues such as bullying, integration and respect for refugees, and informing education authorities of the perspectives of students in relation to schooling.

Australia and New Zealand have been similarly active. All Australian States and Territories have Children's Commissioners, with the exception of South Australia which has a Children's Guardian.[1] Nonetheless, it is seen as important that the Australian Federal Government should take up and harmonise these varying agencies to: ensure that children, from the very youngest to those reaching towards adulthood, can effectively speak up when their rights are violated; review existing laws, propose new policies, conduct research and inquiries; and report to Parliament on the status of children in Australia.

Recently, by establishing the office of a National Children's Commissioner, the Australian Government has taken an important step towards meeting its international obligations to protect and promote the rights of all children and young

---

[1] While a Children's Commissioner works to improve and ensure better services for all children, a Children's Guardian works solely to help improve the services for children in the care of a department, the literature regarding the Children's Guardian does not specify which department, it can be taken that it is any government department concerned with children's wellbeing.

people. Many children and young people in Australia are able to exercise their rights. However, the rights of some children are yet to be recognised and met. For example, these include children experiencing homelessness; children experiencing violence, bullying or harassment; and children who live with a disability, including those living with mental illness. There are also certain groups of children and young people who are less likely to be able to enjoy their full range of rights. These groups include Aboriginal and Torres Strait Islander children; children in out-of-home care; children in detention, including those in immigration detention; and children living in rural and remote areas of Australia.

In some situations, children and young people who are considered to be 'vulnerable' are viewed as in greater 'need' of access to, and exercise of, their rights under the convention. In other instances, the very description as 'vulnerable' seems to obviate the perceived need for access to these rights – almost as if there are many other things that are of more immediate concern for these children and young people, and access to rights is the sort of luxury that can be attended to once more pressing needs have been addressed. Both views situate children and young people's rights as something that can be separated from everyday life and interactions.

The Children's Commission in New Zealand factors in what is seen as important to young people (New Zealand Children's Commission, 2004 – 2008). The Commission:

- Helps the Children's Commissioner in his role standing up for the wellbeing of children and young people in New Zealand/Aotearoa;
- Writes articles for 'Children', the Commissioner's newsletter;
- Provides input into government policy and decisions that affect young people;
- Networks and connects with other reference groups and young people, especially in their region;
- Organises and participates in youth events;
- Develops resources;
- Meets with government officials to provide input and ideas into government work;
- Has national and local involvement with the media; and
- Meets four times a year and has regular communication with the Commissioner and his office. (New Zealand Children's Commissioner, 2004–2008)

A bill to establish a Children's Commissioner in Canada was introduced in 2009, twenty years on from the declaration regarding the rights of the child. Under the bill, a federal Children's Commissioner will promote, monitor and report on the effective implementation of Canada's obligations within the legislative authority of the Parliament of Canada, to advance the principle that children and young people are entitled to special safeguards, care and assistance, including appropriate legal protections.

The Children's Commissioner, still to be established, would also raise awareness of children's rights and children's issues, take special care of First Nation children's issues, liaise with provincial child advocates, and foster collaboration and consultation at all levels.

The UN Convention on the Rights of the Child is the most widely ratified human rights instrument in history (Payne, 2009). However, while it may be said that significant advances have been made in providing organisational means for children's views to be heard through such mechanisms as these Children's Commissioners, further sustaining and developing opportunities for young people to be fully engaged in those social agencies that govern their lives remains a challenge. As we shall later argue, the actualising of these mechanisms cannot be said to have permeated more generally into services such as early childhood education, schooling, health and juvenile justice, in ways that enable children and young people to be genuinely participative in processes of decision-making through their engagement in significant research that investigates issues of importance to them.

For us, as authors of this book, we see ourselves involved in a specific stance, in which we have taken up a position vis-à-vis the expressive, referential, interactional and social implications of children and young people and participatory research. The book brings together not only practical matters associated with developing the capacity of children and young people to be collaborative and responsible in forms of inquiry whose object is to improve their well-being, but it is also designed to raise questions regarding the structural impediments that act to prevent a full realisation of their contributions. We shall argue that these are troubled waters in which to navigate, most particularly with respect to ethical considerations, but, nonetheless, are well worth the energy and output required for a greater and more meaningful inclusion of the contribution of all children and young people, including those who are often left at the margins of various social enterprises.

Children, young people and participatory research

How sobering it is to read the earlier quotes in this introduction; for they would suggest that in spite of the notion that these Rights of the Child should be enshrined in the signatories' political processes and practices, as demonstrated above, it would seem that they are observed more in their absence than in their presence when brought close to practice.

Participatory research that engages children and young people as active, informed and informing agents with respect to different social provisions such as education, health and the law, can well be constructed as a radical means of interrupting this dominant discourse and beginning to address some of the absences in the discussion; for they are no longer silenced and rendered invisible. Participation by young people can take shape in different ways and at different levels. Howard et al. (2002) present a summary of descriptions of participation since 1969, making it clear that the process has been slow, but nonetheless incremental. Shier's (2001: 110) model is particularly useful in considering children and young people's engagement in participatory research because it embodies the nature of commitment required for a project to be successful. He argues that there are five levels of participation, namely: 1) children are listened to; 2) children are supported in expressing their views; 3) children's views are taken into account; 4) children are involved in decision-making processes; and 5) children share power and responsibility for decision-making. He goes on to argue that at each level of participation there are three stages of commitment: openings, opportunities and obligations.

Openings are where there has been a commitment or statement of intent to work in a certain way. It is only an opening, because at this stage, the opportunity to make it happen may not be available. At the second stage, an *opportunity* occurs when the needs are met that will enable the young people to operate at this level in practice. These needs may include resources such as the provision of time, skills and knowledge, maybe through training, development of new procedures or new approaches to established tasks. Finally, an *obligation* is established when it becomes the agreed policy of the organisation or setting that the young people should operate at this level. Later we shall illustrate the ways that these three stages of commitment were created in specific projects.

Useful as models such as this may be, we also need to be alert to a number of the difficulties that may be experienced as we engage with children and young people in participative research (Cammerota and Fine, 2008). Milbourne (2009: 350) asks:

> To what extent do projects simply increase opportunities for young people's inclusion within existing activities and social institutions, satisfying political needs to address youth disengagement? Even where responsive service models which value and respect young people's views are apparent, it is questionable whether this increased participation from young people can be transformative, involving longer-term cultural change and greater impact on existing institutions. Transformative outcomes would imply the potential for community-based and youth-led projects to create sites of resistance and a radical collective habitus based on wider developmental aims. By contrast, research suggests that recent projects may be confined to generating only new sites and forms for young people's accommodation of, and adaption to, normative models of social and political institutions.

The implication is that while many initiatives may have positive outcomes, there are inherent difficulties and dilemmas within contexts that simultaneously seek to liberate and constrain young people and their behaviours, and consequently send mixed messages to those who participate (Christensen and James, 2008).

Children and young people are expected to fit into institutional contexts, in an adult-driven framework. Paying particular attention to work in schools, Fielding (2001) uses a four-fold model of student participation which distinguishes between students as sources of data, students as active respondents, students as co-researchers and students as researchers. In all of these classifications the 'student as researcher' approach is conceived as the most intensive form of participation.

It is important to recognise how children's experiences of childhood vary markedly from one context to another (Collins and Foley, 2008). Variations occur both within and between geographic boundaries; they may be governed by such macro variables as social class, ethnicity, race and gender, and through further considerations of social history and the nature of the places in which children and young people live and learn. We need to consider these different experiences of childhood and how these experiences can impact upon the identity and sense of self-efficacy that are possessed by both individuals and groups. Engaging children and young people in participatory research cannot be fitted into a 'one-size-fits-all' template; there are dilemmas on all sides, not the least being the ways in which participatory research with young people has to be understood in both geographic and institutional contexts. In their study of social participation in Italy and Scotland, Rossi and Baraldi (2009) argued that being young, being a child, is culturally determined and that autonomy and agency are not individual properties, but are socially constructed. Furthermore, they perceived that much depends upon the *visibility* of children and young people if they are to influence policies and practices exercised on their behalf.

Positioning children and young people with regard to participatory research

Regard, for a moment the gerund that is employed as the subject of this subheading. It signals that the 'positioning' is more likely to be done by others rather than the children and young people themselves. This is a reflection of the nature of the power relationships between adults and children. Young people are typically positioned by adults who create the professional and political agenda. These, in turn, are mediated by where children are placed in the social order and the spaces that they occupy. Wyness (2009: 395) suggests that 'while professional adults are committed to creating and sustaining children's spaces, they are equally concerned to locate these spaces within the more conventionally defined structures of children's places'. Enabling children and young people to exercise greater agency is no mean feat and involves negotiating a number of institutional norms and conventions. It is clear that, in the main, while children may exercise a sense of agency within their families and peer groups, when interacting with influential professionals such as doctors, social workers, teachers and lawyers their power is greatly constrained and they are effectively in a minority status (Mayall, 2002). When Aubrey and Dahl (2006) interviewed vulnerable young people regarding the quality and effectiveness of services, they discovered that they were most listened to by their parents, rather than by those who had a responsibility for the design and delivery of those services. Indeed, in a thoroughgoing and complex discussion of needs assessment in children's services, Axford (2010) mapped needs and resources employing standardised instruments and structured case records with no recourse to investigating 'needs' from the young person's point of view. While the design of early childhood services remain largely adult-driven, Clark's (Clark, 2010; Clark and Moss, 2005) investigations provide strong evidence of young children's competence in the design, development and review of early childhood centres and schools. This series of studies stands in contrast to the expectations that services and programmes are designed for, and delivered to, children and young people.

A question that needs to be addressed is to what extent participatory research engaging children and young people is designed to address their interests or needs, or is designed to enable pre-determined processes to be refined. In other words, is participatory research a tokenistic inclusion, or a genuine effort to incorporate the perspectives of children and young people? Participation and consultation are often characterised as being related but they should not be seen as synonymous and whilst 'consultation may be a means of enabling children to participate … it can also be a substitute for participation in that decisions are made without the direct involvement of children' (Hill et al., 2004: 83).

Indeed, in her conceptualisation of different levels of engagement with children and young people, Lansdown (2005a: 14–16) highlights differences between consultation, participatory processes and self-initiation.

Consultation involves the recognition by adults that children and young people have perspectives and experiences that make a valuable contribution to the issues being considered and that these perspectives and experiences are different from those of adults. Consultation elicits information from children and young people that can be used by adults to influence policies and practices that directly affect children and young people. Consultation tends to be driven and controlled by adults. While the involvement of children and young people is confined largely to responding to adult agendas, consultation nevertheless does provide opportunities for the incorporation of the views of children and young people into broader agendas.

Participatory processes move beyond consultation by involving children and young people in the development, implementation, monitoring and evaluation phases of a project. Participatory processes seek to develop partnerships between children and young people and adults and provide opportunities for children and young people to shape the project, both in terms of the processes and the outcomes Lansdown (2005a: 15) suggests that consultation can become participatory when children and young people:

- identify the relevant questions to be asked;
- have input into the methods used in the consultation;
- take on the role of researchers; and
- engage in discussions about the results, their interpretation and implications.

Self-initiated processes 'are those where children themselves are empowered to take action, and are not merely responding to an adult-defined agenda' (Lansdown, 2005a: 15). Through self-initiated processes, children and young people identify and define the areas and methods of investigation. Children and young people themselves adopt the roles of researchers, facilitated by adults.

While each level of engagement has the potential to provide opportunities for children and young people to have input into decisions that affect them (Article 12 of the UN Convention), the balance of participation seems to be weighted in favour of consultation, rather than participation or self-initiation. As a consequence, there are few genuine:

> opportunities for children to become actively involved in the process of influencing decisions, policies and services that impact on their lives. It remains at the level of being 'systems maintaining' rather than 'systems transforming'. And it is the latter that provides a transfer of significant decision-making to children with real opportunities for personal and social development. Furthermore, too little emphasis has been placed on creating opportunities for very young children to demonstrate their capacities. (Lansdown, 2005b: 69–70)

Consider the many services in which children and young people are the 'consequential stakeholders'.[2] They are typically positioned as being children and young people 'doing what adults tell them to do and absorbing what adults have to offer'

---

[2]Groundwater-Smith and Mockler have used this term in a number of publications. For example, Groundwater-Smith and Mockler (2009), where it is understood that young people bear the consequences of decisions that are made on their behalf and deserve recognition as stakeholders in policy setting and decision-making.

(Cook-Sather, 2010: 555). Of all the provisions made for children and young people the one that is most pervasive is that of schooling. Schooling is compulsory and children have little say in where they will go to school and what they will do once they get there. The majority are thoroughly socialised into compliance and acceptance of what the institution has to offer them. When schools choose to depart from this fundamentally instrumental model, students themselves may struggle with becoming more active in taking a measure of responsibility, particularly when it comes to inquiring into their conditions of learning.

Of course engaging in participatory research is not confined to schools. Hart (1997), in discussing community development and environmental care, points out that a further obscuring factor comes into play when, with the best of intentions, what is ultimately offered is a form of tokenism:

> Tokenism is a particularly difficult issue to deal with because it is often carried out by adults who are strongly concerned with giving children a voice but have not begun to think carefully and self-critically about doing so. The result is that they design projects in which children seem to have a voice but in fact have little or no choice about the subject or the style of communicating it, or no time to formulate their own opportunities. (Hart, 1997: 41)

Among the many purposes of this book we shall discuss the range of contexts and practices that involve young people beyond the tokenism that Hart so rightly rejects. While we recognise the problems and dilemmas associated with this discussion of how young people are positioned, we endeavour to outline conditions that will enhance their agency and capability, and examine valid research strategies that will enable those conditions to be met.

Supporting participatory research with children and young people

This introductory chapter has served to provide a rationale for developing participatory research with children and young people. In the chapters that follow we attend to a range of practical issues that need to be addressed by those who wish to support authentic participatory inquiry. We discuss:

> *Chapter 2* – Developing new methodological understandings of social research with children and young people, that regard them as capable and effective reporters of their own experiences and active agents in developing and constructing positive conditions for their lives as a valid social enterprise, and may require some re-framing of current practices that too often see them as the objects of research (Clark, 2005; Danby and Farrell, 2004; Scott, 2008). The chapter addresses: methodological challenges; children and young people as

active agents; considering change and improvement; and re-framing the agenda towards a transformational form of investigation.

Chapter 3 – Ethical questions in relation to participative research with children and young people (Christensen and Prout, 2002), which outline the starting point for research as the ethical relationship between researcher and participants, whether they be children or adults. While recognising the role of institutional protocols for the conduct of research, Christensen and Prout outline the need for researchers to use individual judgement in their everyday ethical practice. The chapter then turns to: institutional protocols for the conduct of research (facilitation and barriers); employing everyday judgement in everyday practice; dilemmas and challenges; assent and dissent; risk and benefit; and trust, respect and reciprocity.

Chapter 4 – Designing a project with young people: investigating the 'researchable question'. This chapter explores the potential for children and young people to be involved across the research process – starting with project design and the identification of researchable questions. We acknowledge issues of power and control, and share examples of research that recognises these. The chapter concludes with a discussion of participation and examples of the multiple ways in which children and young people may participate across the research process. The chapter includes: identifying research questions; what makes a question researchable? issues of power; voice; researching *with* children and young people; differences in participation; and involving children and young people across the research process.

Chapter 5 – A political ecology of access and cooperation. This chapter examines the challenges of access and cooperation within specific contexts. It includes: the nature of context; issues of access and cooperation in context; working with the issues; negotiating access – the importance of time and relationships; creating accessible spaces; making participation accessible; and different ways to participate.

Chapter 6 – Innovative methods. The chapter explores a range of participatory research methods, provides some examples of their use and explores the potential advantages and disadvantages of each. It includes: child-friendly methods; observation; visual/arts-based methods; verbal methods; written methods; multiple methods; a discussion of which methods best suit the purpose of the inquiry; and the relationship between many methods.

Chapter 7 – Issues of impact and sustainability in the context of participatory design and construction. Matters associated with sustainability (see Sinclair, 2004) are discussed. Here the focus will be upon the frailty of some innovation and change that leads to its lack of substance, and the potential for cynicism and lack of authenticity. The chapter covers: broad issues related to impact and sustainability drawing upon a number of environmental projects; moving from consultation to actualization; and the limitations and benefits of engaging with children and young people in developing sustainable projects.

Chapter 8 – Publication and dissemination. The chapter examines who participates in these processes, and a range of forms and means of disseminating the findings, insights and products of participatory research. It includes: who may speak and to whom; performance/theatre and 'speak-outs'; arts exhibitions; online and hard copy reports, including brochures, magazines, comics and posters; and consequences of dissemination and publication, both positive and negative.

Chapter 9 – Action and participation. This final chapter deals with the complications and challenges that arise from taking inquiry forward into action, which matters can be and are acted upon, how and why.

Thus, our objective in writing this book is to explore participatory research opportunities that aim to optimise the engagement of children and young people in an inquiry process. We are mindful of the roles and relationships between children and young people and those adults who wish to facilitate their participation in research. We see that these opportunities will lead to enhancing children's and young peoples' life chances as engaged, active citizens who have an expertise regarding their own lives and the ways in which they are lived. In this way we shall be honouring children and young people, ensuring that the meaning that they make of their lives is recognised and understood.

Key points

- Children and young people are entitled to be *listened to* and *heard* within the context of the United Nations Convention on the Rights of the Child.
- A number of countries have introduced agencies and appointments that work to meet these rights.
- Participatory research provides a means for actualising these rights in constructive and enlightened ways and at different levels of engagement.
- Transcending the conventional positioning of children and young people as lesser, even incapable participants, requires planning, persistence and fortitude.
- Children and young people are involved in a range of human services and their voices deserve to be heard in varying and different contexts.

References

Aubrey, C. and Dahl, S. (2006) Children's voices: The views of vulnerable children on their service providers and the relevance of services they receive. *British Journal of Social Work*, 36: 21–39.

Australian Human Rights Commissioner (2010) Discussion paper. No longer available on the AHRC website.

Axford, N. (2010) Conducting needs assessment in children's services. *British Journal of Social Work*, 40: 4–25.

Barneombudet (2006) Ombudsman for children. www.barneombudet.no/english/communicat/, accessed 1st June, 2011.

Calvert, G. (2008) UNICEF J-RAP. Junior Roundtable on Asia Pacific, NSW Parliament House 9th September, Speaking points (Internal document, NSW Commission for Children and Young People).

Cammerota, J. and Fine, M. (2008) *Revolutionizing education: Youth participatory action research in motion*. New York: Routledge.

Christensen, P. and James, A. (Eds) (2008) *Research with children: Perspectives and practices*. 2nd edition. London: Routledge.

Christensen, P. and Prout, A. (2002) Working with ethical symmetry in social research with children. *Childhood*, 9(4): 477–97.

Clark, A. (2005) Listening to and involving young children: A review of research and practice. *Early Child Development and Care*, 175(6): 489–505.

Clark, A. (2010) *Transforming children's spaces: Children's and adults' participation in designing learning environments*. London: Routledge.

Clark, A. and Moss, P. (2005) *Spaces to play: More listening to young children using the Mosaic approach*. London: National Children's Bureau.

Collins, J. and Foley, P. (Eds) (2008) *Promoting children's wellbeing: Policy and practice working together for children*. Bristol: Policy Press in Association with the Open University.

Committee on Rights of the Child, General Comment 7 (2005) www.2.ohchr.org/english/bodies/crc/docs/AdvanceVersions/GeneralComment7Rev1.pdf (Geneva), accessed 31st March, 2012.

Convention on the Rights of the Child (1990), opened for signature on 20th November, 1989, 1577 UNTS 3 (entered into force 2nd September, 1990) ('Convention'), art 1.

Cook-Sather, A. (2010) Students as learners and teachers: Taking responsibility, transforming education and redefining accountability. *Curriculum Inquiry*, 40(4): 555–75.

Cossar, J., Brandon, M. and Jordan, P. (2011) 'Don't make assumptions'. Norwich: University of East Anglia, Centre for Research on the Child and the Family, for The Office of the Children's Commissioner.

Danby, S. and Farrell, A. (2004) Accounting for young children's competence in educational research: New perspectives on research ethics. *Australian Educational Researcher*, 31(3): 35–49.

Fielding, M. (2001) Students as radical agents of change. *Journal of Educational Change*, 2(2): 123–41.

Groundwater-Smith, S. and Mockler, N. (2009) *Teacher professional learning in an age of compliance*. Rotterdam: Springer.

Hart, R.A. (1997) *Children's participation: The theory and practice of involving young citizens in community development and environmental care.* London: Earthscan Publications.

Hill, M., Davis, J., Prout, A. and Tisdall, K. (2004) Moving the participation agenda forward. *Children & Society,* 18(2): 77–96.

Howard, S., Newman, L., Harris, V. and Harcourt, J. (2002) Talking about youth participation – Where, when and why? Paper presented at the AARE conference, Queensland, Australia.

Lansdown, G. (2005a) Can you hear me? The right of young children to participate in decisions affecting them. Working paper 36. The Hague: Bernard van Leer Foundation. www.bernardvanleer.org/Can_you_hear_me_The_right_of_young_children_to_participate_in_decisions_affecting_them, accessed 7th March, 2010.

Lansdown, G. (2005b) *The evolving capacities of the child.* Florence, Italy: UNICEF Innocenti Research Centre. www.bernardvanleer.org/files/crc/4%20Gerison_Lansdown.pdf, accessed 10th March, 2010.

Mason, J. and Urquhart, R. (2001) Developing a model for participation by children in research on decision making. *Children Australia,* 26(4): 16–21.

Mayall, B. (2002) *Towards a sociology of childhood: Thinking from children's lives.* Buckingham: Open University Press.

Milbourne, L. (2009) Valuing difference or securing compliance? Working to involve young people in community settings. *Children & Society,* 23(5): 347–63.

Mockler, N. and Groundwater-Smith, S. (2011) Weaving a web of professional practice. In T. Wrigley, P. Thomson and R. Lingard (Eds) *Changing schools: Alternative ways to make a world of difference.* London: Routledge, pp. 152–65.

Morrow, V. and Richards, M. (1996) The ethics of social research with children: An overview. *Children & Society,* 10(2): 90–105.

New Zealand Children's Commissioner (2004–2008) www.occ.org.nz/yprg, accessed 1st June, 2011.

Payne, L. (2009) Twenty years on: The implementation of the UN Convention on the Rights of the Child in the United Kingdom. *Children and Society,* 23(2): 149–55.

Rossi, E. and Baraldi, C. (2009) The promotion of children and adolescents' social participation in Italy and Scotland. *Children and Society,* 23(1): 16–28.

Scott, J. (2008) Children as respondents. In P. Christensen and A. James (Eds) *Research with children: Perspectives and practices.* 2nd edition. London: Routledge, pp. 87–108.

Shier, H. (2001) Pathways to participation: Openings, opportunities and obligations. *Children & Society,* 15(2): 107–17.

Sinclair, R. (2004) Participation in practice: Making it meaningful, effective and sustainable. *Children & Society,* 18(2): 106–18.

Wyness, M. (2009) Adult's involvement in children's participation: Juggling children's places and spaces. *Children & Society,* 23(6): 395–406.

TWO

DEVELOPING NEW METHODOLOGICAL UNDERSTANDINGS OF SOCIAL RESEARCH WITH CHILDREN AND YOUNG PEOPLE

This chapter focuses on the rights of children and young people with regard to perceiving them as capable, effective reporters and investigators of their own experiences. We shall argue that, as active agents in developing, constructing and contributing to positive conditions for their young lives, this may require some re-framing of current inquiry practices that too often see them as the objects of research.

It addresses:

- Methodological challenges.
- Children and young people as active agents.
- Developing, constructing and contributing to change and improvement with a focus on current inquiry processes that limit children and young people.
- Reframing the agenda towards a transformational form of investigation.

The methodological challenge

In considering participative research with young people and the forms it might take, we need first to address some of the current debates regarding research methodology in the social sphere. It is important here to make a distinction between 'method' and 'methodology'; a matter that is further discussed in Chapter 6. On the one hand, as Bryman (2005: 27) has so succinctly observed, 'a research method is simply a technique for collecting data'. Of course we could argue that it is much more, in that there is also an interest in the selection of the original case; the analysis of the data; and its interpretation. On the other hand, methodology transcends method in that it encompasses both a family of methods and the thinking, the overarching paradigm that lies behind their selection. This enables them to present as a coherent, interrelated set of procedures. These, in turn, form a discourse about the social practice under consideration. Clearly then, in relation to participative research with children and young people, it is important to first draw on a wider perspective, clarifying the fundamentals of social research.

In a way that illuminates and elucidates the nature of inquiry Waring (2012: 16) has outlined the building blocks of social research, namely: ontology, epistemology, methodology. He poses a series of questions:

- What is the form and nature of the social world?
- How can what is assumed to exist be known?
- What procedures or logic should be followed? and
- What techniques of data collection should be used?

Each question prefigures that which follows. There are, understandably, no ready or simple answers to these powerful concerns. But what is manifest is that when considering participative research with young people a number of ontological positions will be incommensurable with the issues being addressed. So that in effect it can be argued that within the range of paradigmatic approaches to social inquiry some will be more appropriate and accommodating than others. Specifically, this applies to notions of participation and inclusion on the part of those who would have hitherto been regarded as the objects of research rather than active agents with a voice and an investment in its purposes. Positivism, with its mission to discover laws of human behaviour, will embrace a very different apparatus than will interpretative approaches based upon a view of research as a socially critical endeavour. For such an attempt is both constructivist and transformative and allows multi-dimensional narratives to emerge. Thus the methods that are selected within a methodology designed to address participative research with children and young people must be compatible with the intentions of that methodology. In short, methods that are selected need to match the intentions of the fundamental purpose of the research itself.

Participative research, in and of itself, makes a number of demanding claims. It is research within which there is a social contract, that honours and values the multiple voices and perspectives of those who take part. Hitherto, research involving children and young people has often privileged the adult's view of the world, building upon a perception that the adult, being older and more experienced, must necessarily know more of the world of children than they may know themselves.

Nonetheless, we are mindful of the hazards of participative research more generally. Cooke and Kothari (2001) in *Participation: The new tyranny* and Hickey and Mohan (2004) in *Participation: From tyranny to transformation*, remind us of the ways in which social relations, in our case the relations between adults and children, can themselves covertly manipulate and mask the apparently democratic outcomes of participation. After all, participative agency is located within those structures which may govern *who* can act and *how*. For many children and young people, structures, while appearing to act towards their benefit may be more inclined to maintain and strengthen the status quo. As Christens and Speer (2006) have observed:

> The *Tyranny* and *Transformation* books offer two important contributions to other social science disciplines. First, they provide a model of critical and open reflection that should be replicated in disciplines other than international development and on topics other than participation. Second, the insights and issues which are surfaced with regard to participation have applicability to related constructs such as empowerment, planning, social capital and civic engagement. These constructs, as with all constructs, come with implicit assumptions that are often taken for granted.

What may well be taken for granted is that participative research with children and young people is, per se, 'a good thing'. In our writing we seek to enjoin those who wish to engage in participative research with children and young people to be vigilant regarding matters of manipulation and coercion.

Adults may find the notion of participative research discomforting because they may believe that their power and authority have been usurped in the interests of those who are currently experiencing the lived life of childhood. However, as we shall also consistently argue, this enterprise is not one where the adult abdicates from the inquiry, but where the adults, children and young people work in partnership with each other in an endeavour to more fully understand and appreciate relevant life experiences, whether in the school, the family, the workplace or the community. The process moves from a transactional one where children and young people merely provide information to others, to one where there is a capacity to transform their young lives for the better.

As we shall discuss later, particularly in Chapter 5 with its emphasis upon political ecology, and its relation to cooperation and access, children and young people are not a homogeneous group with agreed understandings of their world. Even having a common age is not a determinant of the ways in which they may be engaged in research. Their social experiences will vary from one context to another (Christensen and James, 2008: 170). Also, like the adults with whom they interact, they hold a variety of positions and beliefs. However, we do assert, within the Rights of the Child framework discussed in our opening chapter, that children and young people are affirmed as having the right to hold those with power over them accountable for the ways in which that power is exercised and negotiated, irrespective of the many variables that might influence their lives. Thus it can be argued that a methodology that embraces social research with children and young people is, in effect, one that is rights-based and must be inclusive of methods that do not in any way undermine attempts to misappropriate the voice of the participants (Beazley et al., 2011).

Lolichen (2009: 136) makes the telling observation that what is often characterised as participation is no more than the young people 'taking part' rather than being provided with an opportunity to be 'individuals with their own social and political identity (being) persons with vivid imaginations, deep thoughts, ideas, skills and capacities'. He reports on an Indian non-government organisation, 'Concerned for Working Children', that has pioneered the area of children's rights, especially participation, for the last 25 years and makes the claim that information is the key to effective participation. Others have pointed out that participation is not just a matter of engaging participants in an exchange of information but rather is a cumulative, even gradual process, one that is less directive – moving towards facilitation (Curtin and Murtagh, 2007).

Participation in research is a process in which ownership of the problem is increasingly shared between researchers and researched. In the first instance researchers are likely to own the problem and design the research using methods that enable stakeholders to express themselves. Working directly with stakeholders (including children) and gradually handing over responsibility to them to set the research agenda will change the role of researchers to 'facilitators' and turn the research process into a joint project. (Ennew and Plateau, 2004: 15)

To make this claim concrete we turn to a study undertaken with a cohort of fifteen-year-old girls (Year 9) in an independent girls secondary school in Sydney (Groundwater-Smith et al., 2006) whereby the year was treated as a laboratory within which the students investigated the key matter of 'we shape our environment and environment shapes us'.

CASE STUDY 2.1

As well as the statement (the key provocation) 'we shape our environment and our environment shapes us' applying to their key curriculum studies, in areas as varied as English or Science, it was also encompassed in the requirement for these students to undertake an independent inquiry that would be conducted over the year. A complex formative evaluation of this comprehensive Year 9 innovation was undertaken. The purpose of the study was to identify those elements of the programme that could be developed and improved. It contextualised the innovation in terms of continuous school reform in what may be identified as an 'activist' school. Various forms of evidence were assembled to inform the evaluation including inquiries undertaken by academic researchers, teachers as researchers and the students themselves. A wide range of both quantitative and qualitative procedures were adopted and their complementarities were considered within a discussion regarding the use of mixed methods in a single case. It could be posited that the study was designed to inform a range of stakeholders of the nature and extent of the innovation that had taken place, it drew upon issues in relation to innovation and evaluation in school education, it employed a methodology that honoured the experiences of the participants and used a range of mixed methods to do so. Importantly, in the context of this current discussion, students were enabled to actively participate in the collection, interpretation and analysis of some, but not all of the complex data as research apprentices. The study was increasingly seen as the kind of joint project discussed by Ennew and Plateau, above.

Initially, a student advisory group was convened and met to discuss those parts of the study that most directly involved their peers. Focus group meetings were held on two occasions during the year, with some of their deliberations reported here:

(Continued)

(Continued)

Using focus group inquiry methods and following consultation with the student advisory group two rounds of discussions were conducted with samples of students from each mentor group in March and August.

March Meetings: The discussion was designed as discursive to permit students to express themselves broadly about key elements of their experience.

1. *Independent Project* – Students were requested to describe the Independent Project and the ways in which it related to the Year 9 laboratory key provocation, 'We shape our environment and our environment shapes us'. Did they have concerns regarding the openness of the project? Were students worried about the extent to which they might reveal themselves? Had they identified the audience for the project?
2. *The blog* – What were the communications opportunities offered by the blog? Strengths and weaknesses?
3. *Blocks of learning time* – How were students coping with the longer blocks of learning time? How might teaching and learning be improved within the time frameworks?
4. *Spaces for learning* – How were the assigned spaces for learning working? Were they appropriate? How could they be improved?

August Meetings: Questions were more precise, in line with students having had more experience of the Year 9 laboratory, in particular in relation to being self-directed learners. The student advisory group assisted in recommending the formulation of the questions after they had considered the responses to those posed earlier.

1. How independent do you think you are as a student in Year 9?
2. How independent would you like to be?
3. How can your teachers support you in being independent learners?
4. How does the independent investigation assist you in being an independent learner?
5. Name three major opportunities that this year has offered you.
6. What are the biggest challenges?
7. To what extent are you encouraged to participate in the life of the school beyond the classroom?
8. To whom do you turn when you need to negotiate something that may be difficult for you?
9. What are three key words that you would use to describe a Year 9 student at your school? And, what three words would you use to describe your school?

The process, for this work, was an iterative one with data collection and interpretation informing the next cycle of the evaluation study. The study could be seen to cohere with the first three of five levels of participation that have been put forward by Shier (2001: 110) where the young people are listened to, and supported in expressing their views and seeing these taken into account. While the students were less involved in decision-making processes and the sharing of power and responsibility for decision-making the project was clearly a beginning and this they knew. Nonetheless, Shier's model proved particularly useful in considering the project because it embodied the nature of commitment required for a project to be successful, namely that there was an opening created; that an opportunity occurred; and that there was an obligation to provide conditions that are built into the system. The *opening* created conditions where the young people could express their views regarding their Year 9 experience; the *opportunity* enabled a range of views to be expressed; and the *obligations* were that due weight would be given to the concerns that the students expressed.

Children and young people as active agents

So what are the orientations necessary for children and young people to be active agents in research and inquiry that concerns them?

CASE STUDY 2.2

In October, 2012 Australia was witness to an interesting and some would say a disturbing case whereby the express wishes of four children aged nine to fifteen were negated by a family court judge. An application had been made by the father for an order for the return of the children to Italy pursuant to Family Law (Child Abduction Convention) Regulations 1986, otherwise known as the Hague Convention. Various countries throughout the world (including Australia and Italy) had signed the convention and agree to be bound by it. The convention generally provides that there should be a prompt return of an abducted child to its home country. The mandatory return is subject to the discretion of the court not to order a return if the parent opposing the return can establish:

1 The other parent was not actually exercising rights of custody prior to the removal of the child;
2 The other parent had consented to the removal of the child;
3 There is a grave risk that the child would be exposed to physical or psychological harm;

(Continued)

(Continued)

4 The child objects to the return but at the same time the strength of feeling is beyond mere wishes and the child has a level of maturity to be able to express such a wish. (Tonkin Drysdale Partners, 2012)

The point in recording this case is to draw attention to the ways in which the wishes of the children were taken into account, especially in relation to their rights as children and the fourth point outlined above with respect to preferences, choices and desires. During the course of the hearing the children were interviewed by a Family Consultant, who was nominated as an expert appointed by the court to provide an opinion.

> The Family Consultant told the court that the children identified missing aspects of their lives in Italy, including school, friends and family members. The Family Consultant's expert evidence was that the basis for the girls' objections to returning to Italy was predominantly related to their perception that their father had historically perpetrated violence against their mother. The Family Consultant said that the two younger girls 'lacked the cognitive sophistication for their views to be taken into account fully'. As for the elder girls the Family Consultant said that they 'would lack the ability to truly predict what impact their choices or views would have for their future relationship with their father'. (Tonkin Drysdale Partners, 2012)

The argument put to the court was that the children had been influenced by the need to stay loyal to the wishes of their mother. However, it was the mother's considered view that there was a grave risk to the children in the father's care. It was suggested that the children no doubt believed that there was a danger to them because of what they had been told by the mother and the question was posed, 'But, does this mean that the children were able to make an informed decision about this?'.

Fascinating as the case may be, with multiple perspectives and accounts of the lives of the mother in Australia, of the father in Italy and of the children, what we find of particular interest is the view that it was implied that these young people were unable to make an 'informed decision'. They were not constructed as active agents and competent decision-makers with respect to their own lives. In the ethics chapter of this book (Chapter 3) we shall take up more fully the concept of informed consent and the related concept of 'assent' as they relate to children and young people being participative in research. However, it is important and salient to take up the issue of the capability to process and respond to various forms of information. The implicit assumption in the case reported here was that the girls lacked 'cognitive ability' and 'discernment'. This is strongly refuted by Scott (2008: 96) when she argues that 'there is growing evidence to suggest that the best source of information about issues pertinent to children is the children themselves'. Looking in particular at quantitative research with young people Scott assembles a strong case, based upon a number of studies that demonstrate that careful design features can ensure that the voices of young people can be solicited, evaluated and found trustworthy.

The assumption in the case quoted here is that created by a particular manifestation of developmental psychology that according to James et al. (1998: 15) has 'colonized childhood in a pact with medicine, education and government agencies'. To these vested institutional interests we would add also the law. Such a stance is in contradiction to a broadly sociological one that situates childhood within a series of social constructs that necessarily vary by context. Even the concept of age, so strongly argued in this case, is mediated by age-based cultural contexts that may be a function of social class, gender and ethnicity. An important point to be made is that in research studies concerning children and young people age is a 'social' rather than 'natural' variable (James et al., 1998: 175).

When Lolichen (2009) writes of young people participating in a partnership in local government in India, a partnership built upon their own sense of agency in research, he sees them contributing to the transformation of their lives and the quality of life in their communities. The judgement that they would be too young and immature to make such a contribution can be refuted by their activism. For example, he reports that children in a tiny village were confronted by the problem of alcoholism in their village. When they raised this in a local government meeting they were brushed aside. Their response was to collect and count the number of sachets in which alcohol was packaged and make an estimate of how much was drunk and by how many families. This data provided the children with a springboard for an advocacy restricting alcohol use that would contribute to the overall well-being of the villagers.

While these are examples of cases involving older children we are also alert to the notion that very young people can also be afforded a sense of agency and some control over their lives. For example, Millei and Gallagher (2011) studied pre-schoolers and their perceptions of their bathroom facilities – clearly a sensitive area of concern. They suggested that discussions of bathrooms among very young children form part of the 'null curriculum' in early childhood education; meaning that while much is learned about how to behave in bathroom spaces, it is a covert learning and not made explicit in the teaching practices of centres. They identified that for some young children bathrooms are seen as unsafe and unsatisfactory and that they will avoid their use and can even develop a form of toilet phobia, preferring to wait until they get home to use a more familiar and appropriate facility. Medically and socially, this is an outcome that should be avoided. The researchers set out to work with centre practitioners and the children themselves to form a collaborative team to explore alternatives to the existing bathroom facilities. Children were able to make their own decision about whether to participate and were enabled to provide consent. Data was collected through discussions, stories, incidental talks, drawings, photographs and observations. After some hesitation children were most forthcoming, not only in identifying the various problems associated with privacy and safety, but also pro-actively suggesting solutions. We would argue that this is a holistic methodology that involves not only the range of key stakeholders, but also a selection of methods that can be employed that will enable each voice to be heard.

Clearly, then, from the early years on, it is possible for children and young people to be participative in a range and variety of research endeavours. Harder et al. (2013) as another example, explored the capacities of four-year-old children in Sweden to negotiate and manage their way through a variety of primary health care situations.

Of course we are mindful of the ways in which such accounts can be constructed, and attend to Warming's (2005) distinction between listening to children and young people and giving them authentic agency by acting on their concerns. Also, we are aware that the very concept of 'voice' in terms of consulting and researching with children and young people is highly contested 'largely due to the term's implied universality across individuals and situations' (Parnell and Patsarika, 2014: 100). We need to continually ask ourselves the question, 'whose voice' is being captured here?; as well as asking, 'what is being said and how can it be acted upon?'. Indeed this is a matter that we take up in the final chapters of this book when we write of sustainability and action. We shall offer a number of such examples in our discussion of innovative methods that research designers, whether children or adults, adopt.

Developing, constructing and contributing to change and improvement – current inquiry processes that limit children and young people

In discussing participative methodologies we are also concerned to identify them as purposeful. Working with children and young people, gaining their confidence and supporting them in their inquiries all takes time and should be time well spent. The experiences of children and young people are indisputably many and varied but they all have one thing in common: they are capable of progressive improvement.

CASE STUDY 2.3

A large metropolitan girls high school in Sydney was interested in developing a more inclusive approach for its learners, a number of whom were struggling. They undertook a project *Pedagogical Research: Learning for All* that involved teachers in areas as varied as Design and Technology, English, History and Mathematics education. Many of the school's students who were experiencing difficulties in maths perceived that their needs were not addressed in the mainstream curriculum. A team of maths teachers decided upon a project where they would take the learning in a new direction for their Year 8 (thirteen-year-old) students who were antagonistic towards maths and could not see the purpose in engaging in maths activities. The teachers took an approach to working with data in real time and across real issues. They encouraged their students to be playful and chose to teach the unit in the library, a learning space that was not normally associated with maths teaching. The case is included here, not in terms of detail, but for the processes that were used to gain feedback from the students. They were asked to create simulated 'tweets' and take annotated selfies that demonstrated how they felt about the nature of the particular maths unit; they were asked to 'like', 'comment' and 'share'. It was seen that by using features of social media the process gave permission to students to be more open in their commentary.

Figure 2.1 More of this type of learning please

(Continued)

(Continued)

Figure 2.2 Not so good for me

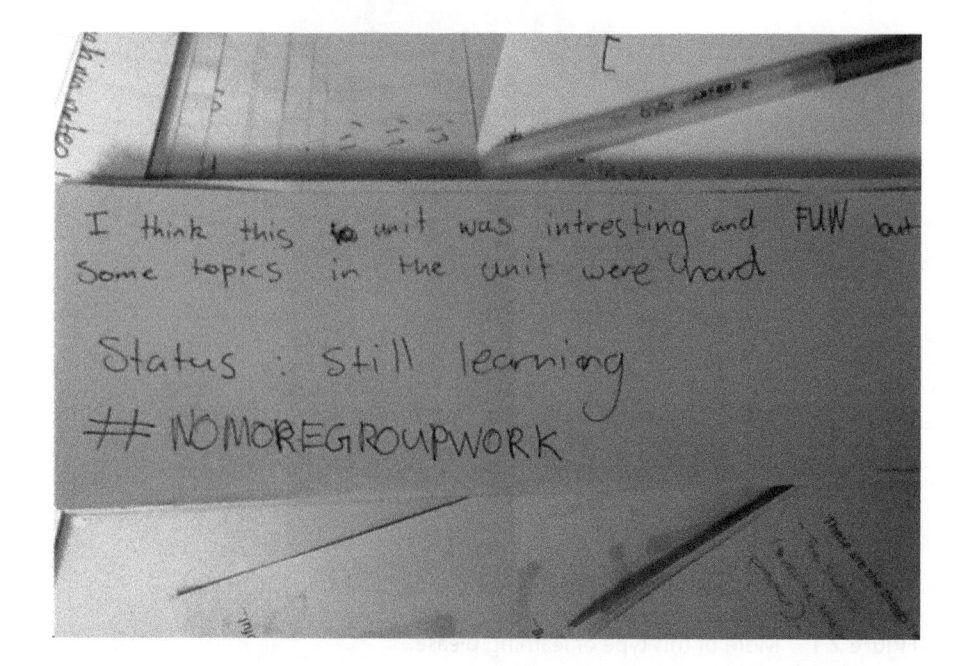

Figure 2.3 Still learning

The maths teachers believed that, following the project, they had a more empathic insight into the students' views and experiences and would be able to build on and redesign learning for them.

Whether we write of the ways in which pre-schoolers engage with the environment in their local park, or how ten-year-old boys cope with bullying in their school, or the impact of isolation and trauma among refugee adolescents, or girls learning mathematics in a new and different context, we are concerned that the conditions in which they find themselves can change for the better. We need to ask ourselves in which ways are children and young people's perspectives capable of being translated into new policy directions? If we think of change and improvement as a policy circuit, then it is claimed that 'children are the least well connected in such circuits' (James et al., 1998: 145). They face a number of obstacles in being listened to and for action to follow their deliberations.

Michael Fielding has been a long-time advocate for young people to have a voice particularly in the matter of their education. Of all the social enterprises encountered by children we would argue that schooling is one of the most enduring and impactful. In the developed world schooling is not a matter of choice, but of compulsion. Indeed, at the urgings of the OECD, the years of attendance are increasing with the school-leaving age taking young people up to seventeen or eighteen years of age. Developing economies are also aspiring to have more children attend school for longer periods of time. Of course we are not arguing against universal education but wish to address Fielding's effort to reclaim education as a democratic project. In the opening chapter that he contributes to *The student voice handbook*, Fielding (2011) argues that there are two typologies that could be employed as an aid to reconceptualising the intentions of those who are advocates for the participation of children and young people in the policies and practices that govern them.

Fielding's first typology is focused upon patterns of partnership, the second argues for a wider institutional framework within which patterns of partnership can be exercised. Drawing upon a range of historical examples Fielding (2011: 10–11) demonstrates that in contrast to basing improvement upon high-performance schooling through market accountability an alternative would be to create a 'person centred education for democratic fellowship'. He eschews the instrumental purposes of employing student voice in order to improve a school for the purposes of ensuring its competitiveness in the marketplace, in favour of a fellowship dimension that informs a holistic way of living and being in a world directed to the common good. In terms of his second typology, that of the institutional framework, he outlines a ten-point plan that connects among other things structures, roles, relationships, practices and accountabilities.

Thus, when we consider engagement with children and young people for the purposes of contributing to change and improvement, we also need to consider why we would argue for particular changes or improvements. Change to what end and improvement for whom? In March, 2009 the BBC reported that a community in Nottinghamshire, UK, had installed pink lighting that would show up 'spotty skin' and thus discourage young people from congregating in local public spaces. The amenity of older members of the community may have been improved, but in ways that angered and alienated the young. In the comprehensive study undertaken by Hatzopoulos and Clancey (2007) the uses made of public spaces by young people were examined as were the many constraints imposed upon their capacity to enjoy them responsibly. Improving public spaces may be an aspiration for some at the cost of the enjoyment of others. Clearly there is much room for negotiation and beneficial discussions.

For many young people, the following are common places to 'hang out' and to be seen: parks, marketplaces, bus and rail interchanges, libraries, shopping centres, beaches/rivers, bicycle pathways, skateboard parks and parking lots (Hatzopoulos and Clancey, 2007: 8) But these are also spaces that other social groups wish to use and may find difficult to share with adolescents, who are often feared for their boisterous and flamboyant behaviour. However, rather than making such spaces unappealing to young people, the recommendations are to find ways of being inclusive of them when seeking to find solutions that will improve those spaces to the benefit of all. Young people, in these circumstances, can well contribute to finding solutions that will ameliorate anxiety and ensure that all users of public spaces feel that they can enjoy themselves and feel safe (Hatzopoulos and Clancey, 2007).

From these varied examples, many more of which will be discussed throughout this book, it is evident that the road to participative research with children and young people, as a process that is genuinely inclusive and democratic, is one that is difficult to negotiate, most particularly when the youngsters themselves are marginalised and lacking in any kind of substantive power. Who will be consulted? How will they be enabled to speak? To what extent will they be fully participative beyond being data sources? Will they have sufficient agency to inform the consequent decisions arising from any inquiry?

Reframing towards the transformational

We have already observed that generally much that passes for participative research with children and young people is transactional rather than transformational. Hart's (1992) oft-quoted ladder of participation argues that early interactions are no more than manipulation, decoration and tokenism; and perhaps it might be admitted that the last of these is at least a step forward. As the ladder is ascended the relationship moves through consultation and the exchange of information towards shared decision-making. These final three steps have been characterised by the New South Wales Commission for Children and Young People as (reading from the bottom of the ladder to the top):

1. Young-people-initiated, shared decisions with adults

   This happens when projects or programmes are initiated by young people and decision-making is shared between young people and adults. These projects empower young people while at the same time enabling them to access and learn from the life experience and expertise of adults. *This rung of the ladder can be embodied by youth/adult partnerships.*

2. Young-people-initiated and directed

   This step is when young people initiate and direct a project or programme. Adults are involved only in a supportive role. *This rung of the ladder can be embodied by youth-led activism.*

3. Adult-initiated, shared decisions with young people

   This occurs when projects or programmes are initiated by adults but the decision-making is shared with the young people. *This rung of the ladder can be embodied by participatory action research.* (New South Wales Commission for Children and Young People, 2008)

Truly transformational inquiry that authentically takes children and young people towards an emancipatory goal is always going to be a major challenge. Understanding the methodological issues, selecting appropriate methods, fostering research skills, developing the capacity to pose researchable questions and facing the troublesome matter of ethics are among but a few of the concerns that will need to be addressed. It is intended that this book will make a contribution that will allow the endeavour of participative research with children and young people to be radically reframed.

Key points

- Reflecting on methodology precedes selecting appropriate methods. When engaged in participative research with children and young people it is essential to select a holistic methodology that sees them as active agents within an authentic inquiry process.
- When undertaking practitioner research with children and young people researchers should be alert to issues of manipulation and coercion and their relation to power and authority.
- Participation is more than 'taking part'; it is a cumulative, planned and resourced process leading to improvement and change that is understood by children and young people to be change for the better.

- Researchers need to be mindful of creating conditions that can ensure when soliciting the agency of children and young people that they are honoured, trusted and respected.

References

Beazley, H., Bessell, S., Ennew, J. and Waterson, R. (2011) Human rights of children in relation to research methodologies. In A. Invernizzi and J. Williams (Eds) *The human rights of children: From visions to implementation.* Surrey: Ashgate Publishing Ltd, pp. 159–78.

Bryman, A. (2005) *Social science methods.* 2nd edition. Oxford: Oxford University Press.

Christens, B. and Speer, P.W. (2006) Tyranny/Transformation: Power and paradox in participatory development. [Review Essay: B. Cooke and Uma Kothari (Eds) (2001) *Participation: The new tyranny* Forum Qualitative Sozialforschung/ Forum: Qualitative Social Research, 7(2): Art. 22. http://nbn-resolving.de/ urn:nbn:de:0114-fqs0602223, accessed 8th January, 2013.

Christensen, P. and James, A. (2008) Childhood diversity and commonality: Some methodological insights. In P. Christensen and A. James (Eds) *Research with children perspectives and practices.* 2nd edition. London: Routledge, pp. 156–72.

Cooke, B. and Kothari, U. (Eds) (2001) *Participation the new tyranny?* New York: Zed Books.

Curtin, M. and Murtagh, J. (2007) Participation of children and young people in research: Competence, power and representation. *British Journal of Occupational Therapy*, 70(2): 67–72.

Ennew, J. and Plateau, D.P. (2004) *How to research the physical and emotional punishment of children.* Bangkok: Save the Children Southeast, East Asia and Pacific Region.

Fielding, M. (2011) Student voice and the possibility of radical democratic education. Re-narrating forgotten histories, developing alternative futures. In G. Czerniawskii and W. Kidd (Eds) *The student voice handbook.* Bingley, UK: Emerald Group Publishing, pp. 3–18.

Groundwater-Smith, S., Martin, A., Hayes, M., Herrett, M., Layhe, K., Layman, A. and Saurine, J. (2006) What counts as evidence: Mixed methods in a single case. Paper presented at the Australian Association for Research in Education, Adelaide, 26th–30th November. www.aare.edu.au/06pap/gro06091.pdf, accessed 20th December, 2012.

Harder, M., Christensen, K. and Soderback, M. (2013) Four-year-old children's negotiation strategies to influence and deal with primary child health care situations. *Children & Society*, 27: 35–47 DOI:10.1111/j.1099–0860.2011.00365.x, accessed 8th January, 2013.

Hart, R. (1992) *Children's participation: From tokenism to citizenship*. International Development Centre. Florence: UNICEF.

Hatzopoulos, P. and Clancey, G. (2007) *Where people and spaces meet: Approaches to public space management*. Surry Hills, NSW Youth Action & Policy Association (NSW) Inc – YAPA. www.yapa.org.au/youthwork/facts/meetingplaces.pdf, accessed 24th December, 2012.

Hickey, S. and Mohan, G. (Eds) (2004) *Participation: From tyranny to transformation*. New York: Zed Books.

James, A., Jenks, C. and Prout, A. (1998) *Theorising Childhood*. Williston, VA: Teachers College Press.

Lolichen, P. (2009) Rights-based participation: Children as research protagonists and partners in mainstream governance. In J. Fiedler and C. Posch (Eds) *Yes they can! Children researching their lives*. Austria: Schneider Verlag Hohengehren GmbH, pp. 135–43.

Millei, Z. and Gallagher, J. (2011) Opening spaces for dialogue and re-envisioning children's bathrooms in a pre-school. Practitioner research with children on a sensitive and neglected area of concern. *International Journal of Early Childhood*, 44(1): 9–29.

New South Wales Commission for Children and Young People (2008) www.youth coalition.net/documents/projects/BRB/sections/Youth%20Participation.pdf, accessed 25th December, 2012.

Parnell, R. and Patsarika, M. (2014) Playful voices in participatory design. In C. Burke and K. Jones (Eds) *Education, childhood and anarchism: Talking Colin Ward*. London: Routledge, pp. 99–112.

Scott, J. (2008) Children as respondents. In P. Christensen and A. James (Eds) *Research with children: Perspectives and practices*. 2nd edition. London: Routledge, pp. 87–108.

Shier, H. (2001) Pathways to participation: Openings, opportunities and obligations. *Children & Society*, 15: 107–17.

Tonkin Drysdale Partners (2012) http://tdplegal.com.au/should-the-court-have-sent-the-girls-back-to-italy/, accessed 21st December, 2012.

Waring, M. (2012) Finding your theoretical position. In J. Arthur, M. Waring, R. Coe and L. Hedges (Eds) *Research methods and methodologies in education*. London: Sage Publications, pp. 15–19.

Warming, H. (2005) Participant observation: A way to learn about children's perspectives. In A. Clark, A.T. Kjorholt and P. Moss (Eds) *Beyond listening: Children's perspectives on early childhood services*. Bristol: Policy Press, pp. 51–70.

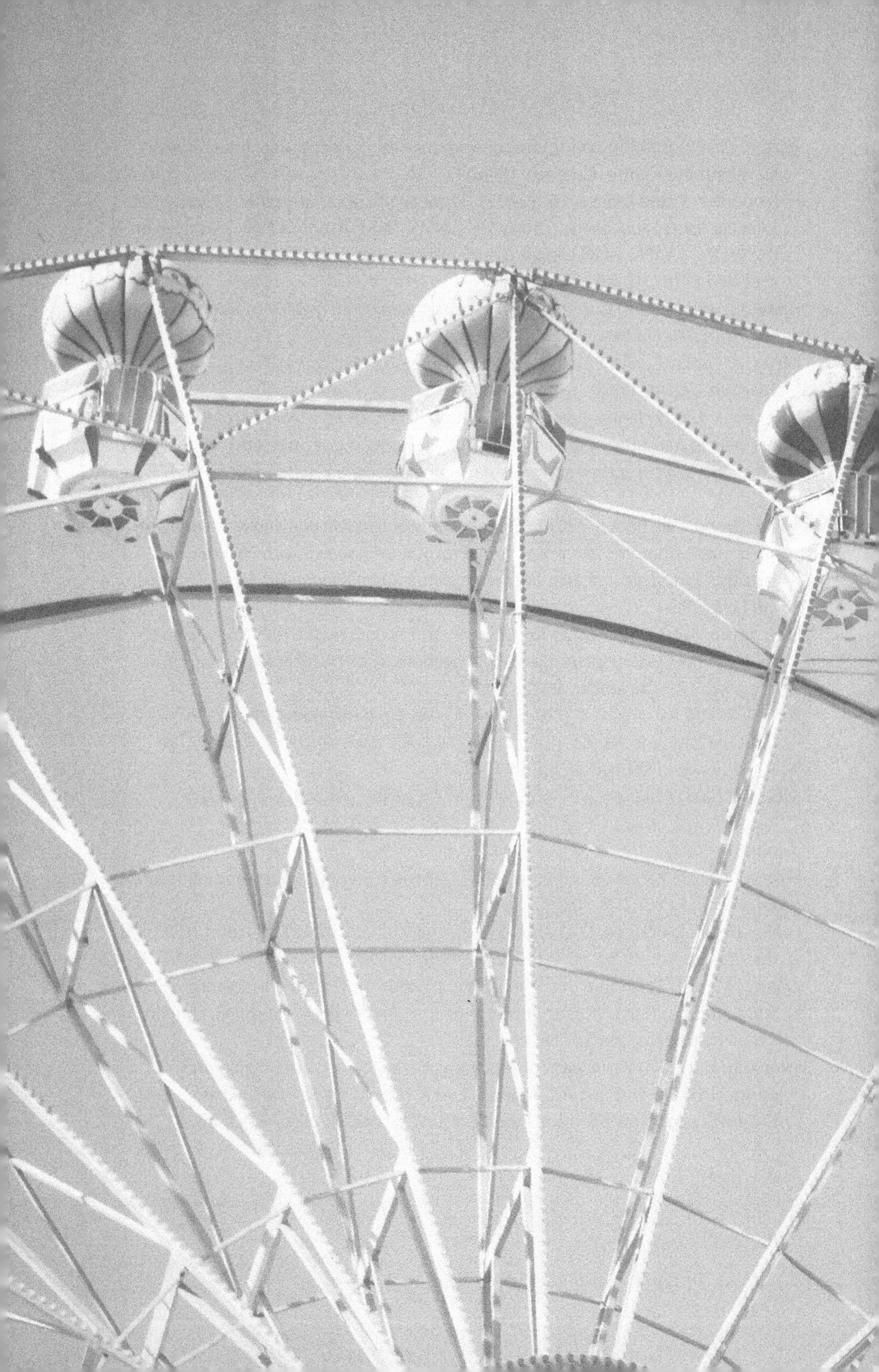

THREE

ETHICAL QUESTIONS IN RELATION TO PARTICIPATORY RESEARCH WITH CHILDREN AND YOUNG PEOPLE

This chapter builds upon notions of ethical symmetry which outline the starting point for research as the ethical relationship between researcher and participants, whether they be children, young people or adults.

It addresses:

- Ethical symmetry.
- Institutional protocols for the conduct of research: facilitation and barriers.
- Employing individual judgement in everyday practice.
- Dilemmas and challenges.
- Assent and dissent.
- Risk and benefit.
- Trust, respect and reciprocity.

As part of a conversation about their participation in a research project, four eight-year-olds commented:

I liked being asked ... like, normally, you don't get a say and you get told *Oh, we're going to put your work in,* and you go *I don't want it to be.* [Here] it's like you get to say *Yes you can* or *No.*

Yeah. You get asked to have your own say.

I think it's good that we get to have our own say because we don't ... Because you listen to us ... we don't get to like go up to the Council and say *Hey I want this and that.*

And especially like how the adults get to have their say, like who they want as the Prime Minister of Australia and then the kids can get their say with what ... The kids can have their say in a certain type of way.

They were all in agreement that being asked about possible participation in research demonstrated respect for them and allowed them to make a choice. Throughout this chapter, we return to conversations with these and other children who shared their perspectives on research participation. More details of these conversations are reported in Dockett et al. (2012b).

Changing views of children and childhood have challenged traditional approaches to research and opened up new possibilities for researching with children and young people. Many of these involve qualitative research approaches which seek to acknowledge and value the social and cultural contexts in which children and young people engage, their ways of knowing and being in the world, as well as the range of people who inhabit these spaces. The changing possibilities for research often highlight complex, interconnected contexts and generate new ground for the interpretation of ethical approaches and principles for research with children and young people.

Most of all, new conceptualisations of children and young people and new research approaches create opportunities for children and young people to guide considerations of the ways in which research can be meaningful and relevant for them, while maintaining commitments to sound ethical principles.

Ethical symmetry

While it is not possible to completely efface asymmetries of power that may be attributable to status and maturity, what is essential in working with children and young people is to promote interactions that ensure justice and respect. We argue that ethics is about relationships, specifically about how participants and researchers relate to one another in morally principled ways that will assist in enacting duties, responsibilities and expectations and contribute to positive change for all involved.

Working in ways that reflect ethical symmetry requires us to acknowledge the multiple ethical issues inherent in research with children and young people, and to develop a set of ethical values – supplementary to institutional protocols – to guide our research and 'provide an anchor' for our practice (Christensen and Prout, 2002: 495). In other words, ethical symmetry involves reflection on the ethical values that guide interactions and the decision-making that occurs within research. The principles of ethical symmetry underpin each element of research – from conceptualising to reporting and advocacy.

Dealing with ethical symmetry requires specific attention. Cahill (2007a, 2007b) in her espousal of engagement with young people in participative action research (PAR) advocates a 'collective praxis approach'; that is, a set of explicit rituals and practices for recognising and working with issues of power within the research process. The project that she reports upon was one developed with six young women aged 16–22, who lived in a New York City neighbourhood. Cahill met with her participants (co-researchers) on a daily basis to undertake a study of the 'everyday lives of young women in the city' (2007a: 300), focusing on stereotypical representations of young people of colour and the lack of financial investment in their neighbourhood, which had resulted in deterioration of local facilities. As a project that was driven by the group it was not possible to anticipate exactly how it would progress and what shape it would take; what was essential was that a collective praxis approach underpinned the interactions. The co-researchers employed a range of methods including a series of mapping devices (mental maps, social maps, visual maps) and daily focus group discussions. Through these, they were involved in data collection, data analysis and the presentation of research findings. 'The research process was complicated, cyclical, and "layered" and each turn pushed us to ask new questions and re-think our interpretations' (2007a: 301). In this context, the enactment of 'collective praxis' was essential.

The approach embodied a relationship between dialogue, critical reflection and action and drew upon what Cahill named as 'rituals' especially as they related to writing and reflection. In circumstances such as these, the issue of symmetries of power were addressed through processes of dialogue, truth telling and a respect for others.

Habermas (1979: 97) writes 'Dialogue is a gentle, but obstinate, never silent, although seldom redeemed claim to reason'. It requires respect, truth, open mindedness, and a willingness to listen and risk one's own preconceptions, fixed beliefs, biases and prejudices. It requires fundamental procedures that try to reduce overt and subtle forms of power. As Linklater (2005: 148) observes, 'dialogue is an unfinished and unfinishable journey'.

In research with young children, attention to ethical symmetry requires us to acknowledge children's competence as well as their rights to have a view on things that matter for them. In practice, this could involve seeking children's assent – agreement to participate – in addition to parental consent, and the use of research methods that provide options and choices about participation. It could also require attentiveness to children's actions, as well as their words, as they engage in research activities, and ongoing opportunities for children to re-assess their participation (Dockett et al., 2012a).

Throughout this book we consistently address issues in relation to symmetries of power. One of the challenges in the context of drawing attention to ethical concerns is to ask ourselves how open and unexpected processes such as those outlined above can be governed by the various institutional protocols for the conduct of participative research with children and young people.

Institutional protocols: facilitation and barriers

Institutional ethics committees are tasked with assessing the appropriateness of proposed research. In doing so, they clearly have a responsibility to face such dilemmas in their deliberations as they seek to serve the interests of research participants, researchers and the institution itself, as well as society at large; interests that may both conflict and intersect. At the heart of their work must lie concerns to promote research that has merit and integrity, reflects the principles of justice, minimises potential harm and respects individual rights to privacy and confidentiality, as well as each individual's right to make an informed choice about research participation.

It can be supposed that many of the research proposals encountered by institutional ethics committees will be hypothesis-driven and will outline a research route with a clear demarcation of what will be undertaken when and how. What can be more difficult for these committees to deal with are inquiry processes that are collaborative and participative. In such cases, proposals are necessarily rather more like a framework of what is to be achieved than a set list of procedures. Where ethics committees are unused to such applications, collaboration may be necessary in order to provide ongoing input about the progress of research and issues that arise. This is particularly the case when institutional ethics committees favour a risk-averse approach, or when the prevailing discourse positions children and young people as vulnerable and in need of protection (Graham and Fitzgerald, 2010).

Institutional ethics committees have important roles in raising awareness of ethical issues and monitoring research standards (Alderson and Morrow, 2004). However, there is more to conducting ethical research than gaining the approval of the institutional ethics committee; gaining such approval does not guarantee that all aspects of the research will be conducted in an ethical manner. Ethical dilemmas are generated throughout research and need to be addressed as they arise. While the guidelines of an institutional ethics committee can provide useful starting points, researchers have a responsibility to be reflexive and critical as they address situational ethics – the issues that arise in the socio-political and cultural contexts in which the research is conducted (Ahsan, 2009).

Balancing the interests of the institution, the researchers and participants can be difficult, but not insurmountable. Gorman (2007: 16) points out that however much a researcher and ethics committee may disagree 'it would be difficult to disagree on the importance of "respect for persons"', being a 'regard for the welfare, rights, beliefs, perceptions, customs and cultural heritage, both individual and collective of persons involved in research'.

Employing individual judgement in everyday practice

At the beginning of this chapter we wrote of ethical relations as they apply to symmetries of power and the positioning of children and young people through dialogue and interaction. In encounters with children and young people these ideals may be mediated through practical forms of engagement that perceive them, nonetheless, as social actors, capable of evaluating and judging their everyday circumstances. They are seen as having a voice in the matters that affect them. But the exercise of their activism is neither easy nor uncomplicated.

Ethical decisions will continue to be made well after a proposal has been approved by the relevant institutional ethics committee. In many instances the material provided to ethics committees will not provide the information needed to make these decisions. Rather, 'researchers may have to rely on their own personal judgements in their everyday ethical practice' (Christensen and Prout, 2002: 489). These judgements derive from, and contribute to, a set of ethical values that guide our stance as researchers. Situational ethics emphasise the context-specific nature of research and the need for researchers to interpret ethical regulations within these contexts. Such interpretation relies not only on the principles of ethical regulation, but also on the basis of the relationships between researchers and participants (Gilligan, 1982). These approaches do not ignore the importance of ethical regulation. However, they balance this by urging researchers to make decisions based on the notion of care for research participants in specific contexts.

As one example, the research team involved in a recent project working with children and families described as having complex support needs, developed an ethical stance that included commitments to recognising the strengths of participants and ensuring that the research would not be reported in ways that contributed to the further marginalisation of participants (Dockett et al., 2009). This stance guided the research methods used, as well as the ways in which data were generated, analysed and reported. When researching with groups described as vulnerable in some way – a description often applied to children and young people – it is often easy to fall into the habit of confirming stereotypes, for example by reporting things that children cannot do or do not understand. Adopting an ethical stance based on strengths can provide an 'anchor' for practice, as we make everyday decisions by reference to this stance.

In another example, Viviers and Lombard (2013) describe a set of thirteen ethical principles to guide participatory research with children and young people. These include: recognising participation as a right affirmed in international conventions, such as the Convention on the Rights of the Child (United Nations, 1989); respecting children's views and input; communication and information-sharing with children and young people, before, during and after participation; and the roles of adults in facilitating participation.

Reflecting the principles of both institutional and situational ethics, and drawing on a wide range of research and expertise, Graham et al. (2013: 3) present an Ethics Charter, 'an aspirational statement of seven commitments written for researchers and others who engage in research involving children, and who are committed to fulfilling their responsibility to undertake ethical research, irrespective of context'. The commitments to guide ethical research with children are:

- Ethics in research involving children is everyone's responsibility;
- Respecting the dignity of children is core to ethical research;
- Research involving children must be just and equitable;
- Ethical research benefits children;
- Children should never be harmed by their participation in research;

- Research must always obtain children's informed and ongoing consent;
- Ethical research requires ongoing refection.

Dilemmas and challenges

Ethical concerns with respect to participative research with children and young people may be characterised as dilemmas. On the one hand, if we seek to protect vulnerable children and young people, it may be the case that we are, in effect, patronising them, not giving them sufficient credit to imagine themselves as powerful and responsible. On the other hand, if we believe them to be strong and invulnerable we may be underestimating their fragility and susceptibility. We need to ask ourselves, 'do we believe children and young people to be competent, that is competent to make decisions and competent to provide valid data,

Table 3.1 Possible challenges and dilemmas in research with children and young people

Situation	Dilemma
Children and young people indicating a desire to be involved in research, but parents/guardians withholding consent	Is the consent of children and young people sufficient to include them in research? What legal standing do children and young people have in relation to consent?
Children and young people disclosing information that could suggest potential harm	Does the information constitute evidence of potential harm? Should the situation be reported to relevant authorities? Would this constitute a breach of the trust relationship you have established with participants?
Adults (parents, teachers) insisting that children and young people participate in research	While this may increase the number of participants, what are the implications for the data generated? How do we respect the preferences of children and young people? Does the initial insistence mean that children and young people at least hear about the research and have the opportunity to participate?
A participant engages in the project almost to the end, but then withdraws their consent to participate	The data already contributed may be important and very relevant. Can it still be included? Should you try to convince the participant to stay with the project?
Over time you have developed a strong positive relationship with participants. They ask you to keep working with them even though the project has finished	What is your exit strategy? How can you continue to provide support, but not create dependency?

or do we see them as incapable informants, untrustworthy even?' Or would it be better to see them as 'different' rather than 'lesser' (Morrow, 2004: 10).

Multiple dilemmas arise in research with children and young people. Resolution of these may involve reference to ethical guidelines, laws or the ethical stance adopted by researchers. In addition, some professions have developed Codes of Ethics that can be used to guide decision-making (see, for example, British Educational Research Association, 2004). It is possible that some dilemmas are not resolved, or that what appears to be resolution masks an uncomfortable compromise.

Examples of possible dilemmas in research with children and young people are given in Table 3.1.

In developing the compendium for the Ethical Research Involving Children (ERIC) project, Graham et al. (2013) present multiple case studies, each of which details the ethical challenges encountered in the research and the choices made in response to these. The inclusion of reflexive questions and considerations promotes ongoing discussion about these case studies and encourages researchers to revisit their own, and others', experiences of ethical challenges and dilemmas.

Edwards and Mauther (2012: 26) have outlined the following series of questions for researchers to consider as they encounter ethical challenges and dilemmas in research. In responding to these questions, they urge researchers to reflect upon possible courses of action and their accountability for these.

- Who are the people involved in, and affected by, the ethical dilemma raised in the research?
- What is the context for the dilemma in terms of the specific topic of the research and the issues it raises personally and socially for those involved?
- What are the specific social and personal locations of the people involved in relation to each other?
- What are the needs of those involved and how are they interrelated?
- Who am I identifying with, who am I posing as other, and why?
- What is the balance of personal and social power between those involved?
- How will those involved understand our actions and are these in balance with our judgement about our own practice?
- How can we best communicate the ethical dilemmas to those involved, give them room to raise their views, and negotiate with and between them?
- How will our actions affect relationships between the people involved?

Assent and dissent

A central principle of ethical research is the right to make a choice about participation. When research involves children and young people, the legal right to provide consent for participation often rests with parents or guardians, rather than the potential participants themselves. This derives from an age-based approach to competence (Morrow and Richards, 1996), which assumes that children below a specific age are not competent to make informed decisions about research participation. Challenges to this approach question its universal application in the face of considerable diversity among children and young people. Not only does this diversity include ability and experience, but it also extends to the social and cultural contexts in which children and young people are located. Among other things, our fixation on chronological age can blind us to differences. As Morrow asks (2013: 151) 'what's in a number anyway?'.

It is important to question any assumption that there is a comprehensive and inclusive model for obtaining informed consent and that this model can be reduced to an age criterion. There are serious limitations associated with expectations that children and young people constitute a homogeneous group. Is the Indigenous child living in a remote community in Central Australia in the same position to provide informed consent as the alienated teenager residing on the fringe of a large Spanish city?

An alternative is to consider children's competence in terms of their experiences and contexts (Mason and Urquhart, 2001), recognising that competencies are evolving, rather than fixed, and will vary according to context. In addition, Lansdown (2005: ix) notes that 'children's capacities can differ according to the nature of the rights to be exercised'. Focus on the individual and the experiences and understandings they bring to the research context leads to the realisation that children of the same age may well require different information, or different explanations, in order to reach an informed decision about research participation. Regarding children as individuals within a particular social context has resulted in changed perceptions of competence (Heath et al., 2007). For example, in the context of relationships with familiar and trusted others, children can demonstrate competence beyond that demonstrated in unfamiliar contexts, or individually (Cocks, 2006).

Where children and young people are considered unable to provide consent, many researchers invoke the concept of assent, whereby all are asked explicitly to indicate their own agreement to participate in research. Typically, this occurs after parents/guardians have been asked to provide consent. In this context, assent is defined as 'an explicit, affirmative agreement to participate, not merely the absence of objection' (Vitiello, 2003: 89). Figure 3.1 provides an example of one strategy used to seek informed assent from children in their first year of school (Dockett et al., 2012b). This example provides clear indications of the child's decision not to participate.

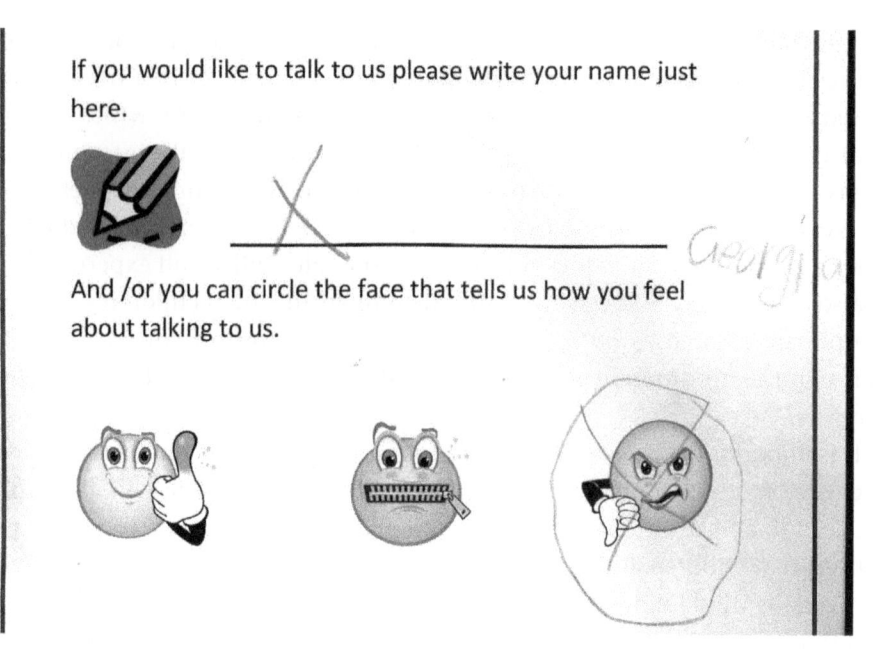

If you would like to talk to us please write your name just here.

And /or you can circle the face that tells us how you feel about talking to us.

Figure 3.1 Indicating dissent

Assent is often regarded as an ongoing process, where children and young people have the right to revoke or renegotiate participation throughout the research. Providing or renegotiating assent can involve researchers attending to the behaviours and actions of children and young people, as well as their verbal interactions.

Conversations about their decisions to participate in research, or not to do so, suggest that there is an emotional, as well as a practical, element to their decisions. The following comments are taken from a conversation with a group of five-year-old children who were discussing their decisions about research participation. They had been asked about their decisions to share some of the materials they had been working on as part of a study of child-friendly communities (Dockett et al., 2012b: 821–2).

Child 1:   [I decided] to share. I said ... I decided to ... and I changed my mind.
Child 2:   I'm saying no 'cause I'm allowed!
Researcher: How did you feel when you made your decision to share or not to share [your data]?
Child 1:   Sad, sort of ... it's because I really wanted to but I was a bit shy. I didn't change my mind [not to share].

Comments from two children in the upper primary years of school (aged about 8 years) also highlighted the emotional elements of their decisions about research participation:

I wanted to pull out a few times like, because things weren't going like I planned to do it, and I got scared but then I got really, like good ...

It was like sometimes I got nervous, like should I or should I not, but what I wasn't sure of ... what would happen when I handed it over ... I said it to myself ... but when I finished I felt OK.

Acknowledging the importance of assent also involves recognising that children and young people may choose not to participate by indicating dissent (Dockett et al., 2012b). Voluntary participation involves an active decision to take part. However, it can be undermined by a number of things, including perceived obligations to adults and a sense of how those adults will react to decisions to withdraw. Where they know that adults have sanctioned participation, children and young people may feel obliged to participate (David et al., 2001).

If we accept that children and young people have the competence and the rights to make informed decisions about research participation, we reach into a different arena. Here we may need to speculate upon their life circumstances and the extent to which they are congruent with the expectations of the researcher. Have their social, religious, economic, gendered and cultural conditions provided them with the necessary background and understandings to reflect upon that which they are giving consent to? In turn, have the same variety of conditions satisfactorily provided the researcher with the communicative capacity required to formulate their intentions in a sufficient and transparent mode?

Decisions about consent and assent occur within the context of relationships, whether they be with researchers, family, friends or significant others. Informed decisions require the provision of appropriate, accessible information, interactions to ensure that the information is understood and a recognisable response that affirms acceptance.

In their Australian study of children and young people's experiences of homelessness, Moore et al. (2008) established a Children's Reference Group to guide their project and to provide advice and feedback to the researchers. Conversations with this group addressed all aspects of the research, including the rights of participants. The starting point for discussions was a rights page that outlined the rights of research participants, communicated through text and images. These rights included the right to *stop participating at any time*. Workshop activities where participants discussed these rights, their interpretation and possible application, had the tangible outcome of changes to wording for the rights page as well as generating a strong sense from both researchers and participants of shared understandings about rights and responsibilities. This provided the basis for informed decisions about participation.

It is not only the potential participants who have rights to know about the research: those who provide consent also need to have access to information that promotes informed decisions. In her extensive work with pre-school-age children, Margaret Carr has emphasised the centrality of the family and the need for them to be taken respectfully through any processes that require their consent (personal communication). This respect is at the core of the Learning Stories approach (Carr and Lee, 2012), which utilises strong connections between children, educators and family to explore children's learning. Inherent in this approach is recognition that families are the protectors of the safety (physical, social and emotional) of their children and that their decisions focus on what is considered to be best for their children. However, such an approach does not resile from seeking input from children and promoting their agency to provide assent, or dissent.

Margaret's work is also guided by commitments to open communication with children and families, using language that is appropriate, but not patronising, and to the generation of data that are 'fit for purpose'; that is, data that are necessary for the matter being investigated. In much research involving children and young people, there is a tendency for researchers to generate or collect large amounts of data. This latter commitment reminds us that there needs to be a purpose for the generation of data, and that data generated for one purpose cannot be used for other purposes without negotiation with participants.

Risk and benefit

Researchers have obligations to act in ways that bring benefit (beneficence) and avoid doing harm (non-maleficence) (Beauchamp and Childress, 2008). Achieving balance between these principles is important, as we seek ways to ensure that we avoid harm but, at the same time, make a positive difference. Such a balance is challenging as it can be difficult to define potential harm in advance and because what constitutes harm is often individualistic.

Actions to address beneficence and non-maleficence include researchers assessing potential risks or discomfort for participants, reflecting sensitivity in interactions with participants, and considering the social and cultural impacts of the research. While there may be limited physical risks involved in some research, there remains the potential for social/emotional distress or discomfort for some children and young people, depending on the subject of the research and the research approaches taken.

Several researchers have argued that the emphasis of institutional ethics committees on risk-minimisation, particularly in relation to research with children and young people, has had the effect of limiting the possibilities for these groups to participate in research. This is despite a range of evidence reporting the beneficial effects of such participation. One paradoxical consequence is that perceptions of risk for children and young people may be limiting their access to the benefits of research participation. While recognising the importance of harm minimisation, Graham and Fitzgerald (2010: 141) have cautioned against 'gate-keeping children out of research purely on the basis of potential risk' and argued that the potential benefits of participation deserve greater attention.

Trust, respect and reciprocity

When we situate research ethics within relationships, issues of trust, respect and reciprocity demand our attention. While these clearly apply to our relationships with participants, they also relate to our interactions with ethics committees and other gatekeepers.

Many gatekeepers may be involved when researchers seek to engage children and young people in research. For example, research in schools requires negotiations with educational systems, principals and teachers before discussions can occur with parents or children. Any of these groups may act as gatekeepers who facilitate or hinder access to potential participants.

Gatekeepers are often portrayed in the role of blocking access to research participants. Indeed, this may well be the case as gatekeepers make decisions about the participation of children and young people, possibly citing reasons such as the sensitivity of the research, children's perceived competence or interest and the potential disruption the research may cause. In these situations, it is possible that children and young people who may wish to be involved (or to make a choice about their own involvement) may not have the opportunity to do so (Heath et al., 2007). Regardless of the reason for gatekeeping, Scott (2005: 137) reminds us that 'attempts to crash through the gate' rarely resolve the issue. Building trusting and respectful relationships with all involved is regarded as a much more effective, longer-term strategy to promote research engagement.

Gatekeepers can also be facilitators of research: they can provide a familiar and trusted mediator between participants and researchers, and gatekeepers' knowledge of social and cultural contexts, language or cultural protocols means that they can be critical partners in research. Reporting on research with children in New Zealand, Suaalii and Mavoa (2001: 39) have described the importance of researchers moving away from the individualistic framework that often underpins approaches to research, replacing this with recognition of the 'respective principles of collective ownership and responsibilities lived by Maori and migrant Pacific groups'. This can only be achieved when researchers build positive relationships with families and communities.

Relationships based on trust and respect are characterised by confident expectations that those involved will interact with integrity and consistency. In research relationships the foci of these expectations are issues of privacy and confidentiality. One way of promoting confidentiality in research is to mask the identity of participants and the location of the research by using pseudonyms. Anonymity may prevent negative consequences arising from the identification of participants and promote participants' comfort in sharing information, knowing that it will not be directly attributable to them, or related to their location, in the dissemination of research (Grinyer, 2002). In relation to children and young people, a further argument for the use of pseudonyms is that participants may not be aware of the consequences (long- and short-term) of having their identity connected with specific data. As well, the use of pseudonyms is regarded as a means of protecting the identity of others who may be mentioned in the research and who may be identifiable through their connections with participants (Wiles, 2013).

However, just as some adults have questioned the use of pseudonyms, some children and young people have rejected the notion of using a name other than their own (Conroy and Harcourt, 2009). There have been questions about why it is acceptable for researchers to claim authorship of publications when those who contributed the data are represented by pseudonyms, and questions about who has the authority to speak to specific data, particularly when it reflects social and cultural knowledge of a group or community (Gubrium and Harper, 2013).

In the conversations about research participation, children reflected on being asked to provide a pseudonym. While many of the children enjoyed the exercise of choosing a different name, or even inventing a name, some argued cogently for using their own names (Dockett et al., 2012b: 819):

Child 1: Some people were proud to put their name on it.
Child 2: Yeah. I put my name on it and I felt a lot better when I put my name on it ... just so people know that little girl actually had a say and she was proud to do it.
Child 3: I was confident to put my name on it 'cause I want people to know I did it and so no one can copyright it.

Arguments against the anonymisation of data must be balanced with the protection that can be afforded by pseudonyms. In other words, it is not sufficient for researchers to use the names or locations of participants without considering the potential consequences that may arise.

It can be challenging to anonymise all data. For example, visual data – including drawings, collages, photographs or video – may be recognised outside the research context and this can lead to identification of both participants and locations (Wiles et al., 2011). Pixilation of features may counter this to some extent, but there may also be other visual clues in the image that lead to recognition. Whatever decisions are made about anonymity and ways to promote this, it is important that participants are aware of the ways in which data will be reported. In the case of children and young people, this awareness needs to extend to those who have signed the consent forms.

In research, confidentiality is taken to mean that the identity of research participants will be protected and that specific information contributed by participants will not be disclosed in ways that may identify them (Iphofen, 2009). This can be a contentious issue in research with children and young people, partly because of the possibility that some children may disclose information that leads to the intentional breaking of confidentiality. This could occur if there is disclosure related to abuse or neglect, or where participants are deemed to be at risk of harm. To address this, some researchers invoke the notion of 'limited confidentiality' (Noble-Carr, 2006), where children are informed of what information will be regarded as confidential and what, if any, will be reported.

Other risks to confidentiality come from the expectations of adults (such as teachers and parents) that they have the right to know what children and young people have said or done within the research (Hill, 2005). Some studies report that both children and adults expect this to occur. For example, Christensen and Prout (2002: 486), describe research in a school where teachers questioned the researcher about what children had said, 'as if a promise of confidentiality to children could be bracketed out, or superseded ... that it was not to be taken all that seriously'. In the same vein, the Children's Reference Group established by Moore and colleagues (2008), raised concerns about confidentiality, noting particularly that breaches of confidentiality by adults often had minimal consequences.

In New Zealand the Treaty of Waitangi that finally reconciled the Maori people and the European invaders acts as a form of guidance for ethical participative research, with its principles including partnership and active participation. Time and again, New Zealand researchers engaged in participative research, whether with children and young people or broadly with the community, turn to the Treaty for wise counsel. Partnerships are seen as forming the foundation of an obligation to act in good faith and make informed decisions through consultation. Embedded in the Treaty is the concept of reciprocity (Lee et al., 2013). The approach requires researchers to pay attention to: noticing, recognising, responding, recording and re-visiting, and builds upon relationships and holistic development that strengthen the child, the family and the community. Such relationships are at the core of ethical approaches to research with children and young people.

A range of key ethical issues require consideration when developing procedures for authentic participative research with children and young people. At one level, researchers will need to meet the guidelines and regulations set out by the relevant institutional ethics committee. At another level, researchers need to rely on situational ethics, and be alert to ethical issues that emerge during the research as well as a range of strategies to address these. Working from both levels should make it possible for researchers to develop an ethical protocol that will 'enable gatekeepers to feel secure in allowing access to the children they are responsible for' (Leeson, 2007: 140).

Key points

- Adopting approaches based on ethical symmetry requires the consideration of both the requirements of institutional ethical committees as well as the everyday ethical interactions and decisions in which researchers engage.
- These considerations provide the basis for addressing, but not always resolving, ethical dilemmas that arise during research.
- Ethical research is based on relationships – both with potential participants (children and young people) and those who work with and care for them.
- Ethical relationships are characterised by trust, respect and reciprocity.

References

Ahsan, M. (2009) The potential and challenges of rights-based research with children and young people: Experiences from Bangladesh. *Children's Geographies*, 7: 391–403.

Alderson, P. and Morrow, V. (2004) *Ethics, social research and consulting with children and young people*. Barkingside: Barnardos.

Beauchamp, T. and Childress, J. (2008) *Principles of biomedical ethics*. 6th edition. New York: Oxford University Press.

British Educational Research Association (2004) *Revised ethical guidelines for educational research*. www.bera.ac.uk/publications/ethical-guidelines, accessed 16th August, 2013.

Cahill, C. (2007a) Doing research with young people: Participatory research and rituals of collective work. *Children's Geographies*, 5(3): 297–312.

Cahill, C. (2007b) The personal is political. *Gender, Place and Culture*, 14(3): 267–92.

Carr, M. and Lee, W. (2012) *Learning stories: Constructing learner identity in early education*. London: Sage.

Christensen, P. and Prout, A. (2002) Working with ethical symmetry in social research with children. *Childhood*, 9(4): 477–97.

Cocks, A. (2006) The ethical maze: Finding an inclusive path towards gaining children's agreement to research participation. *Childhood*, 13(2): 247–66.

Conroy, H. and Harcourt, D. (2009) Informed agreement to participate: Beginning the partnership with children in research. *Early Child Development and Care*, 179(2): 157–65.

David, M., Edwards, R. and Alldred, P. (2001) Children and school-based research: 'Informed consent' or 'educated consent'? *British Educational Research Journal*, 27(3): 347–65.

Dockett, S., Einarsdóttir, J. and Perry, B. (2012a) Young children's decisions about research participation: Opting out. *International Journal of Early Years Education*, 20(3): 244–56.

Dockett, S., Perry, B., Kearney, E., Hampshire, A., Mason, J. and Schmied, V. (2009) Researching with families: Ethical issues and situations. *Contemporary Issues in Early Childhood*, 19(4): 353–65.

Dockett, S., Perry, B. and Kearney, E. (2012b) Promoting children's informed assent in research participation. *International Journal of Qualitative Studies in Education*, 26(7): 802–28. doi.org/10.1080/09518398.2012.666289, accessed 31st March 31, 2014.

Edwards, R. and Mauther, M. (2012) Ethics and feminist research: Theory and practice. In M. Birch, T. Miller, M. Mauther and J. Jessop (Eds) *Ethics and qualitative research: Theory and practice*. 2nd edition. London: Routledge, pp. 14–28.

Gilligan, C. (1982) *In a different voice: Psychological theory and women's development*. Cambridge, MA: Harvard University Press.

Gorman, S. (2007) Managing research ethics: A head-on collision? In A. Campbell and S. Groundwater-Smith (Eds) *An ethical approach to practitioner research*. London: Routledge, pp. 8–23.

Graham, A. and Fitzgerald, R. (2010) Children's participation in research: Some possibilities and constraints in the current Australian research environment. *Journal of Sociology*, 46: 133–47.

Graham, A., Powell, M., Taylor, N., Anderson, D. and Fitzgerald, R. (2013) *Ethical research involving children*. Florence: UNICEF office of Research–Innocenti. http://childethics.com, accessed 2nd April, 2014.

Grinyer, A. (2002) The anonymity of research participants: Assumptions, ethics and practicalities. *Social Research Update*, 36. http://sru.soc.surrey.ac.uk/SRU36.html, accessed 4th August, 2013.

Gubrium, A. and Harper, K. (2013) *Participatory visual and digital methods*. Walnut Creek, CA: Left Coast Press.

Habermas, J. (1979) *Communication and the evolution of society*. London: Heinemann.

Heath, S., Charles, V., Crow, G. and Wiles, R. (2007) Informed consent, gatekeepers and go-betweens: Negotiating consent in child- and youth-oriented institutions. *British Educational Research Journal*, 33(3): 403–17.

Hill, M. (2005) Ethical considerations in researching children's perspectives. In S. Greene and D. Hogan (Eds) *Researching children's experience: Approaches and methods*. London: Sage, pp. 61–86.

Iphofen, R. (2009) *Ethical decision making in social research*. Basingstoke, UK: Palgrave Macmillan.

Lansdown, G. (2005) *The evolving capacities of the child*. Florence, Italy: UNICEF Innocenti Research Centre. www.bernardvanleer.org/files/crc/4%20Gerison_Lansdown.pdf, accessed 15th September, 2013.

Lee, W., Carr, M., Soutar, B. and Mitchell, L. (2013) *Understanding the Te Whãriki approach: Early years education in practice*. Abingdon, UK: Routledge.

Leeson, C. (2007) Going round in circles: Key issues in the development of an ethical protocol for research involving young children. In A. Campbell and S. Groundwater-Smith (Eds) *An ethical approach to practitioner research*. London: Routledge, pp. 129–43.

Linklater, A. (2005) Dialogic politics and the civilising process. *Review of International Studies*, 31(1): 141–54.

Mason, J. and Urquhart, R. (2001) Developing a model for participation by children in research on decision making. *Children Australia*, 26(4): 16–21.

Moore, T., McArthur, M. and Noble-Carr, D. (2008) Little voices and big ideas: Lessons learned from children about research. *International Journal of Qualitative Methods*, 7(2): 77–91. http://ejournals.library.ualberta.ca/index.php/IJQM/article/view/1941/1362, accessed 3rd October, 2013.

Morrow, V. (2004) The ethics of social research with children and young people – an overview. www.ciimu.org/wellchi/reports/wsh1/pdfs/pd%20securizats/morrows.pdf, accessed 14th May, 2013.

Morrow, V. (2013) What's in a number: Unsettling the boundaries of age. *Childhood*, 20(2): 151–5.

Morrow, V. and Richards, M. (1996) The ethics of social research with children: An overview. *Children & Society*, 10(2): 90–105.

Noble-Carr, D. (2006) *Engaging children in research on sensitive issues*. Institute of Child Protection Studies, Australian Catholic University and ACT Department of Disability, Housing and Community Services. www.acu.edu.au/icps, accessed 3rd September, 2013.

Scott, D. (2005) Inter-organisational collaboration in family-centred practice: A framework for analysis and action. *Australian Social Work*, 58(2): 132–41.

Suaalii, T. and Mavoa, H. (2001) Who says yes? Collective and individual framing of Pacific children's consent to, and participation in, research in New Zealand. *ChildreNZ Issues*, 5(1): 39–42.

United Nations (1989) *Convention on the rights of the child*. New York. www.unicef.org/crc, accessed 15th October, 2013.

Vitiello, B. (2003) Ethical considerations in psychopharmacological research involving children and adolescents. *Psychopharmacology*, 171(1): 86–91.

Viviers, A. and Lombard, A. (2013) The ethics of children's participation: Fundamental to children's rights realization in Africa. *International Social Work*, 56(1): 7–21.

Wiles, E. (2013) *What are qualitative research ethics?* London: Bloomsbury Academic.

Wiles, R., Coffey, A., Robison, J. and Heath, S. (2011) Anonymisation and visual images: Issues of respect, 'voice' and protection. *International Journal of Social Research Methodology*, 15(1): 41–53.

FOUR

DESIGNING A PROJECT WITH CHILDREN AND YOUNG PEOPLE

INVESTIGATING THE 'RESEARCHABLE QUESTION'

This chapter explores the potential for children and young people to be involved across the research process – starting with project design and the identification of researchable questions. We acknowledge issues of power and control, and share examples of research that recognises these. The chapter concludes with a discussion of participation and examples of the multiple ways in which children and young people may participate across the research process.

It addresses:

- Identifying research questions.
- What makes a question researchable?
- Issues of power.
- Voice.
- Researching *with* children and young people.
- Differences in participation.
- Involving children and young people across the research process.

Identifying research questions

There are many definitions and many ways of conceptualising participatory research with children and young people. Several typologies have been outlined in Chapter 1. These provide one means to consider the ways in which children and young people may be involved across the research process. While recognising the importance of these descriptive frameworks, there are also calls for more nuanced or sophisticated models of participation that reflect the complexity of efforts to engage with children and young people in research (Graham and Fitzgerald, 2010; McCarry, 2012; Thomas, 2012; Tisdall, 2013). Such models recognise the transformative potential of participatory research, but also acknowledge that much of this research is highly managed by adults, heavily imbued with power relationships and that participation often remains 'a way of talking about rather than doing research' (Cooke and Kothari, 2001: 32).

Identifying appropriate questions is a critical step in any research. Deciding on research questions is often seen to be the starting point for initiating a research project. However, before research questions can be established, we contend that much needs to occur. This includes developing an awareness of the area or topic to be researched and, when researching with children and young people, understanding the relevance, importance or priority of the research topic for them. Such understanding comes from dialogue with children and young people and recognition of the importance of insider knowledge (Gubrium and Harper, 2013).

In some instances, children and young people are encouraged to identify research questions and, with appropriate training, to undertake research themselves. For example, the Children's Research Centre (Kellett, 2005, 2011) has developed a programme of research training for children and young people that equips them with a range of research skills, including some background in framing research questions. The development of a 'think sheet' which helps children and young people identify their areas of research interest and narrow this down to researchable questions is a key aspect of the approach.

Perusal of the archives of the Children's Research Centre (www.open.ac.uk/researchprojects/childrens-research-centre) reveals a wide range of research initiated and undertaken by children and young people, in response to questions they have identified as relevant and meaningful for them. These include investigations of food choices for school dinners, children's views about religion, social media sites, the impact of classroom environment and young people's awareness of poverty in Africa.

A recent study of cyberbullying designed and undertaken by young people (Tarapdar et al., 2013), also illustrates the power of young people framing and asking questions that matter for them. These researchers argue that young people ask different questions from adult researchers and pursue research addressing these using different language and approaches, generating different data, analysis and conclusions.

It is often the case that research questions have to be decided in advance of applications to funding bodies and/or institutional ethics committees. In many cases, it can be very difficult to consult with potential participants prior to making these applications. A consequence is that research questions and projects will often be decided well before children and young people are involved. One interpretation of this situation could be that any such research is not genuinely participatory as it has not involved children and young people in all phases of the process. An alternative interpretation is that participation can mean different things for different people in different contexts: participation can be enacted in different ways.

What makes a question researchable?

Researchable questions derive from uncertainty about an issue or issues. When children and young people are engaged in participatory research, the research purpose needs to be meaningful for them, as well as researchers. In other words, children and young people need to regard the topic as relevant, worthy of investment and likely to lead to change.

The research context, potential participants, availability of time and resources, as well as the perceived sensitivity of the issues, the overarching philosophy or research paradigm, the preferred methods, the innovation and/or novelty of the project as well as its relevance and perceived value are among the many elements that impact on the researchability of a particular question.

A second issue relates not to the researchability of a question, but to who decides what is to be researched. Clearly, there are ethical issues to be considered, and institutional ethics committees have guidelines about the nature of research that is considered acceptable and appropriate. As well, if research is to be funded, the priorities of funding bodies may influence the research focus and approach.

Beyond this, participatory research must involve discussion with the community within which we want to work. There will be occasions when these discussions cannot occur before funding and ethical approval has been attained. However, it is critical that some engagement with the community occurs at a point before the research focus becomes fixed.

The notion of community is broad. It may include seeking advice from children and young people and it also may include consultation with a geographic or cultural community. Research undertaken in Indigenous contexts, for example, requires 'an ethical undertaking to work with the community, define the research topic, agree on conduct, share analysis of findings, and the distribution of outcomes' (Wilson and Wilks, 2013: 145).

The importance of working with the community is emphasised by Wilson and Wilks (2013), who describe the processes of integrating consultation with a local Australian Aboriginal community with the requirements of a university ethics committee, to create a space for the involvement of Aboriginal children and young people in research about their learning experiences at school. Cognisant of the importance of working with the local community, these researchers established a two-stage process, first seeking approval from the university ethics committee to undertake a feasibility study with members of the local Aboriginal community in order to propose, discuss and establish guidelines for the research. This was undertaken as a deliberate strategy to position the community and 'its needs, perspectives, practices and values at the forefront of the research' (Wilson and Wilks, 2013: 146). As a result, an agreed research design was generated, and an ongoing consultative structure put in place, enabling community members to act as a reference group and monitor the research. Only when these processes were in place did the researchers then submit another ethics application outlining the agreed research elements.

In a similar example, Roberts et al. (2013) describe the process of seeking advice from a group of young people about a proposed doctoral research project. Initial institutional approval was gained to talk with the young people to ascertain their views about the proposed topic, preferred strategies for investigating it, and the ways in which they might be willing to be involved in the research. Their advice provided the basis for the development of the full research proposal. The young people have continued to be involved in the project as an advisory group.

Ethical commitments to work with the community are central to research involving Maori participants. This is seen in calls to ensure that such research is 'based on Maori perspectives and on Maori positions on issues and concerns ... consistent with Maori values and beliefs; validates Maori knowledge; is widely acceptable to Maori communities; and supports Maori aspirations' (Te Maro, 2010: 47). Key elements of this approach are respect and collaboration – suggesting the importance of working with the community in order to establish not only what is to be researched, but also how this is done (Ritchie and Rau, 2008; Smith, 2012).

The same respectful consultation and negotiation with children and young people is evident across a range of projects supported by the Centre for Children and Young People (Graham and Fitzgerald, 2010) and the Institute of Child Protection (Moore et al., 2011). As well as consultation with a range of children and young people about research focus and design, a youth consultative committee – Young People Big Voice – has an integral role in the research of the Centre for Children and Young People, while specific reference groups have been established for projects undertaken with the Institute of Child Protection.

One of the challenges acknowledged by these, and other, groups relates to the representativeness of those who participate in advisory or reference groups. While there is much support for working with these groups, there is also caution about considering children and young people as a homogeneous group and expecting that children and young people are experts on any but their own lives (Scourfield, 2010).

Issues of power

One of the features of participatory research with children and young people is its claim to redress some of the power differentials identified in other research. Indeed, some of the early aims related to participatory research included empowering children and young people and challenging 'unequal power relations' through use of 'child-friendly' methods (Barker and Weller, 2003: 36). While these have been admirable aims, more recent conceptualisations of power and power relations have moved away from notions of power as a commodity, possessed by some (adults, researchers), exercised over others (children, research participants) and subject to re-distribution. In their critique of power relations, Cooke and Kothari (2001) acknowledged that adults do seem to have more power than children and young people, but emphasised that children and young people themselves are not powerless. Rather they urged recognition of the many ways in which power is exercised by children, young people and adults, through points of resistance and confrontation, as well as compliance.

Recent discussions of power in research with children and young people draw on Foucault's (1983) notion of 'power as a diverse, ambivalent web of relations, rather than a unidirectional force of domination' (Gallagher, 2008: 144), emphasising the dynamic, shifting and multiple layers in which power is evident in interactions between and among children, young people and adults. As a result, power is conceived of as a form of action, exercised in multiple ways, by all participants. This can include resistance, disobedience and subversion, as well as compliance. In several circumstances, resistance can be regarded as a positive exercise of power. However, it is important to remember that while resistance can be liberating for some, it can also marginalise others. Viewed in this way, power can be regarded as both productive and repressive (Foucault, 1983), offering opportunities for action, but also constraining possible actions. Power is dynamic and relational, and often complicated.

Examples of children and young people exercising power through action can be noted in the ways they adopt, change or redirect the tasks in which they are engaged. For example, young children involved in a drawing activity have been observed to draw and talk about the topic at hand, but then scribble all over the drawing. Other children are very adept at non-replies to questions that have been asked, even when they have agreed to participate. Still others have a knack of turning all interactions back to their favourite topic, and young people are quite capable of contributing non-responses, or irrelevant responses to questionnaires.

In an investigation of their local community, the girls in Figure 4.1 were eager to participate in a photo tour of local sites, which they had helped to plan. At one point, they were observed taking multiple photos of each other leaning

Figure 4.1 Playing the game

over a sign in the park. This activity resulted in a great deal of laughter as they prompted each other to take up different poses. When adults accompanying the tour happened to pass nearby the girls quickly redirected their cameras to different features of the park. As the adults moved away, they resumed their game.

Edwards and Mauther (2002: 27) urge that 'rather than ignoring or blurring power positions, ethical practice needs to pay attention to them'. Participatory research does provide opportunities to do this, as we attend to the many ways in which all participants enact relationships. However, we need to be wary of assuming that participatory research necessarily negates issues of power.

Holland et al. (2010) addressed these issues in their project entitled *(Extra)ordinary Lives*, which was conducted in the Cardiff (Wales) area and aimed to explore the ordinary, everyday lives of young people who were looked after by the local authority in foster, residential or kinship care. The researchers conceived of power as dynamic and relational. They sought to understand the 'between-ness' of the various manifestations of power in a variety of situations and encounters ranging from car journeys to conversations within the home. They gathered rich longitudinal data with a small group of eight young people and were interested in their everyday relationships, cultures and identities in different contexts, and, in particular, how they managed and negotiated these in relation to their positioning. While not reporting on the findings of this complex study, we cite it here as an example of the range of challenges and dilemmas that it generated, including: the impact that the participants had upon one another, such that they at times spoke over and disrupted the rights of their peers; the breaches of confidentiality in spite of seeking for participants to analyse only their own data; and, finding ways to integrate many different narratives into a complex whole.

Among other studies that have highlighted issues related to power, Porter and her colleagues (2010) described the dangerous potential of power in their study of children's mobility in sub-Saharan Africa. The project aimed to generate evidence to improve children's mobility and transport access, and through this, to improve access to health and education services. One element of the project involved children as researchers, interviewing their peers. The researchers indicated that the political arena of their work positioned it as 'suspect – even dangerous' from the perspectives of some adults in light of traditional social positions within some communities, with the potential to 'subvert the traditional view of children's proper role as supporters, not leaders' (Porter et al., 2010: 217).

Voice

One of the signs of the shift in the conceptualisation of power is seen in problematisation of the terms *voice, children's voices* and *listening to children's voices*.

While the principles underpinning much of this work remain, there is growing recognition that voice has become a trope and, sometimes, a mask for adult interpretation of children and young people's perspectives. Critics note that reporting children and young people's voices often involves adults making some judgements about interpretations, as well as what is reported and how – in effect mediating between participants and audience (I'Anson, 2013; Tisdall, 2012). James (2007: 264–5) argues that:

> although children's words quoted in research may be 'authentic' – in that they are an accurate record of what children have said – it remains the case that the words and phrases have been chosen by the researcher and have been inserted into the text to illustrate an argument or underline a point of view. The point of view being presented is, therefore, the view of the author, not that of the child.

What does it mean to listen to children's voices? At a methodological level, Tangen (2008) proposes that it requires genuine and active listening (Rinaldi, 2005), with adult researchers needing to learn how to listen, not just to words, but also to the many ways in which children and young people express themselves. Interpreting and reporting also require a great deal of considered reflection, balancing researcher and participant perspectives, contextual influences, as well as individual and social dynamics.

Researching *with* children and young people

Participatory research with children and young people has been conceptualised in many ways. A range of typologies and frameworks have been described and these have been influential in guiding practice around participation. Some of the best known typologies are: Hart's (1992) ladder of participation, which outlined eight rungs of participation, starting with three forms of non-participation and leading to the highest level of collaboration between adults and children and young people; Treseder's (1997) realignment of the top five levels of Hart's ladder into a circle to demonstrate that different forms of participation did not necessarily reflect a hierarchy; and Shier's (2001) focus on the roles of adults in promoting different levels of participation. More recently, Lansdown (2005: 14) has proposed three levels of participation – encompassing consultative, participatory and self-initiated processes – with each considered to be 'valid and [to] necessitate a commitment to listening to children and taking them seriously, but allow[ing] for differing degrees of actual engagement'.

Drawing on several typologies, Table 4.1 presents an overview of potential forms of participation and what this participation might look like at different

Table 4.1 Forms of participation

Type of participation	Form of participation		
	Children and young people are consulted about the research	Children and young people and adults collaborate in the research	Children and young people have ownership of the research
Research design, development, and planning	Adults seek perspectives of children and young people and may reflect these in research decisions	Children and young people have opportunities to be involved in research decisions. Decisions are adult-led, but views of children and young people do influence research directions and outcomes	Adults act as facilitators as children and young people build research skills, identify research areas and undertake research
Timing of participation	Consultation at key decision-making points	Throughout the research	From the initiation through to research completion and dissemination
Data generation	Children and young people provide advice on data generation – for example, how data is generated, who participates and when	Data are co-produced by children and young people and adults. Children and young people may be involved in designing data collection tools and in data generation	Children and young people determine what data is generated, how, when and by whom
Data analysis	May provide advice about data analysis and interpretation	Adults and children and young people collaborate in data analysis	Children and young people guide data analysis
Reporting and dissemination	Children and young people may be consulted about the report or plans for dissemination	Children and young people may participate in planning strategies for reporting and dissemination. May also have a role in designing the report format and in disseminating results	Children and young people are considered to be owners of the research and take the lead in reporting and dissemination

points in the research process. These reflect Lansdown's three levels, renamed to incorporate elements of several typologies. The columns of the table consider each of these levels and what researching with children and young people may involve. One of the aims of the table is to illustrate the range of ways in which children and young people may be involved in research.

Consulting with children and young people: an example

The recent redevelopment of the Australian Museum provided opportunities to consult young children about their experiences and expectations of the museum space (Dockett et al., 2011). Consultation took many forms as children as young as two years, and their carers, chose to engage in a range of arts-based activities, such as drawing, painting and construction, as well as conversations, photo tours and the compilation of journals about their visits and interactions. On a page in his journal (Figure 4.2), Angus (aged four) dictated the following comment to his mother, to accompany a photograph he had taken. In response to being asked about what he liked best at the Museum, he replied:

> Looking at crocodiles. Because they snap and I like them. I like the dead ones because I can touch them. But I want to make it real.

What I like the best of all at the museum

Figure 4.2 Looking at crocodiles

Children, young people and adults collaborating in research

Collaboration can occur in co-construction of data. In the following example, Figure 4.3, young people were invited to collaborate with their teacher to generate data about the ways in which they travelled to school. The young people worked with the teacher to design a survey and distribute this to their peers. When the data were collated, they designed the format for the presentation of the research. The PowerPoint presentation was set on automatic play and other children and young people were invited to view it.

Figure 4.3 Reporting the transport survey

Children and young people having some ownership of research processes

Children and young people can build research skills in many ways. The children in Figure 4.4 are engaged in a process of sorting waste into the categories of recyclables and non-recyclables. Their participation includes elements of conducting the research and data generation. In presenting their results, they commented on the ways they had chosen to categorise and analyse their data.

As research tools, typologies that reflect a participation hierarchy have been criticised for promoting a linear representation of participation, based on the assumption that more intense participation is necessarily better or more genuine than lower levels of participation. There is also concern that such models regard children and young people as homogeneous groups, masking diversity.

Figure 4.4 Sorting recyclables from non-recyclables

Further, there is concern that issues of power are considered in terms of power between children and adults, rather than emphasising the complex, multi-layers of power relations between and among children, young people and adults.

Typologies can both limit and extend the ways in which we consider participatory research. If they are applied rigidly, it is possible to reduce participatory research to a series of steps or actions to be applied across contexts, or to enact research in ways that promote divisions between children and adults. However, typologies can also be used to provoke critically reflective practice as researchers and/or participants examine their actions and expectations, their positioning and assumptions. They can also remind us that multiple forms of participation may be involved within the same project; that the nature of participation can change over time; and that boundaries between the different levels of participation are often blurred.

Differences in participation

In seeking a more nuanced understanding of research with children and young people, several researchers have questioned the assumption that the aspiration of participatory research involves children and young people at all levels, all the time (Graham and Fitzgerald, 2010; Thomas, 2012; Tisdall, 2013). McCarry (2012: 65) argues:

if researchers want to involve young people in an empowering and collaborative way, we have to be more flexible and accommodating ... [and question] the models of participation which assume that the greater the level of involvement the more inclusive and empowering it is for young people, and the stronger the research is as a result.

Such views recognise that participation can, and will, be different for different individuals or groups, may change over time and may even involve different levels of participation at the same time. In other words, participation is not an *all or nothing* phenomenon. Nor is it necessarily *better* than other forms of research (Gallacher and Gallagher, 2008).

Regardless of the topic or approach, effective participatory research with children and young people must reflect standards of good quality research. This includes being grounded in ethical practice, generating data that is systematic and valid, and using appropriately rigorous strategies for analysis. In addition, participatory research with children and young people is based on genuine respect for participants, with regard for their knowledge and expertise (Beazley et al., 2011). Further, it is underpinned by commitments to reporting and dissemination that aim to make a positive difference (Dockett and Perry, 2014).

These elements are echoed in several key themes identified by Graham and Fitzgerald (2010) from their work in Australia, where children and young people sought:

1. Respect – as individuals who could make valuable contributions. Expectations of respect included having opportunities to make choices about participation, and having those choices respected.
2. Genuine opportunities to participate and, through this, to generate change. Participation was linked to a clear purpose, for participants as well as for researchers.
3. Access to information in order to make informed decisions both about and within the research.
4. Opportunities to engage in shared decision-making, rather than assuming responsibility for decision-making.
5. Opportunities to engage in collective and collaborative processes.

These researchers frame children and young people's participation as a process of recognition 'of who they are (their identity), of their place in social and political life (their status) and of what they have to say (their voice)' (Graham and Fitzgerald, 2010: 348).

Involving children and young people across the research process

Participation is sometimes seen at the beginning of the research process, when children and young people may be consulted about the topic or their interest,

Table 4.2 Children and young people's participation across the research process

Research process	Collaboration/participation	Ethical issues	Knowledge generation
Research design, development and planning	Who plans/designs the research? What questions are investigated? Who decides these? Are research questions developed collaboratively? How does research as a practice, reflect collective action? What opportunities are there for capacity building, to enable children and young people to develop the skills needed to participate in the research in multiple ways?	How are the requirements of ethics committees explained, interpreted and met? How are the principles for everyday ethical practice developed and implemented? What role do community ethics play in the design of the project?	Are research goals developed collaboratively? How are decisions made about what is worth researching, what is researchable, and what will lead to change? Who makes these decisions? What is interesting and important to those involved?
Data generation	Who generates data? Who participates? What processes promote opportunities for participation?	Who participates? What training/support is provided for those generating data? What ethical principles apply? What processes are in place to seek consent/assent? How are these processes interpreted? What opportunities are included for ongoing reflection about ethical issues?	How are insider and outsider perspectives reflected? Do participants guide what data is produced? Are there opportunities for the interplay of participant, researcher and other perspectives?

Research process	Collaboration/participation	Ethical issues	Knowledge generation
Data analysis	How are participants involved in discussion and analysis of the data? How is this facilitated? For example, is there opportunity for the participatory editing of visual and/or verbal texts?	Who participates in data analysis? How is this promoted? What skills are needed for facilitators to make this possible and fair? What opportunities exist for discussion of how the data is to be presented, interpreted and used in next phases of research? Role of researchers	What is documented? How is this presented? What opportunities are included for the negotiation of meaning, such as member checking, or seeking input from a reference group?
Dissemination and reporting	Are there opportunities to develop multiple research products, with multiple research authors, designed for multiple audiences? Who makes decisions about audiences and outcomes? Is reporting regarded as an opportunity to gauge the impact of research?	Who owns the data? Who can/has the authority to speak to the data and for participants? How is the data presented? In what forms? How are issues of confidentiality, anonymity and privacy resolved?	Who has access to the knowledge generated? Does reporting reflect accessible language and/or approaches? Does reporting include affective and aesthetic elements? How can informed action occur as a result of the research? What recognition is afforded to children and young people as a result of their participation in research?

Adapted from Gubrium and Harper (2013): 21–2

or at the end, when results may be presented and their reactions sought. While this may promote some genuine engagement from children and young people, it could easily become tokenistic. An alternative is to consider how children and young people may be involved across the process of research. This is not to suggest that all children and young people should engage in the same ways, or even all phases of the project. Rather, we pose a number of questions to be asked at each phase of the research, with the aim of challenging practice that can be taken for granted, and exploring opportunities for children and young people to participate in research in meaningful ways. These questions are presented in Table 4.2, in relation to elements of the research process and the principles of collaboration/participation, ethics and knowledge generation.

These questions – and the responses they provoke – reflect growing recognition of the complexity of participatory research with children and young people, and accept that the concept of researching with children and young people will involve 'a wide range of different phenomena in different social settings: private and public, structured and unstructured, formal and informal' (Thomas, 2012: 463).

Key points

- There are many ways of conceptualising participatory research with children and young people, and many ways of considering how children and young people may participate in research.
- The focus of participatory research with children and young people needs to be relevant, meaningful and interesting for them.
- Participatory research involves connection and consultation with relevant communities.
- Power relations in research are often complex and multi-layered. It is not simply the case that adults exert power over children and young people. Participatory research does not necessarily overcome issues of power.
- The problematisation of voice in participatory research with children and young people has prompted attention to active listening and to exploration of the mediating role of adults in this research.

References

Barker, J. and Weller, S. (2003) 'Never work with children?': The geography of methodological issues in research with children. *Qualitative Research*, 3(2): 207–27.

Beazley, H., Bessell, S., Ennew, J. and Waterson, R. (2011) How are the human rights of children related to research methodology? In A. Invernizzi and J. Williams (Eds) *The human rights of children: From visions to implementation*. Farnham, UK: Ashgate, pp. 159–78.

Cooke, B. and Kothari, U. (2001) The case for participation as tyranny. In B. Cooke and U. Kothari (Eds) *Participation: The new tyranny.* London: Zed Books, pp. 1–15.

Dockett, S., Main, S. and Kelly, L. (2011) Consulting young children: Experiences from a museum. *Visitor Studies,* 14(1): 13–33.

Dockett, S. and Perry, B. (2014) Participatory rights-based research: Learning from young children's perspectives in research that affects their lives. In O. Saracho (Ed.) *Handbook of research methods in early childhood education.* Charlotte, NC: Information Age Press.

Edwards, R. and Mauther, M. (2002) Ethics and feminist research: Theory and practice. In M. Birch, T. Miller, M. Mauther and J. Jessop (Eds) *Ethics and qualitative research: Theory and practice.* 2nd edition. London: Routledge, pp. 14–28.

Foucault, M. (1983) The subject and power. In H.L. Dreyfus and P. Rabinow (Eds) *Michel Foucault: Beyond structuralism and hermeneutics.* Chicago, IL: University of Chicago Press.

Gallacher, L-A. and Gallagher, M. (2008) Methodological immaturity in childhood research: Thinking through 'participatory methods'. *Childhood,* 15(4): 499–516.

Gallagher, M. (2008) 'Power is not an evil': Rethinking power in participatory methods. *Children's Geographies,* 6(2): 137–50.

Graham, A. and Fitzgerald, R. (2010) Progressing children's participation: Exploring the potential of a dialogical turn. *Childhood,* 17(3): 343–59.

Gubrium, A. and Harper, K. (2013) *Participatory visual and digital methods.* Walnut Creek, CA: Left Coast Press.

Hart, R. (1992) *Children's participation: From tokenism to citizenship.* Geneva: UNICEF International Child Development Centre. www.unicef-irc.org/publications/100, accessed 2nd September, 2013.

Holland, S., Renold, E., Ross, N. and Hillman, A. (2010) Power, agency and participatory agendas: A critical exploration of young people's engagement in participative qualitative research. *Childhood,* 17(3): 360–75.

I'Anson, J. (2013) Beyond the child's voice: Towards an ethics for children's participation rights. *Global Studies of Childhood,* 3(2): 104–14.

James, A. (2007) Giving voice to children's voices: Practices and problems, pitfalls and potentials. *American Anthropologist,* 109(2): 261–72.

Kellett, M. (2005) *How to develop children as researchers.* London: Sage.

Kellett, M. (2011) Empowering children and young people as researchers: Overcoming barriers and building capacity. *Child Indicators Research,* 4(2): 205–19.

Lansdown, G. (2005) *Can you hear me? The right of young children to participate in decisions affecting them.* Working paper 36. Bernard van Leer Foundation, The Hague. www.bernardvanleer.org/Can_you_hear_me_The_right_of_young_

children_to_participate_in_decisions_affecting_them, accessed 5th August, 2013.

McCarry, M. (2012) Who benefits? A critical reflection of children and young people's participation in sensitive research. *International Journal of Social Research Methodology*, 15(1): 55–68.

Moore,T., Saunders, V. and McArthur, M. (2011) Championing choice – lessons learned from children and young people about research and their involvement. *Child Indicators Research*, 4: 249–67.

Porter, G., Hampshire, K., Bourdillon, M., Robson, E., Munthali, A., Abane, A. and Mashiri, M. (2010) Children as research collaborators: Issues and reflections from a mobility study in sub-Saharan Africa. *American Journal of Community Psychology*, 46: 215–27.

Rinaldi, C. (2005) *In dialogue with Reggio Emilia: Listening, researching, and learning*, New York: Routledge.

Ritchie, J. and Rau, C. (2008) *Whakawhanaungatanga – partnerships in bicultural development in early childhood care and education*. www.tlri.org.nz/tlri-research/research-completed/ece-sector/whakawhanaungatanga%E2%80%94-partnerships-bicultural-development, accessed 31st September, 2013.

Roberts, M., Perry, B. and Dockett, S. (2013) Involving young people as partners in research: Reflections on a learning experience. Unpublished manuscript.

Scourfield, P. (2010) A critical reflection on the involvement of 'experts by experience' in inspection. *British Journal of Social Work*, 40: 1890–907.

Shier, H. (2001) Pathways to participation: Opening, opportunities and obligations. *Children & Society*, 15: 107–17.

Smith, L.T. (2012) *Decolonising methodologies: Research and Indigenous peoples*. 2nd edition. London: Zed Books.

Tangen, R. (2008) Listening to children's voices in educational research: Some theoretical and methodological problems. *European Journal of Special Needs Education*, 23(2): 157–66.

Tarapdar, S., Kellett, M. and Young People (2013) Cyberbullying: Insights and age-comparison indicators from a youth-led study in England. *Child Indicators Research*, 6: 461–77.

Te Maro, P. (2010) Involving children and young persons who are Maori in research. In J. Loveridge (Ed.) *Involving children and young people in research in educational settings* pp. 47–66. www.educationcounts.govt.nz/publications/schooling/80440/chapter-3, accessed 3rd July, 2014.

Thomas, N. (2012) Love, rights and solidarity: Studying children's participation using Honneth's theory of recognition. *Childhood*, 19(4): 453–66.

Tisdall, E.K.M. (2012) The challenge and challenging of childhood studies? Learning from disability studies and research with disabled children. *Children & Society*, 26: 181–91.

Tisdall, E.K.M. (2013) The transformation of participation? Exploring the potential of 'transformative participation' for theory and practice around children and young people's participation. *Global Studies of Childhood*, 3(2): 183–93.

Treseder, P. (1997) *Empowering children and young people: Training manual.* London: Save the Children.

Wilson, K. and Wilks, J. (2013) Research with Indigenous children and young people in schools: Ethical and methodological considerations. *Global Studies of Childhood*, 3(2): 142–52.

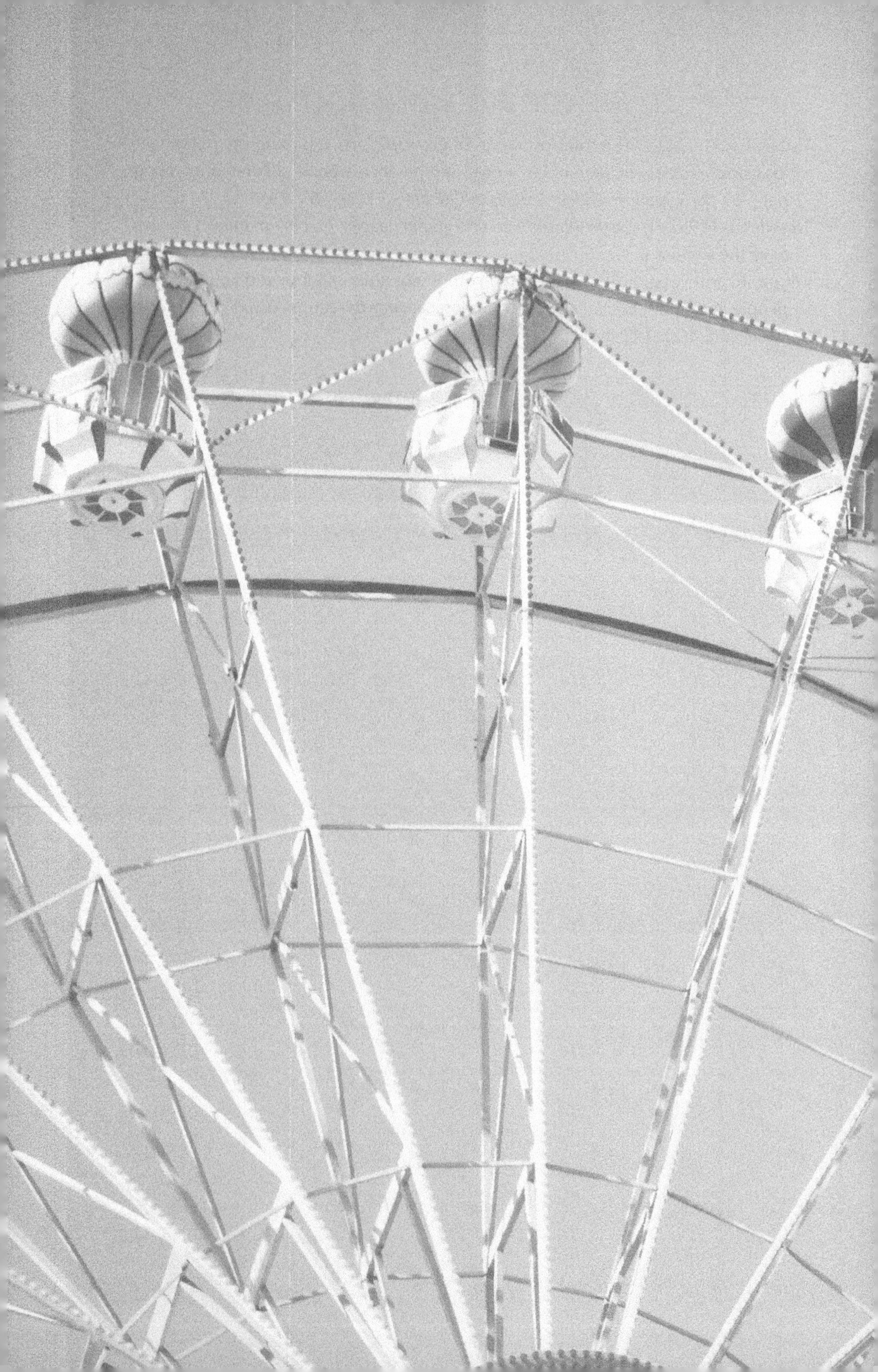

FIVE

A POLITICAL ECOLOGY OF ACCESS AND COOPERATION

This chapter focuses on issues of access and cooperation that are fundamentally questions of who participates, where, in what ways and to what ends. While collaboration is a hallmark of participatory research, researchers have highlighted the barriers of specific contexts in terms of power relations, the difficult circumstances of particular groups and how the focus of inquiry may delimit participation. In this chapter we conceptualise the research context as multi-dimensional and comprising a political ecology.

It addresses:

- The nature of the context: researching with children in educational, community and social contexts in terms of political ecology.
- Access and cooperation in context.
- Working with issues of access and cooperation.
- Negotiating access: the importance of time and relationships.
- Creating accessible spaces.
- Making participation accessible.
- Different ways to participate.

The nature of the context: researching with children in educational, community and social contexts

Researchers work with children and young people in a broad range of contexts, including early childhood settings, schools, children's and youth services, hospitals, nursing homes, juvenile justice facilities, immigration detention, family services, out of home care, sports clubs, workplaces and online communities. These are very different contexts to work in and perhaps more importantly, they are not first and foremost places of research. For children and young people they are places to work, learn, play, fear, find comfort, be confined, miss home and get well. Research sites are social contexts related to personal circumstances, social status, identities and the everyday forms of participation that are routine for children and young people in these settings. In turn, the social context of the setting is shaped by the distribution of resources that reflects broader social structures underpinning privilege and disadvantage. These are often most visible at the local level in geographical patterns of neighbourhood and community resources, including the available services for children and young people. In the broader geography of globalising markets, patterns of service access (such as access to schools, hospitals and recreation centres) and the regulatory control of young lives (e.g. criminalisation and detention) are patterned in circuits of poverty and wealth at the level of families, nations and regions (Fine and Ruglis, 2009; Raco, 2009). Who has access to public and private resources will be evident in the social identities of children and young people in any specific setting. As organisations in which adults have responsibility for the care of young people, these settings are institutional as well as social and geographical contexts. In turn, the cultural practices and protocols of the institution are shaped by legal and policy mandates and the 'commonsense' of professional frameworks, codes of practice, accountabilities and regulatory requirements.

One way of conceptualising the research context is in terms of a 'political ecology'. France et al. (2012) adopt this frame for situating young people's accounts of their relations to crime in poor and high-crime areas in England. Political ecology draws on Bronfenbrenner's (1977) idea that children grow up within nested systems of influence and Bourdieusian analysis of the distribution of power, status and opportunities through the positioned accrual of capital, especially in its cultural, social and symbolic forms (Bourdieu, 1997). The latter has been an important framework in educational research in accounting for children and young people's highly differentiated experiences of schooling – of learning, achievement, relations with peers and teachers and access to resources (Mills, 2008). It is argued that inequitable outcomes are embedded in the logic of practice that privileges dominant languages and codes of White middle-class culture such that working-class children who bring different cultural capital and 'funds of knowledge' (González et al., 2005) may have their right to education diminished (Thomson, 2002; Zipin, 2009). Out of school contexts, comparative studies have shown how family practices in relation to education map onto the institutional logic through differential capacity to enrich children's schooling preparedness. Ball (2010: 161) sums up the resultant contrast of pre-schoolers' educational experience: 'The lives of these children in the two class groups were, with some very minor, internal variations, starkly and almost absolutely different'.

Clearly, children and young people accrue different and unequal 'participatory capital' (Wood, 2013) related to the relative power embedded in class, race, gender, age, sexual identities, 'dis'/abilities and a host of other forms of structured exclusion and inclusion in specific community, social and institutional contexts. As France et al. (2012) argue, these are shaped by policy that creates and puts children into categories such as 'special needs', 'at risk', 'anti-social', invisibly 'getting by' or 'high achievers' that infuse identities and may elicit young people's mobilisation of participatory capital as compliance, resistance or struggling to find their way through multiple service systems; while majority-world children may struggle to find services adequate to their needs and identities outside diminishing stereotypes of passive service recipients (Nieuwenhuys, 2007). At organisational level, how professionals respond to accountability pressures to 'boost' student achievement, 'break the cycle' of 'persistent offending' or 'protect vulnerable children' is critical in shaping the scope for everyday participation and young people's exercise of agency. In combination, then, the contextual specificities of research may enable or delimit the roles of children and young people. Weis and Fine (2012) argue that we need to bring a 'critical bifocality' to research. This entails looking for the structural conditions and global patterns that hold the heterogeneity of young people. In the specific research setting, this may include researcher sensitivity to the social and political processes of the immediate micro-ecology, while looking for the influence of macro-logics of inclusion and exclusion seeping into the setting and relational dynamics.

Researchers' positioning is similarly a constituent of context. How researchers enter research settings depends on our position and relationship to them. Practitioners who initiate research in their schools and community organisations and 'outsider' researchers may hold similar aims to build emancipatory knowledge, strengthen inclusive practices and contribute to social change, yet we may encounter different tensions in gaining access and cooperation. While much participatory research deliberately collapses 'insider' and 'outsider' status (Fine, 1994) through reconceptualising the notion of the researcher – with and as participants – this dichotomy often persists in the exercise of power within the contexts of participatory research.

Access and cooperation in context

Researchers have highlighted a number of tensions between their inclusionary intent in working with children and young people and the required negotiation of power relations in particular contexts. These tensions are often related to enactments of institutional authority, but also to how young people are differentiated through discourse and practice, and how researchers, gatekeepers and children actively influence the shape of the research. In short, who 'owns' the research matters in terms of who gets to participate and how children and young people engage with the research.

Gatekeeping in contexts

As institutions, schools, health facilities and community organisations may exercise their gatekeeping authority to facilitate or deny access to researchers and participants. Sime's (2008) research with Scottish children and young people living in poverty aimed to address their exclusion from decision-making in policy and service improvement by seeking their views of the services they used in their local communities. However, initially gaining access to the ten- to fourteen-year-olds in primary and secondary schools at times proved difficult as school managers self-excluded some schools entirely and, in others, limited access to selected groups of students. Negotiating access in community settings may be subject to similar or greater levels of gatekeeping power exercised by adult authorities. Health researchers typically need to negotiate multiple authorities to work with young people in hospital settings. In addition to university and hospital ethics committees, Bishop's (2008) doctoral research within an Australian children's hospital involved obtaining permissions from the heads of all departments, nursing unit managers, team leaders and a comprehensive security clearance before inviting parental and participant consent. In all, there were ten levels of gatekeeping. Access in commissioned research may be more readily facilitated with the support and cooperation of professionals enlisted by the host organisation (Lambert et al., 2013). However, there are often many intermediary decision-makers between researchers and young participants, sometimes resulting in long delays to the research schedule.

The dynamics of gatekeeping may be intense when children and young people belong to particularly marginalised groups. Where demographics such as geographic area, age and gender are important to the selection of particular children, multiple permissions to initially identify the children before inviting them to participate may also mean that some are excluded because they have left the hospital or community programme, are no longer accessing a particular service or are transient service users by virtue of their circumstances. Professionals working with those who are homeless, living on the streets, excluded from school or in care may be more protective in their advocacy because these young people have already experienced diminished rights and resources in their communities. Professionals are acutely aware of children and young people's personal struggles to deal with issues that have brought them into vulnerable or institutionally dependent situations (Kendrick et al., 2008). Researchers have also found that parents and carers may see the research as another unwelcome 'welfare' intervention that exposes them to others' judgements (Moore et al., 2009) or staff may block access because they regard children in vulnerable circumstances as not having the capacity to participate (Mason, 2009). In a range of research contexts, young people may be excluded because they are assigned to social categories that have been discursively incapacitated. This has especially been the case until quite recently for children and young people with disabilities, where the very categorisations are a form of gatekeeping, not only in research but in children and young people's rights to participate in society (Slee, 2008).

Within a political ecology perspective, it is recognised that important factors beyond the immediate context shape the way institutional authority is exerted. Stalker et al. (2004) suggest that the extensive range of permissions required for hospital-based research with children in the UK were not only related to consideration of children's wellness to participate, but also related to recent media attention to a case of unethical practice involving a children's hospital, and to heightened risk management related to child protection in institutional settings more broadly. Ensuring as far as possible our own and participants' safety is a prominent issue where research is conducted in community contexts of conflict and violence. Decisions about researcher safety may also be subject to higher authority, as was the case for Winton (2007) who was recalled to the UK from her doctoral research in Guatemala due to a violent incident in the area where she was working. While she was acutely conscious of negotiating exposure to risks, Winton would have preferred to stay on and suggests there is a need for more open discussion of responses to danger that explore beyond 'obligatory risk assessment' (2007: 511).

Within institutional settings, professionals' duty of care situates them as responsible for the well-being of the young and for maintaining control over what happens within the institution. In addition to the demands of busy everyday routines and event schedules in schools, and health and community centres, Sime (2008) and Nolas (2011) have noted that performance pressures on schools and services within increased regulatory accountabilities may influence access decisions and conditions of participation. Top-down policy 'initiatives' may require teachers, youth workers and other professionals to incorporate student voice and participatory projects into externally driven reforms (Rudduck and Fielding, 2006). In this political climate, cooperative work to expand children and young people's access to decision-making roles may be seen as burdensome or another required box to tick. In poor majority-world countries, the pressures on teachers, social workers and other professionals are perhaps more complex, as their own work conditions, remuneration and the ongoing difficulty of addressing young people's everyday basic needs such as food, clothing and health care may leave little space for the 'luxury' of participating in research (Nieuwenhuys, 2007). Gatekeeping in these contexts may be a complicated response to the 'outsider' minority-world researchers who represent potential access to greater resources for the organisation and community but also potentially tighter regulatory control (Jeanes and Kay, 2013; Nieuwenhuys, 2007; Ray and Carter, 2007).

In these varied contexts, then, some children and young people have no opportunity to shape the services they use or depend on and the related policy frameworks (Theron and Malindi, 2010), while others may have limited scope to refuse. Ironically, external pressures may influence some gatekeepers to exert pressure *for* children's participation, for example in community services funded by majority-world sponsors. Undertaking doctoral research in Bangladesh, Ahsan (2009) found that officials in schools and community organisations instructed children to participate or told them that the research would help solve community problems related to their ethnic minority status. Further, as a former employee of a donor organisation, Ahsan was positioned as holding authority that might be important to the future prospects of both community and particular organisations. In this case, young people's free choice to participate was seriously constrained. We ought to be concerned about and resist these instances of authoritative power exercised over children and young people. Whilst recognising the constraints of difficult contexts, we need to find ways to push back against the political pressures that exclude, and effectively constitute systemic and symbolic violation of, children and young people.

Constraints on cooperation

While institutional power is commonly encountered in negotiating access to conduct research, it may extend beyond initial access to decisions that impinge on the researcher's intended ways of working with participants. Researchers have highlighted the tensions of negotiating the focus of participatory inquiry in terms of institutional control of the agenda, and how institutional categories and the structured spaces of schools and community organisations influence children and young people's participation.

The topic or focus of the research may be vetoed or delimited by gatekeepers, as was the case in the Youth In Focus (a North Californian non-government organisation) health project that worked with young people in seven school-based clinics (Suleiman et al., 2006). Working in small teams, young people surveyed their peers and decided on their team focus, with all projects aiming to improve the clinic services and student access to them. One team's plan to focus on condom access was initially approved, then made subject to parental consent by the school authorities who made it clear to the team that many staff and parents were opposed to it. Dentith et al.'s research with adolescent girls on gender and sexuality (2009; 2012) encountered similar institutional control as Las Vegas school principals vetoed a proposed after-school club where girls would plan their own research agenda, even though parental consent had been granted. In these and other cases, powerful interests reach into and shape the scope of young people's participation. Resistance to the Las Vegas plan was explained in terms of the girls' potential critique of the local sex industry and affront to the powerful religious right and corporate interests. Internal pressures from external accountabilities such as inspections or performance outcomes may also mean that school authorities may be less inclined to see the value of the research (Sime, 2008).

Even as participation and researching *with* children and young people has become the 'new orthodoxy' (France, 2004: 177), schools and community services may respond in ways that limit the scope for transformative practice that challenges the 'normative models of social and political institutions' (Milbourne, 2009: 351). Some researchers have then questioned the meaning and effects of 'cooperation' throughout the research process, as children and young people are themselves caught up in the pressures to perform, produce, tick boxes and achieve strategies in the context of service performance targets, insecure funding and managerialist policy 'ownership' of outcomes and outputs (Milbourne, 2009; Nolas, 2011). These are particularly salient issues that underline the interrelatedness of power, purposes and whether children and young people do in fact access benefits and opportunities by participating in research.

Children and young people's cooperation

While gatekeeper and staff perceptions of the benefits of the research may limit or open up the scope of inquiry, young people's own interests, time and experience of settings are key to how they participate. The realities of children and young people's own schedules and interests may mean they decline to participate or that their level of their engagement is sporadic. For example, extracurricular activities in schools may clash with the 'spaces' made available for the research (Suleiman et al., 2006); and youth services often involve fluid membership where attendance may be dependent on other activities available in the community such as sport, or just 'hanging around' with mates in the park or local streets (Bottrell, 2007; Nolas, 2013). In community contexts, who 'owns' the space is also an important consideration in terms of young people's engagement. A youth centre may seem to be a safe, friendly venue appropriate for research, yet it may be a place where territorial conflicts play out such that for some young people it will not feel safe to enter (France, 2004). Moreover, youth services may not attract particular groups who are marginalised in their communities – for example young people involved in problematic substance abuse (Coupland and Maher, 2005; Daley, 2013); or groups who prefer to carve out their own cultural spaces that are less restrictive (Milbourne, 2009).

Within the constraints and scope afforded by gatekeepers and researchers, children and young people control their own participation. Children and young people are responsive when there is scope for them to contribute to the research agenda, though some may not be overly enthusiastic at what they perceive to be another adult-centric enterprise (Percy-Smith, 2010). Within the research process, off-putting, irrelevant or overly 'sensitive' topics may elicit refusal or resistance. Voting with their feet is not uncommon with young children through to older teenagers. Researchers have referred to children simply walking away from the group or activity (Bessell, 2009), refusing to talk or subverting the process. Discussing the use of participatory video with young people in a youth club, Nolas (2011: 1199) points out how young people's interpretation of participatory methods may be at odds with the researcher's. Looking 'through the lens of popular culture', young people were not so interested in dialogical and relational exploration, but in the DVD product itself and an opportunity to star on camera or create the kind of video diaries familiar from reality television shows. In his Masters fieldwork on children's perception of school spaces, Gallagher (2008) found that the six- and seven-year-olds resisted the model-building activity he initiated and prioritised their own fun with the building blocks. Their resistances included refusing to be part of a group, drifting in and out of the activity and appropriating his notebook to write notes to him and sometimes insults to peers. His attempts to bring order to the process without coercion left Gallagher feeling uncomfortable about his regulatory role and 'policing' a group where some children monopolised the activity to the exclusion of others, along dominant gender lines.

When children and young people are situated in vulnerable circumstances, they may withdraw if it appears the project may reveal their marginalisation or expose aspects of themselves, their kin or community that outsiders may judge or misinterpret (Kendrick et al., 2008). The setting may also reinforce young people's consciousness of the excluded identities assigned to them. Fox's (2013) analysis of the relational dynamics of young people excluded from school reveals how the institutional discourses and practices of schooling seeped into the informal setting of the Scottish youth project where her doctoral research was based. Although in a different setting, young people and adults still identified and were positioned as students and teachers. It was unsurprising, then, that young people who had resisted school and been excluded would also resist participating in what appeared to be just more 'work'. Self-managing participation within a research context, with the support of family or friends or that arranged by the researcher and institutional personnel may, however, be important to children and young people experiencing a sense of control over their lives within circumstances of vulnerability or marginalisation (Bishop, 2008). Children in hospital, or homeless and young people who have experienced violence and abuse, have clearly articulated their willingness and capacity to manage the vulnerability of speaking about their lives because they want to 'make a difference' – for others in similar circumstances and to stimulate institutional, social and policy change (Bishop, 2008; Daley, 2013; Tucker, 2013).

Working with issues of access and cooperation

The range of research projects discussed in this chapter and throughout the book indicates the interest and commitment of researchers to working *with* professionals and young participants across diverse contexts. In some cases, researchers' intentions to include particular groups of children and young people have not been realised due to institutional refusal or constraints. Whether and how institutions and individuals respond to invitations to participate, or indeed initiate research within their schools and communities, depends on the range of contextual factors, including: prior experience of consultations, university researcher projects and action for social change; perceived benefits to children and young people and the organisation; and external pressures. However, some participatory researchers have argued that institutional resistance should be unsurprising, not only because critical research agendas are discomforting. They also include 'sensitive' or 'controversial' issues and the casting of critical eyes in contexts that may expose and interrogate the conditions of marginalisation, including how institutional practices contribute to them. Similarly, children and young people's resistance or divergent cooperation may take researchers, participants and professionals out of our comfort zones as we enter into 'complex pre-existing relations of power' (Gallagher, 2008: 147) and indeed shape them through our collective participation (Plows, 2012).

Given that layers of power and authority may need to be negotiated, time and relationships emerge as significant features of accessibility. Torre (2005: 254) argues that creating democratic participatory spaces within schools and community sites requires deep engagement with the contexts and consequences of diverse and differently dis/empowered groups coming together in 'contact zones'. Relationally, this involves setting up comfortable, safe spaces and agreements around respectful discussion so that trust may flourish. In considering the layers of access and cooperation discussed above, we might extend this notion of contact zones to include the groundwork of negotiating with institutions, services and communities.

The challenges of access and cooperation are not 'one-off' issues. Embedded in contexts, power and positioning, they are ongoing dimensions of the research process. Researcher reflections on negotiating with gatekeepers, professionals, communities and young participants highlight the importance of collaborative ways of working. The following discussion of how researchers work with issues of access and cooperation does not intend to suggest a set of 'solutions', because the research contexts are diverse and contextual specificities that shape research practice are not always neatly transferrable from one context to another. Nevertheless, there are invaluable practical insights shared in researchers' reflections on dealing with some of the challenges outlined in the forgoing discussion.

Negotiating access: the importance of time and relationships

Taking time to establish and strengthen relationships is essential not only to specific projects but to the broader aims of participatory research for social inclusion and social change. Reflecting on community-based projects centred on youth participation, Milbourne (2009: 354) sums up the importance of trust in three key elements: 'young people trusting adults; adult power-holders trusting young people and the need to promote wider trust in young people's abilities'. Establishing trust requires honest acknowledgement of constraints as well as possibilities that pertain to the historical and contemporary marginalisation of young participants and their communities.

From the perspective of marginalised communities, taking time to pay respect to the 'proper authority' (Hammersley and Traianou, 2010) of community leaders and elders holds particular significance because their history typically involves the lack of community rights afforded to dominant groups. In Indigenous communities, the assertion of community control over the conduct of research aims to redress historically skewed power relations of dispossessing research, and it is important to follow established protocols in seeking young people's involvement. In conducting health research with Indigenous young people, Mooney-Somers and Maher (2009) underline the importance of cooperating with Indigenous health services and community organisations. Taking time to establish partnerships is 'a way of ensuring research is responsive to community needs, conducted in a culturally appropriate manner, and beneficial to the community' (Mooney-Somers and Maher, 2009: 112). In many cultures, it is a mark of respect to seek children's participation through community and faith leaders (Green and Kearney, 2011). In these contexts, gaining access is a two-way process that aims for more equitable participation. Critical engagement with contact zones is both necessary groundwork and essential throughout the project for strengthening participants' individual and collective identity.

The relationships of researchers and the organisations they work with are often built over months or years before a project begins. This groundwork typically reflects and enables the focusing of participatory aims and processes and ultimately ensures that benefits of participation are equitably distributed (Sanders and Munford, 2009). Discussing the emergence of three youth projects that were school-, home- and community-based, Nygreen et al. (2006) detail the community building through dialogue originating in their experiences and observations of youth marginalisation. The school-based project involved a team of five students and graduates and Nygreen a former teacher at the school who had moved into a university research position. The Participatory Action Research Team for Youth (PARTY) met weekly over a year to share their experiences and reflect on the issues affecting the lives of young people of the school community. This dialogue was concerned with forging relationships and building shared understanding, across their differences of age, race, class and gender. Additionally in their first year they surveyed and interviewed students and staff of the school to gain a broader understanding of significant issues for their community. This work then informed the development of curriculum that enabled 'students to think critically about social justice issues and engage in action for social change' (Nygreen et al., 2006: 111).

Indeed, time and relationships are crucial if we aim to shift relations of power and enable *young authority* to emerge in critical voices and action. Bolzan and Gale (2011) propose that participatory projects may provide an 'interrupted space' in which marginalised young people can experience the world differently, out of their usual routines, and subsequently, through reflection, may forge resilient and more powerful identities. They describe how the projects based in urban and rural youth centres 'spluttered and staggered along for a few months, whilst the groups attempted to find their voice and identify something they wanted to work on' (Bolzan and Gale, 2011: 6). Over the eighteen-month period of project work (which included Indigenous boys training show-jump sheep dogs; and homeless youth producing a magazine), the groups relied less and less on the youth workers who acted as a resource for their work, though taking control involved some struggle as they came to terms with really having responsibility for *their* social action. In parallel, the adults struggled with relinquishing control, not being so ready to solve problems and to trust young people as knowledgeable and competent contributors to their communities.

Creating accessible spaces

Researchers have highlighted many practical ways of making participation accessible to children and young people. Creating safe and congenial spaces is a common theme in participatory research. This may involve providing food and drinks and recreational activities as a focus for building rapport and informally beginning to find out about the interests and issues children may wish to address (Brown et al., 2009). The timing of the research needs to fit with children and young people's routines and, keeping in mind the differential distribution of family and community resources, France (2004) additionally reminds us that we need to consider how young people will travel to the site and home if we are working outside schools, or in after-school clubs and organisations that are not part of the children's everyday routines.

As noted above, however, choosing settings that are 'friendly' to children and young people may be inclusive for some, but not for others who do not have an established relationship with a particular service or centre-attending peer group. Yet the service organisation may still be a worthwhile place to begin. Faced with the dilemma of excluding homeless young people who are not attached to a particular service, Pain et al. (2002) gained the assistance of youth workers and agency staff to identify a range of locations such as lunch clubs where young people were likely to be contactable. They also increased the time they spent in street locations, taking advice and introductions from young people and conducting group sessions and individual interviews in the nearest convenient place. Daley (2013) found that recruiting young people through a welfare programme supported her aim of balancing protection and respecting vulnerable young people's self-determination. Professionals were trusted people the young people would go to if they needed support. Spending time at the centre was also a valuable way of learning about the contexts of young lives.

Accessibility takes on particular significance in researching with children and young people with disabilities. Researchers working from a social model of disability have identified the 'double meaning' of accessibility as physical and social access to sites, and inclusion of children and young people with disabilities as participants and researchers. Both dimensions are important to the aims of emancipation and shifting relational power toward eliminating the predominant notion of 'mainstream' as an essence of disabling culture (Stevenson, 2010). The young 'Vipers' aged 12–21 who took a lead role in the Voice Inclusion Participation Empowerment Research (VIPER, 2012) project in England, identified the opportunity to socialise and have fun, and the selection of fully accessible home-base and fieldwork settings as supportive of their participation. In their role as researchers, the Vipers were concerned with the physical, social and authoritative access within community services. They found that some services still offered very inadequate facilities such as rooms where only one wheelchair could fit; but more importantly, there was limited scope for participation that the young people thought really mattered. For example, their analysis showed that young people with disabilities rarely had opportunity to influence service policies or have some control over decision-making agendas. Younger children were especially invisible in these processes. However, when afforded opportunity, young people had initiated important service changes including improved physical access, sport and recreational programmes, sex education, 'Stay Safe' cards and establishment of a new supported self-advocacy service.

Making participation accessible

Researcher reflexivity includes conscious focus on the distribution of power within the research space and deliberative attention to enabling diverse voices. Rather than seeing sporadic or drifting participation solely as resistance, researchers have highlighted the importance of working with flexible roles and processes that respond to the different ways children and young people may prefer to participate. Negotiating the research agenda is important groundwork if the project is to sustain the interest of and accrue benefits to young participants (Minkler, 2012). Inviting children and young people to identify the personal, institutional, local or global issues they would like to bring into the project initiates the co-inquiry of researching *with* children and young people. As detailed in Chapter 6, there are many participatory methods to facilitate developing focus questions and the research design. Wicks and Reason (2009) argue that in opening up the 'communicative space' we need to pay attention to the emotions that arise in the process of forming groups: 'The challenge here is to help people feel free, comfortable and able to contribute, while at the same time providing a sense of challenge and stimulation.' (Wicks and Reason, 2009: 249). Working out research questions together should give clear shape to the inquiry whilst each participant should be able to sense that the agenda is theirs. This is not to suggest a fixed set of questions or agenda. Participatory researchers also expect to re-think research questions and projects as they unfold and young participants take the opportunity to frame or re-frame the research problem (Torre and Fine, 2006) and possible methods of inquiry. Involving children and young people in these important decisions (and others throughout the project) 'does more than just tell young people that they have rights; it encourages them to enact them' (Daley, 2013: 5).

Flexible approaches to researcher roles are a feature of inclusive participatory research. Across different contexts and with heterogeneous groups in an early childhood service, school or community centre, including different options for participation may ensure there are opportunities for all participants to contribute meaningfully. For example, in a peer interviewing project, Schäfer and Yarwood (2008) found that switching roles of interviewer, interviewee and camera operator was engaging for the children and helped them to develop understanding of the process from different perspectives, thereby appreciating their work as researchers in more complex ways. The varied educational backgrounds of the children also meant that some were immediately confident interviewers and interviewees while working in close collaboration with peers, and that the researchers assisted others to hone their questions. Children's experimentation and initiatives may inform how we should adapt the methods, media, groups or spatial arrangements within the research site. For example, some researchers argue for the importance of research training prior to children and young people taking part in the research. Yet it may be that jumping straight into experimenting with peer interviewing, for example, may be what children and young people need to do – testing their own inventiveness whilst socialising and having fun. The researcher's attitude and how we respond may help to establish a culture of risk-taking that is a condition for children and young people's innovations. When researchers and participants enter the research space with openness to different ways of working, all may benefit through gaining confidence, skills and deeper appreciation of both research and participation. As Stevenson (2010: 47) advocates, this openness means that in her co-research with young people with intellectual disabilities, young people's 'voices are continually in earshot, their presence felt, and their influence brought to bear at most stages of the research journey'. Researchers have also highlighted their reflexive attunement to group members' life experiences in specific contexts such that participation may elicit vulnerabilities. 'Checking in' with participants for their responses to the experience of participation, specific research processes or discussions and their suggested changes of process or follow-up, are ways of 'using the learnings from the research to change the process of research where it is needed' (Burkett, 2012: 28).

As Torre (2005) suggests, attending to power and/in the research process takes commitment, trust and willingness to talk about one's life experience and reflect on how it links to others' within the social relations of positioned privilege and marginalisation.

According due recognition to inequality structures that permeate research locales, sites and situations as embodied identities, researchers have underlined the importance of facilitating children and young people's critical appreciation of their lifeworlds and contexts. If participatory research is to achieve its aim of empowering children and young people to be confident participants in society (well after the project is finished) and to be actors for social justice, the educative dimensions of the research should not be confined to children and young people's training in methodologies and organising into action teams. At times we may fall into expecting children and young people to be experts on all aspects of their lives and local ecologies, and be reticent to 'impose' our own expertise. However, it is the bringing together of all our partial knowledges and pushing our own and participants' knowledge boundaries that makes for deeper understanding of the issues (Torre, 2005). The expert knowledge that researchers and professional collaborators (including teachers and service workers) bring to the discussion, mapping, photo-voice or other activity contributes to enabling young participants to locate individual and collective experience in relation to systems, policies and social processes. This may begin with or include analysis of institutional and local context, laying the foundation for devising actions for change. As Suleiman et al. (2006: 127) argue, 'To truly create social action, young people must have a sense of power to achieve change and understand the context of their community'.

Marginalised children and young people have often been the focus of participatory research for developing empowerment through deep understanding of contexts. However, connecting the micro-ecologies of classrooms and youth clubs to local and global patterns requires attention to understanding privilege. The issue of empowerment, then, is examined and appreciated from differently positioned perspectives so that children and young people can identify the intersecting patterns of access to health, housing, education, recreation and employment and 'begin to uncover the need, and practical methods for systematic social change' (Suleiman et al., 2006: 129). Stoudt et al.'s (2012) participatory project, 'Polling For Justice', deliberately brought together young New Yorkers of diverse backgrounds, including students attending wealthy elite and poor urban schools; young people identified as lesbian, gay, bisexual, transgender, queer or questioning sexualities; and homeless, formerly incarcerated and immigrant youth. Working with activist researchers, educators, social workers and lawyers, they explored and documented young people's differentiated experiences of education, health and criminal justice, by social group and localities. These processes are not concerned with achieving some consensus of worldview; but when guided with care, respect and reflexivity, challenging our comfort zones and working with resistance as a resource, the shared understandings across difference may serve to counter-hegemonically legitimise 'marginal' knowledge and prompt solidaristic responses to and through the collective analysis, into social action.

Different ways to participate

There is no one right way to approach participatory research because the contexts of participants, researchers and projects are diverse and need to be negotiated in specific sites, locales, social circumstances and within the given structures of authority, power and interrelated purposes. While much has already been said in earlier chapters about different ways children and young people participate in research, here we wish to turn back this issue to researcher positioning, with a focus on student-researchers to consider how the scope for their participation may be constrained by position and practical matters.

Student-researchers' access to collaborative work is increasingly supported by inclusion on research teams within university faculties; yet the tradition of academic research education remains predominantly individualised, particularly in student research for Honours, Masters and Doctorate degrees. In various ways, the formal structures may present challenges to working with children and young people in participatory ways. Reflecting on her doctoral research, Fox (2013: 11) problematises the dominant model of researcher expertise that 'requires the researcher to act alone, to construct knowledge which they must state is their "own work" and to be hugely more invested in the life of the research than other subjects'. This form of distancing researchers and participants and the dominance of 'traditional' forms of data collection and its presentation diminish the scope for more fluid and 'non-conformist' processes, and may then present challenges to gaining support for participatory research. In many ways, these issues are more pressing within increasingly widespread pressures on academic researcher performance ('outputs'), policy and organisational demand for 'evidence' that frequently valorises what is quantifiable, and the burgeoning of privatised 'fast' research with which university researchers must compete (Brownlee and Irwin, 2010; Clark, 2011). In this context, there is on the one hand 'a yearning for public, participatory, post-colonial feminist science to gather evidence for justice' (Fine, 2012: 15) that emanates from researchers working on small projects in marginal quarters to practitioners and activists in large-scale social movements. On the other hand, the academic status of participatory research in many institutions is the product of inappropriate appraisal by positivist criteria or incorrect charges that it lacks reliability and validity. These issues may be more difficult to negotiate in some contexts than others. For example, Bergold and Thomas (2012) point out the near impossibility of doctoral research in psychology using participatory methods being approved by German universities. As Sánchez (2009) notes, participatory research that includes advocacy and social action may be perceived to be inferior to other methodologies and necessitate the diversion of the researcher's attention to formal doctoral or tenure requirements and the pursuit of 'meaningful' research – pressures that appear to be in tension and may not be readily resolved.

Student-researchers also recount practical constraints of schedules and funds. Time is a key consideration in participatory research, often a scarce resource for academic researchers and may be especially problematic for student-researchers. For example, conducting an action-focused participatory project may be untenable for an Honours student who must complete her thesis within one year. For both practitioner and academic researchers, the time schedules of commissioning and host organisations may result in challenges that are balancing acts of ideals and practicalities. Similarly, the resources required may be out of reach or be a cause of further tension with ethical priorities. For example, it is increasingly common for youth organisations to require participant remuneration. This expectation is acknowledged as a right to appropriate wages for co- and peer-researchers (Smith et al., 2002) and rewards for participants in marginalised and sometimes 'over-researched' communities. However, student-researchers' access to particular groups of children and young people may then be dependent on their access to project funding (Daley, 2013). Where the student-researcher's faculty or university proactively supports postgraduate students this may not be such a challenge; similarly, philanthropic foundations provide small grants, though again this is not uniformly widespread or accessible.

Within the time and resourcing constraints on student research, especially for one-year Honours or Masters projects, researchers may need to consider how they may nonetheless adopt participatory methods that are inclusive and offer real opportunities for children and young people to benefit from participating. There may not always be time or opportunity to involve children and young people in the research design, but certainly we can devise ways of inviting them to enter into the process beyond tokenism. Atkins' (2013) approach, although involving research with mainly sixteen- and seventeen-year-olds in low-level post-compulsory education is relevant to working with children and young people more broadly. As a starting-point, Atkins worked with self-selected groups and asked 'questions such as "What do I need to ask you to find out about your lives and what is important to you?" "What sorts of things could we do together that would help me understand your lives?"' (Atkins, 2013: 147). This was a fruitful approach to generating a list of issues important to the young people that were then used to shape the final questions for group and individual interviews.

There may be no short-cuts to creating safe spaces for research with children and young people, and particularly with those in vulnerable circumstances. Taking time to establish rapport with professionals will be as important as developing relationships with the children and young people. However, in addition to pre-arranging the support of agency staff as needed, building debriefs into interview or focus group guides or the daily activities of the project can be a valuable way of checking in with participants as to how they are feeling about the work. As Burkett (2012: 27) suggests, 'The very nature of community-based research means that, despite our best efforts, our research methods sometimes have unintended consequences in certain communities with whom we work'. The debrief can also be a useful guide as to what may need to be adapted in terms of the processes and direction of the project (Burkett, 2012).

Putting one's research into context as a contribution to knowledge building and social change is a way of perhaps alleviating some of the tensions experienced in short-term research. A perusal of Student Action Teams' projects in Victoria, Australia, highlights the value of young researchers' social action in their schools and communities. Over a period of fourteen years, many projects have made a significant contribution to addressing racism, bullying, environmental issues, and health and safety in local communities (Australian Student Participation Resource & Information Network, 2013; also Walsh and Black, 2011). Similarly, in community development programmes of participatory research there are often a number of projects that contribute to the broad aims of building knowledge that is creating change for and by the community. Over time, small projects and the cumulative effects of collective efforts can and do make a difference. As we will see in Chapter 8, the 'products' of participatory research in relation to publications and dissemination take many forms, and a short-term 'traditional' Honours or postgraduate study may make a significant contribution to participants and organisations as well as establishing a foundation for a longer trajectory in participatory research.

Clearly, issues around access and cooperation when engaged in participatory research with children and young people are multi-faceted and deserve close and careful attention by all who are involved.

Key points

- Contexts and power relations, in terms of political ecology and participant heterogeneity, are complex and deserve close attention at all times during the inquiry process.
- Gatekeepers in institutions, whether adults or children and young people have an influence on who is able to participate and in what manner, particularly when attending to the needs of those who are vulnerable and marginalised.
- Many initiatives for participative research are the result of externally driven reforms that place additional burdens on those negotiating cooperation and access.
- Children and young people themselves have agenda that can well influence the kinds of cooperation that they are willing to offer.
- Time and relationships are significant variables when negotiating cooperation and access, including hospitable spaces and flexible arrangements.
- Establishing trust among and between participants needs to take account of the very real constraints that various parties face, and takes time to put into place and maintain.
- Particular attention needs to be given to access and cooperation when working with children and young people with disabilities so that their presence and perspectives are always kept in view.
- Flexibility is an essential feature of inclusive participatory research ensuring that the inquiry is responsive rather than following a fixed, predetermined route. There is no one 'right way' to approach participatory research involving children and young people, in spite of a dominance in academic settings of positivist models of research.
- One year Honours or Masters projects work within severely limited institutional constraints and will need to consider ways of making adjustments while still honouring the contribution that children and young people may make to their inquiries.

References

Ahsan, M. (2009) The potential and challenges of rights-based research with children and young people: Experiences from Bangladesh. *Children's Geographies*, 7(4): 391–403.

Atkins, L. (2013) Researching 'with', not 'on': Engaging marginalized learners in the research process. *Research in Post-Compulsory Education*, 18(1–2): 143–58.

Australian Student Participation Resource & Information Network (2013) *Student action teams.* http://asprinworld.com/student_action_teams, accessed 15th July, 2013.

Ball, S. (2010) New class inequalities in education: Why education policy may be looking in the wrong place! Education policy, civil society and social class. *International Journal of Sociology and Social Policy*, 30(3–4): 155–66.

Bergold, J. and Thomas, S. (2012) Participatory research methods: A methodological approach in motion. *Forum: Qualitative Social Research*, 13(1): Art. 30, January, np.

Bessell, S. (2009) Research with children: Thinking about method and methodology. In Australian Research Alliance for Children and Youth and the NSW Commission for Children and Young People, *Involving children and young people in research [electronic resource]: a compendium of papers and reflections from a think tank co-hosted by the Australian Research Alliance for Children and Youth and the NSW Commission for Children and Young People on 11 November 2008*, pp. 17–24. Woden ACT: ARACY and NSW CCYP.

Bishop, K. (2008) From their perspectives: Children and young people's experience of a paediatric hospital environment and its relationship to their feeling of well-being. Doctoral thesis, University of Sydney. http://ses.library.usyd.edu.au/handle/2123/3962, accessed 2nd October, 2013.

Bolzan, N. and Gale, F. (2011) Using an interrupted space to explore social resilience with marginalized young people. *Qualitative Social Work*, Online First, DOI: 10.1177/1473325011403959.

Bottrell, D. (2007) Dealing with disadvantage: Resilience and the social capital of young people's networks, *Youth & Society*, 40(4): 476–501.

Bourdieu, P. (1997) The forms of capital. In A. Halsey, H. Lauder, P. Brown and A. Stuart Wells (Eds) *Education: Culture, economy and society.* Oxford: Oxford University Press, pp. 46–58.

Bronfenbrenner, U. (1977) Toward an experimental ecology of human development. *American Psychologist*, 32(7) 513–31.

Brown, J., Collits, P. and Scholfield, K. (2009) Involving young people in research: Lessons from the 10MMM Project in south western Victoria. In Australian Research Alliance for Children and Youth and the NSW Commission for Children and Young People, *Involving children and young people in research [electronic resource]: A compendium of papers and reflections from a think tank co-hosted by the Australian Research Alliance for Children and Youth and the NSW Commission for Children and Young People on 11 November 2008*. Woden ACT: ARACY and NSW CCYP, pp. 38–48.

Brownlee, P. and Irwin, J. (2010) Research frontiers and border crossings: Methodology and the knowledge industry. In L. Markauskaite, P. Freebody and J. Irwin (Eds) *Methodological choice and design: Scholarship, policy and practice in social and educational research*. Dordrecht: Springer, pp. 277–91.

Burkett, I. (2012) Commentary 2. In S. Banks and A. Armstrong (Eds) *Ethics in community-based participatory research: Case studies, case examples and commentaries*. Durham: National Coordinating Centre for Public Engagement and the Centre for Social Justice and Community Action, Durham University, pp. 27–8.

Clark, T. (2011) Gaining and maintaining access: Exploring the mechanisms that support and challenge the relationship between gatekeepers and researchers. *Qualitative Social Work*, 10(4): 485–502.

Coupland, H. and Maher, L. (2005) Clients or colleagues? Reflections on the process of participatory action research with young injecting drug users. *International Journal of Drug Policy*, 16(3): 191–8.

Daley, K. (2013) The wrongs of protection: Balancing protection and participation in research with marginalised young people. *Journal of Sociology*, OnlineFirst, 8 May, DOI: 10.1177/1440783313482365, 1–18.

Dentith, A., Measor, L. and O'Malley, M. (2009) Stirring dangerous waters: Dilemmas for critical participatory research with young people. *Sociology*, 43(1) 158–68.

Dentith, A., Measor, L. and O'Malley, M. (2012) The research imagination amid dilemmas of engaging young people in critical participatory work. *Forum: Qualitative Social Research*, 13: Art. 17.

Fine, M. (1994) Working the hyphens: Reinventing self and other in qualitative research. In N. Denzin and Y. Lincoln (Eds) *Handbook of qualitative research*. 1st edition. Thousand Oaks, CA: Sage, pp. 70–82.

Fine, M. (2012) Troubling calls for evidence: A critical race, class and gender analysis of whose evidence counts. *Feminism & Psychology*, 22(1): 3–19.

Fine, M. and Ruglis, J. (2009) Circuits and consequences of dispossession: The racialized realignment of the public sphere for U.S. youth. *Transforming Anthropology*, 17(1): 20–33.

Fox, R. (2013) Resisting participation: Critiquing participatory research methodologies with young people. *Journal of Youth Studies*, 16(8): 986–99.

France, A. (2004) Young people. In S. Fraser, V. Lewis, S. Ding, M. Kellett and C. Robinson (Eds) *Doing research with children and young people*. Los Angeles: Sage/Open University, pp. 175–90.

France, A., Bottrell, D. and Armstrong, D. (2012) *A political ecology of youth and crime*. Basingstoke, UK: Palgrave Macmillan.

Gallagher, M. (2008) 'Power is not evil': Rethinking power in participatory methods. *Children's Geographies*, 6(2): 137–50.

González, N., Moll, L. and Amanti, C. (2005) *Funds of knowledge: Theorizing practices in households, communities and classrooms.* New York: Routledge.

Green, A. and Kearney, J. (2011) Participatory action learning for self-sustaining community development: Engaging Pacific islanders in Southeast Queensland. *Australasian Journal of University–Community Engagement*, Autumn: 46–68.

Hammersley, M. and Traianou, A. (2012) *Ethics and educational research.* British Educational Research Association on-line resource. www.bera.ac.uk/category/keywords/ethics, accessed 2nd October, 2013.

Jeanes, R. and Kay, T. (2013) Conducting research with young people in the global South. In K. te Riele and R. Brooks (Eds) *Negotiating ethical challenges in youth research.* New York: Routledge, pp. 19–30.

Kendrick, A., Steckley, L. and Lerpiniere, J. (2008) Ethical issues, research and vulnerability: Gaining the views of children and young people in residential care. *Children's Geographies*, 6(1): 79–93.

Lambert, V., Coad, J., Hicks, P. and Glacken, M. (2013) Social spaces for young children in hospital. *Child: Care, Health & Development*, early view article, DOI: 10.1111/cch/12016.

Mason, J. (2009) Strategies and issues in including children as participants in research on children's needs in care: A case study. In Australian Research Alliance for Children and Youth and the NSW Commission for Children and Young People, *Involving children and young people in research [electronic resource]: a compendium of papers and reflections from a think tank co-hosted by the Australian Research Alliance for Children and Youth and the NSW Commission for Children and Young People on 11 November 2008.* Woden ACT: ARACY and NSW CCYP, pp. 89–95.

Milbourne, L. (2009) Valuing difference or securing compliance? Working to involve young people in community settings. *Children & Society*, 23(5): 347–63.

Mills, C. (2008) Reproduction and transformation of inequalities in schooling: The transformative potential of the theoretical constructs of Bourdieu. *British Journal of Sociology of Education*, 29(1): 79–89.

Minkler, M. (2012) *Community organizing and community building for health and welfare.* 3rd edition. New Brunswick, NJ: Rutgers University Press.

Mooney-Somers, J. and Maher, L. (2009) The Indigenous Resilience Project: A worked example of community-based participatory research. *NSW Public Health Bulletin*, 20(7–8): 112–17.

Moore, T., McArthur, M. and Noble-Carr, D. (2009) Taking little steps: Research with children – a case study. In Australian Research Alliance for Children and Youth and the NSW Commission for Children and Young People, *Involving children and young people in research [electronic resource]: a compendium of papers and reflections from a think tank co-hosted by the Australian Research Alliance for Children and Youth and the NSW Commission for Children and Young People on 11 November 2008.* Woden ACT: ARACY and NSW CCYP, pp. 99–106.

Nieuwenhuys, O. (2007) Participatory action research in the majority world. In S. Fraser, V. Lewis, S. Ding, M. Kellett and C. Robinson (Eds) *Doing research with children and young people*. Los Angeles: Sage, pp. 206–21.

Nolas, M. (2011) Reflections on the enactment of children's participation rights through research: Between transactional and relational spaces. *Children and Youth Services Review*, 33(7): 1196–202.

Nolas, M. (2013) Exploring young people's and youth workers' experiences of spaces for 'youth development': Creating cultures of participation, *Journal of Youth Studies*, DOI: 10.1080/13676261.2013.793789.

Nygreen, K., Kwon, S. and Sanchez, P. (2006) Urban youth building community. *Journal of Community Practice*, 14(1–2) 107–23.

Pain, R., Francis, P., Fuller, I., O'Brien, K. and Williams, S. (2002) *'Hard to reach' young people and community safety: A model for participatory research and consultation*. Report. London: Policing and Reducing Crime Unit, Home Office.

Percy-Smith, B. (2010) Councils, consultations and community: Rethinking the spaces for children and young people's participation. *Children's Geographies*, 8(2): 107–22.

Plows, V. (2012) Conflict and coexistence: Challenging interactions, expressions of agency and ways of relating in work with young people in the Minority World. *Children's Geographies*, 10(3): 279–91.

Raco, M. (2009) From expectations to aspirations: State modernisation, urban policy, and the existential politics of welfare in the UK. *Political Geography*, 28: 436–44.

Ray, P. and Carter, S. (2007) *Understanding and working with children in the poorest and most difficult situations*. London: Plan UK.

Rudduck, J. and Fielding, M. (2006) Student voice and the perils of popularity. *Educational Review*, 58(2): 219–31.

Sánchez, P. (2009) Chicana feminist strategies in a participatory action research project with transnational Latina youth. *New Directions for Youth Development*, 123, Fall: 83–97.

Sanders, J. and Munford, R. (2009) Participatory action research. In L. Liebenberg and M. Ungar (Eds) *Researching resilience*. Toronto: University of Toronto Press, pp. 77–102.

Schäfer, N. and Yarwood, R. (2008) Involving young people as researchers: Uncovering multiple power relations among youths. *Children's Geographies*, 6(2): 121–35.

Sime, D. (2008) Ethical and methodological issues in engaging young people living in poverty with participatory research methods. *Children's Geographies*, 6(1): 63–78.

Slee, R. (2008) Beyond special and regular schooling? An inclusive education reform agenda. *International Studies in Sociology of Education*, 18(2): 99–116.

Smith, R., Monaghan, M. and Broad, B. (2002) Involving young people as co-researchers: Facing up to the methodological issues. *Qualitative Social Work*, 1(2): 191–207.

Stalker, K., Carpenter, J., Connors, C. and Phillips, R. (2004) Ethical issues in social research: Difficulties encountered gaining access to children for hospital research. *Child: Care, Health & Development*, 30(4): 377–83.

Stevenson, M. (2010) Flexible and responsive research: Developing rights-based emancipatory disability research methodology in collaboration with young adults with Down Syndrome. *Australian Social Work*, 63(1): 35–50.

Stoudt, B., Fox, M. and Fine, M. (2012) Contesting privilege with critical participatory action research. *Journal of Social Issues*, 68(1): 178–93.

Suleiman, A., Soleimanpour, S. and London, J. (2006) Youth action for health through youth-led research. *Journal of Community Practice*, 14(1–2): 125–45.

Theron, L. and Malindi, M. (2010) Resilient street youth: A qualitative South African study. *Journal of Youth Studies*, 13(6): 717–36.

Thomson, P. (2002) *Schooling the rustbelt kids: Making the difference in changing times*. Crows Nest, NSW: Allen & Unwin.

Torre, M. (2005) The alchemy of integrated spaces: Youth participation in research collectives of difference. In L. Weis and M. Fine (Eds) *Beyond silenced voices: Class, race, and gender in United States schools.* revised edition. Albany, NY: State University of New York Press, pp. 251–66.

Torre, M. and Fine, M. (2006) Researching and resisting: Democratic policy research by and for youth. In S. Ginwright, P. Noguera and J. Cammarota (Eds) *Beyond resistance! Youth activism and community change.* New York: Routledge, pp. 269–85.

Tucker, S. (2013) Considerations on the involvement of young people as co-inquirers in abuse and neglect research. *Journal of Youth Studies*, 16(2): 272–85.

VIPER (2012) Voice Inclusion Participation Empowerment Research. UK: Alliance for Inclusive Education, the Council for Disabled Children, NCB Research Centre and the Children's Society. http://viper.councilfordisabledchildren.org.uk/, accessed 6th September, 2013.

Walsh, L. and Black, R. (2011) *In their own hands: Can young people change Australia?* Melbourne: ACER Press.

Weis, L. and Fine, M. (2012) Critical bifocality and circuits of privilege: Expanding critical ethnographic theory and design. *Harvard Educational Review*, 82(2): 173–201.

Wicks, P. and Reason, P. (2009) Initiating action research: Challenges and paradoxes of opening communicative space. *Action Research*, 7(3): 243–62.

Winton, A. (2007) Using 'participatory' methods with young people in contexts of violence: Reflections from Guatemala. *Bulletin of Latin American Research*, 26(4): 497–515.

Wood, B. (2013) Participatory capital: Bourdieu and citizenship education in diverse school communities. *British Journal of Sociology of Education*, DOI: 10.1080/01425692.2013.777209, 1–20.

Zipin, L. (2009) Dark funds of knowledge, deep funds of pedagogy: Exploring boundaries between lifeworlds and schools. *Discourse: Studies in the Cultural Politics of Education*, 30(3): 317–31.

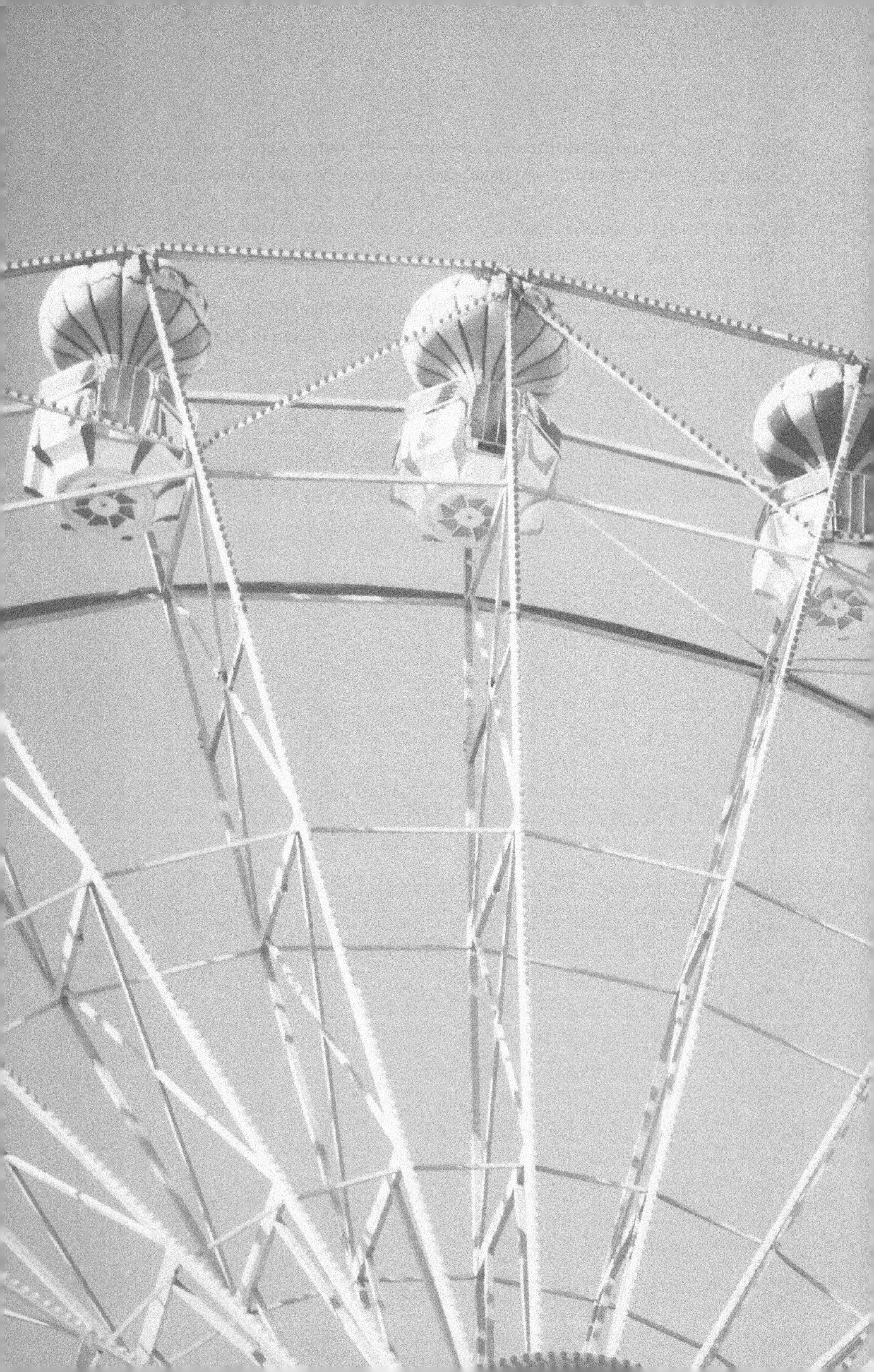

SIX
INNOVATIVE METHODS

This chapter explores a range of participatory research methods, provides some examples of their use and explores the potential advantages and/or disadvantages of each. We argue that the methodology underpinning research, rather than the methods themselves, is critical in promoting the participation of children and young people.

It addresses:

- Child-friendly methods?
- Observation.
- Visual/arts-based methods.
- Verbal methods.
- Written methods.
- Multiple methods.
- Which method/s?
- Choosing methods.

Focus on the participation of children and young people in research has resulted in the development and refinement of a wide range of research methods. Sometimes methods have been adapted for use with children and young people; other times specific methods have been developed. The range of methods used in research with children and young people is extensive and includes the use of interviews and focus group methods; visual methods, such as photography, drawing and mapping; role play and other drama; the use of social media; and combinations of these.

Underpinning the discussion in this chapter is recognition that while methods are important, it is the underlying theoretical base – the methodology – that largely determines how these are used and if/how they are likely to support the participation of children and young people. In arguing that a focus on methods sometimes overtakes consideration of the rationale for their adoption, Bessell (2009: 17) notes that 'the world of methods has become so fascinating and now offers such opportunity for innovation that we sometimes lose sight of *why we choose* particular methods and, more importantly, *how we use them*'. As we discuss a range of methods, we urge consideration of both methodology and methods.

In this chapter, we consider methods as 'techniques and procedures for gathering and analysing data' (Corbin and Strauss, 2008: 1). The previous chapters have explored elements of methodologies that inform research with children and young people. These elements are critical in determining appropriate methods. As one example, Dockett et al. (2011a) outline a theoretical framework that incorporates focus on children's agency, children's rights and citizenship, as well as ethical symmetry. Using this framework, they describe a process of matching methodology and methods, with the aim of ensuring that the choice and implementation of methods provides opportunities for children to exercise choice, provide informed assent, engage in data collection decisions and data analysis, and contribute to the reporting and dissemination of research.

Child-friendly methods?

There has been considerable debate about whether research with children and young people requires new and/or different methods from research with adults. Arguments for child-centred methods cite children and young people's competence and experiences as different from those of adults, with the consequence that different methods are required to match these. Contrary views also focus on competence, but propose that the competence of children and young people is the reason that new methods are not required (Christensen and James, 2008a). Between these positions is recognition that methods ought to be fit for purpose; that is, that appropriate methods are required for all research and all participants (Punch, 2002). In other words, there are moves towards person-centred, rather than child-centred, methods (Clark, 2011; Waite et al., 2010). While such methods seek to match the interests and preferred communication modes of children and young people, it remains critical that researchers explore the benefits and challenges of any method, ensuring that those chosen are neither tokenistic nor patronising in their assumption that traditional methods are inappropriate.

Methods underpinning participatory research with children and young people regard knowledge as generated intersubjectively through interactions and relationships. Appropriate methods build trust and rapport between researchers and participants, show regard for the competencies of each and promote opportunities to demonstrate these. Numerous studies incorporate multiple methods, recognising that there are many preferred ways of communication. Sound research incorporates critical reflection on methods and any assumptions underlying these, as well as their implementation and effectiveness. Such reflection is not the province of researchers only; the input of children and young people is also important.

In the following discussion, we describe methods individually. However, much research uses multiple methods or incorporates elements from a range of methods. Rather than aiming to provide comprehensive coverage of every possible method, we confine our discussion to introducing some of the more widely used methods, some benefits and challenges associated with each, and some examples of the ways in which these have been employed in research with children and young people.

Observation

Observation remains a powerful means of engaging with young children in ways that respect their independence, interests and capacity to make choices. Observation by a known and trusted adult can provide insightful and sensitive information about children's preferences and interests. In research with older children and young people, participant observation provides opportunities to become familiar with potential participants and their contexts. Sustained observation is

Table 6.1 Observation: opportunities and challenges

Potential opportunities	*Potential challenges*
• Is less disruptive than other methods • Does not rely on verbal interactions • Is promoted as an appropriate method for researching with young children • Seeks to observe people in authentic, naturalistic settings • Can be flexible and adapted to specific contexts • Seeks to access lived experiences of those being observed • Can be used to complement other methods, considering what is said as well as what is done • Promotes exploration of context • Extended observation provides time and opportunity to explore emergent issues or themes • Sustained participant observation can build relationships leading to greater acceptance and access to information	• Questionable whether it is possible to know the experiences of others • Sustained observation can be time-consuming • Limited observation may miss relevant data • Older children and young people may be more aware of, and sensitive to, the presence of an observer than younger children • There can be potential conflict between the roles of observer and researcher • Participant observers may assume access to a common understanding of events or situations

Examples

MacArthur et al. (2007) report an ethnographic study of the experiences of disabled children in several New Zealand schools. As participant observers, researchers observed classroom and playground interaction over several years.

Corsaro (2003) adopted the role of 'untypical adult' in his participant observations of pre-schoolers. Children's actions were not constrained by concerns that he would act as a teacher.

White et al. (2007) video-recorded the actions and interactions of children aged one to two years over a single day. They used excerpts as prompts for conversations with parents and caregivers about children's play and learning.

Richman (2007) posted a request for information and then adopted the role of non-participant observer in her study of young people's postings to internet chat rooms.

often a feature of ethnographic studies. The nature of observation links to the status of researchers as insiders or outsiders and their access to insider knowledge. Whether positioned as insiders or outsiders, participants or non-participant observers, researchers who utilise observation in participatory research with children and young people do so in an overt, rather than covert, manner. Some examples of the uses of observation in research with children and young people, along with an overview of potential opportunities and challenges associated with this method, are included in Table 6.1.

Visual/arts-based methods

Many of the 'child-friendly' methods adopted have drawn on visual or arts-based approaches. These approaches seek to be inclusive, promoting the engagement of a diverse range of children and young people. They rely on participants being willing to show, as well as talk about, issues of importance for them. Many approaches combine words with drawings, photographs, maps, charts, role play, construction or other media. The inclusion of text – explanation, interpretation or narrative – is important as the artefact alone can be interpreted in multiple ways which may not reflect the meanings intended by the creator.

Figure 6.1 Drawing in the sand

Drawing

Methods incorporating drawing can take many forms, using a range of materials and approaches, including draw and write activities (Sewell, 2011), emphasis on drawing and reflection (Einarsdóttir et al., 2009), and the use of prompts such as rainbows and clouds (Pimlott-Wilson, 2012). The materials used and contexts in which drawing takes place can also be many and varied (Figure 6.1).

Figure 6.2 The Reflections task

Drawings that make comparisons can prompt a range of discussions. In one study, Groundwater-Smith et al. (2011) have examined children's notions of learning in different contexts through their drawings. In another, Einarsdóttir et al. (2007) describe the Reflections task, inviting children to reflect through drawing and/or writing on their first year of school, using the prompts 'When I started school I ...' and 'Now I ...' (Figure 6.2).

Table 6.2 Drawing: opportunities and challenges

Potential opportunities	Potential challenges
• Can be less confronting than more formal approaches such as interviewing – for example, does not require eye contact with researchers • Can establish rapport and set up a relaxed interaction	• Drawings can be altered – so the meaning and intent may not be clear, or may change over the interaction • Cannot assume that all participants enjoy or choose to draw

Potential opportunities	Potential challenges
• Can act as prompts for conversations, help recall events, and serve as organisers for narratives	• Drawings may reflect an easy or quick way to complete a task, rather than tapping into relevant issues
• Focus on non-verbal, as well as verbal expression	• Prompts may be too open or vague
• Activities can be open-ended	• Participants may produce 'expected' or stereotypical drawings
• Drawings can take time, and do not demand a quick response	• In group contexts, drawings can be copied, producing social rather than individual processes
• Participants can change drawings during the activity – exercising some control over what is included and how	• Drawings are situated within specific contexts, time and culture, as well as the materials available
• Drawings, and the materials used, are often familiar to children and young people	• Analysis of images alone may misrepresent the intentions of the drawer
• Participants can elaborate drawings with written text and narrative	• A single drawing provides a snapshot view – a point in time, rather than changing perceptions of feelings

Examples

Children's (aged five to twelve) perceptions of care were investigated using draw-your-day and circles-of-closeness methods (Eldén, 2013). These highlighted the multiplicity of children's perspectives.

Christensen and James (2008b) report asking ten-year-olds to record how/where they spent their week. The children were asked to fill in a circle in any way they chose to represent the week and then to reflect upon how they completed the chart. Some ignored the circle altogether and developed a different way to represent the week.

Winter (2010) has used the concept of reality boxes to explore children's self-perceptions. On the outside of a box, children are asked to draw images of themselves that reflect how they think they are viewed by the outside world. Images on the inside reflect how children feel about themselves.

Drawings can also be a powerful means of eliciting stereotypes and discussion around these. Studies where participants have been invited to 'draw a scientist' (Chambers, 1983) or 'draw a teacher' (Weber and Mitchell, 1995) provide examples. Potential opportunities and challenges associated with drawing as a research method are outlined in Table 6.2.

Photography

Photography is generally used in one of three ways in research with children and young people (Banks, 1995; Holm, 2008): participants take photos about some aspect of their life or experiences (Figure 6.3); researchers document events and share these with participants (Figure 6.4); or pre-existing images are used to elicit responses.

Figure 6.3 Photographing the local environment

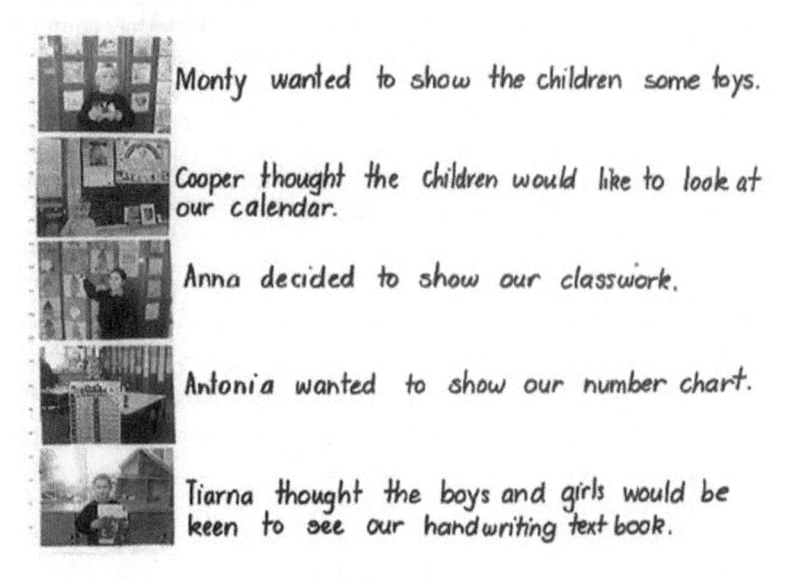

Monty wanted to show the children some toys.

Cooper thought the children would like to look at our calendar.

Anna decided to show our classwork.

Antonia wanted to show our number chart.

Tiarna thought the boys and girls would be keen to see our handwriting text book.

Figure 6.4 Teacher's recording of the data contributed by school children who were planning a visit to the nearby pre-school class to share what they knew about school

BMX Track

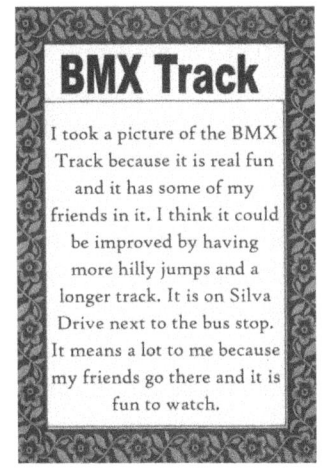

I took a picture of the BMX Track because it is real fun and it has some of my friends in it. I think it could be improved by having more hilly jumps and a longer track. It is on Silva Drive next to the bus stop. It means a lot to me because my friends go there and it is fun to watch.

Figure 6.5 BMX track

Anzac Memorial

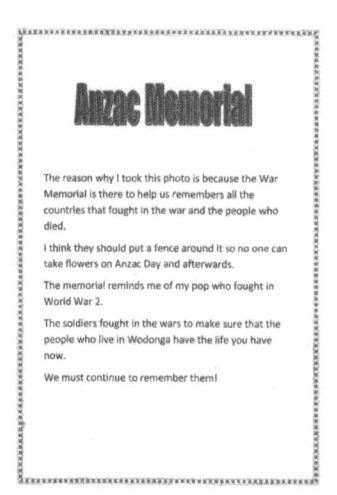

The reason why I took this photo is because the War Memorial is there to help us remembers all the countries that fought in the war and the people who died.

I think they should put a fence around it so no one can take flowers on Anzac Day and afterwards.

The memorial reminds me of my pop who fought in World War 2.

The soldiers fought in the wars to make sure that the people who live in Wodonga have the life you have now.

We must continue to remember them!

Figure 6.6 Anzac memorial

Photo-elicitation, or photo-voice, consists of taking photographs around a theme; generating a narrative around the photographs; and sharing the photographs and narrative with a broader audience. In Figures 6.5 and 6.6, two young people share their favourite places through photo-voice.

In the UK, *PhotoVoice*, working in partnership with other charities, non-government and community organisations has developed a number of participatory and digital storytelling methods for, among others, children and young people to build advocacy for social change, particularly in conditions where they would otherwise be socially excluded. For example, *PhotoVoice* worked with six young people from Action for Children's Southwark Young

Carers group, exploring how they felt the United Nations Declaration on the Rights of the Child affected their lives and the lives of other young people in the UK. A sample of their work can be found at www.slideshare.net/PhotoVoice/rights-cameras-action. A number of international photo-voice projects are discussed in Chapter 7.

In an innovative use of photography with children and young people, Herssens and Heylighen (2012) designed a photo-ethnographic study involving children and young people born blind. Children and young people participated with researchers in photo tours, photographing their experiences of their school environment. While accepting that the taking of photographs by those with limited or no vision seems paradoxical, the researchers argue that the use of digital cameras provided a means for communication about the children and young people's

Table 6.3 Photography: opportunities and challenges

Potential opportunities	*Potential challenges*
• Participants are often familiar with the technology and eager to use it • Digital technology is readily available and accessible • Participants can control what is photographed and how • Photographs can be deleted and re-taken until the desired outcome is achieved • Photographs can help evoke information, feelings or memories that would not otherwise be accessible	• Some technology is not readily accessed by all potential participants • Equipment both supports and constrains photography – for example, battery life, camera capacity, shutter speed • Photographs can involve recognisable people and places – challenging confidentiality and privacy • Who owns the photographs and can use/publish them? • Photographs are situated within specific contexts, time and culture, as well as the equipment available • Photographs are always socially constructed • Analysis of images alone may misrepresent the intentions of the photographer. Analysis needs to look beyond the image

Examples

Photo-elicitation was used by Cremin et al. (2011) to explore the views of thirteen- and fourteen-year-old British pupils on identity and schooling. Participants took photos with disposable cameras, made poster presentations and created individual scrapbooks consisting of photographs and text around these.

Young children (aged six to seven years) in Einarsdóttir's (2005) study of Icelandic pre-schools used either disposable or digital cameras to record what was important for them in the pre-school environment. The different equipment and the nature of the task using this equipment led to the children taking and reporting on different types of photographs.

sensory experiences of their school. Researchers developed a semi-structured questionnaire to guide the photography, focusing for example, on 'Take a picture of the place in or around the institute which you feel is the most pleasant'. The questions acted as prompts for photos and provided a context for conversations about the photo and the reasons for taking it. Researchers noted not only the way in which children and young people managed the camera, but also the images themselves and the triggers for taking these. For example, the act of pushing the button on the camera was described as both a haptic and auditory experience, as well as confirmation that the photograph had been taken. The images themselves reflected tangible triggers – where objects were touched, smelt or heard before being photographed – as well as intangible triggers – such as photographing a room equipped with judo mats because of the feelings of safety and freedom associated with a space in which the children and young people could move, run and play without being hurt. In this study, photography resulted in a series of 'non-visual sensory images' (Herssens and Heylighen, 2012: 119), where the processes of taking the photos and the rationale behind this was more important than the visual product. Some examples of photography as a research method, along with potential challenges and opportunities, are noted in Table 6.3.

Video/digital story telling

The increasing availability of video-recording equipment and editing software has seen an increase in the use of video and/or digital storytelling. Uses of video are many and varied, often mirroring the use of photography as participants video aspects of their own lives and experiences and generate narratives to accompany these; researchers use video to document events and share these with participants; and pre-existing videos are used to elicit responses from participants. The purposes underpinning children and young people's use of video and/or digital storytelling include documentation for personal reasons – such as creating a narrative about their own lives or generating a personal video diary; social reasons – such as recording family or social life and interactions; and producing a documentary video or story that reflects their lives or provokes political awareness (Muir, 2008).

Video diaries often involve providing video cameras and inviting participants to collect video data about some aspect of their lives over an extended period of time (Noyes, 2004). Just as in other research interactions, the strength of the data generated depends on the relationships between the researcher and participants. At the very least, there needs to be a high level of trust: from the participants that the researcher will value their contribution and treat it – and them – with respect; and trust from the researcher that the data have been contributed voluntarily and as described – that is, it has not been posed or acted (Buchwald et al., 2009). Potential opportunities and challenges associated with video and digital storytelling are reported in Table 6.4.

Table 6.4 Video/digital storytelling: opportunities and challenges

Potential opportunities	Potential challenges
• Children and young people often have high levels of technological skill and knowledge and may be encouraged to participate in research that involves this • Videos are often a familiar format • For those making regular video-recordings, the camera can take on the persona of a sympathetic listener • Video enables the study of both verbal and non-verbal expression • Children and young people may feel positive about research that offers them the opportunity to use valuable equipment • Video production occurs over an extended time, providing opportunities to revisit or reflect upon the data • Video can facilitate the expression of feelings and ideas that are hard to verbalise • Video can be taken without the researcher's presence • Video provides the opportunity to make choices about what to leave in or edit out	• Videos and home movies can take on ritualised forms – depicting situations and events that perpetuate stereotypes • The ready availability of video equipment and technology can promote the representation of idealised family life – everyone wants their family to look like the one on television • Making videos can be resource intensive • Equipment, and skill in using it, influences the generation of data. For example, battery life, shutter speed, memory capacity all influence the data generated • Video can capture a great deal of data, but also miss a great deal • The amount of data generated through video is extensive and analysis can be challenging • It can be difficult to translate video to text – either for analysis or reporting • There are ethical challenges in protecting the privacy and identity of participants • The images captured on video can be difficult to interpret on their own – context and interpretation of participants is important

Potential opportunities

Potential challenges

- There is no opportunity to immediately follow up on something that is shared on a video diary
- It can be difficult to verify video data or to verify the identity of a blog author
- Having no immediate access to participants means that there is no opportunity to intervene if necessary – for example, if the research provokes strong emotions or reactions
- If the video diary is developed over time, it can be difficult to ensure privacy. For example, if the diary is completed at home, can other family members access it?

Examples

Working with a group of young people in South Africa, Reed and Hill (2010) have promoted digital storytelling as a way to explore and share the challenges they face in their lives. A combination of skills-building workshops, the digital story making process and the support of facilitators resulted in young people being confident and competent to tell their stories.

Hwang (2013) worked with eight- to fifteen-year-old siblings of autistic children to produce home videos of what life was like for them.

Young people in Chalfen and Rich's (2004) study followed a specific protocol in using video cameras to document their illness and the way it impacted on their lives. The aim was to generate video narratives to teach their medical specialists about their illness and to share their experiences, knowledge and understanding of the impact of illness on their lives.

Tours and mapping

The notion of 'walking alongside' participants has a long history in ethnographic research, as researchers seek to 'observe, experience and make sense of everyday practices' (Clark and Emmel, 2010: 1). Walking interviews have been a feature of the *Connected Lives* project in the UK, where researchers have sought to understand the sense of place and neighbourhood connectedness felt by young people.

Participatory mapping also has a long history, as researchers have sought to access knowledge and experiences of social as well as geographic locations. Participatory mapping techniques are often used in conjunction with other methods, such as interviewing. Emmel (2008: 3) emphasises the importance of the 'tangibility of the map', which serves both as a record of the interaction and as an opportunity to revisit features recorded on the map for further elaboration or exploration.

Jim's map (Figure 6.7) details his views about what is needed in his community. His ideas are elaborated in both the map and his accompanying narrative:

> ... we need a school for the kids to learn. We need a police station so the baddies don't go into any houses at night. We need street lights so that the car can see where they are going at night. We need an army base for the army to help the police. We should have a swimming pool and a playground joined to the school. We also need a fire station otherwise the fires will burn the land down.

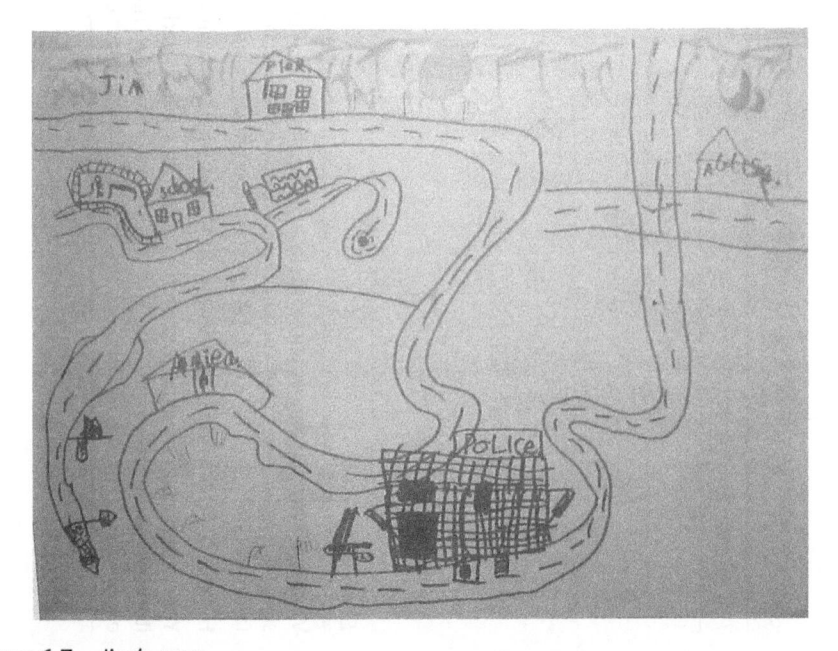

Figure 6.7 Jim's map

When used in combination, tours and mapping provide a range of opportunities for children and young people to take the lead in research as they guide researchers and assemble maps to document environments, spaces and/or associated emotions and personal responses.

Maps can be of many types, including:

- *Transect or walking maps* where adults walk with children along a pre-determined route and discuss features as they walk.
- *Physical maps* of an area.
- *Social maps*, plotting social and demographic data.
- *Relational maps*, plotting key people or institutions and locating these in order of importance or relevance.
- *Mobility maps*, which document where people go, how often and for what purposes.

Examples of these forms of mapping, along with an overview of potential opportunities and challenges, are included in Table 6.5.

Table 6.5 Tours and mapping: opportunities and challenges

Potential opportunities	*Potential challenges*
• Participants have direct involvement in the construction of artefacts and associated meanings • Involves sensory as well as verbal modes of interaction • Can document emotional, as well as physical, associations	• Can be a lengthy process • Focus can be on the artefact, rather than on the meanings and interpretations of the map makers • Requires access to a range of resources and equipment • Some maps can have implications for surveillance of children and young people

Examples

Five-year-old children led tours of their school. They photographed places of importance and located these on large pieces of paper. They glued the photographs in place, interacted, drew and engaged in role play as they created the map. Their final map reflected a 'multi-layered artefact' which incorporated a range of modes of documentation (Clark, 2011).

Christensen et al. (2011) used ethnographic fieldwork, global positioning technology and an interactive questionnaire completed by mobile phone to map the mobility of ten- to thirteen-year-old Danish children.

Children aged eight to 12 years walked their neighbourhood, and planned and curated a tour for adult participants in an Australian study reported by Hickey and Phillips (2013).

A wide range of other arts-based methods have been employed across research with children and young people. These include the provision of *construction materials* to focus attention on the research topic (Figure 6.8) and *collages*, or *moodboards*, where materials are collected and incorporated into one artefact;

116 PARTICIPATORY RESEARCH WITH CHILDREN AND YOUNG PEOPLE

and *role play* where participants adopt a role or persona to share perspectives about a specific event or situation. Potential challenges and opportunities associated with these methods are noted in Table 6.6.

Figure 6.8 Constructing an 'ideal' school

Table 6.6 Collage, role play and construction: opportunities and challenges

Potential opportunities	*Potential challenges*
Collage	
• As a projective technique, this method can tap into emotions and abstract ideas, without needing to put these into words first • Documentation of the process, as well as the product, can provide rich data	• Can be a lengthy process to collect images and construct the collage or moodboard • Choice of images may be constrained by what is readily available, with the consequence that the artefact may reflect stereotypes or idealised images • Using pre-existing images may promote conformity to social expectations. Also raises issues of authenticity – does the artefact reflect individual and/or social contexts? • The artefact generated is open to many interpretations. Analysis needs to be undertaken in collaboration with participants • Issues of ownership of the artefact
Example	
Pimlott-Wilson (2012) encouraged young people to create moodboards using images from magazines, newspapers, brochures and other available material.	

Potential opportunities	*Potential challenges*
Role play	
• Role play and other projective techniques can tap into emotions and abstract ideas, without needing to put these into words first	• Some participants will not be comfortable with role play • It may be difficult to distinguish between role play and pretend play

Example

Four- to six-year-old Singaporean children used persona dolls to share their experiences of friends, race and identity (Jesuvadian and Wright, 2011).

Construction

• Can be less confronting than more formal approaches such as interviewing – for example, does not require eye contact with researchers • Can establish rapport and set up a relaxed interaction • Can act as prompts for conversations, help recall events, and serve as organisers for narratives • Focus on non-verbal, as well as verbal expression • Activities can be open-ended	• Some participants may feel that construction materials are 'childish' or 'toys' and choose not to engage with them • Participants may be easily distracted from the research topic • Can be difficult to distinguish between responses to research prompts and imaginative play • Analysis without accompanying dialogue may misrepresent the intentions of participants • Need to consider the appropriateness of the construction materials for the research task • Some construction materials may have stereotypical uses, or expected uses in specific contexts

Example

Pimlott-Wilson (2012) conducted semi-structured interviews with five- to six-year-olds as they used Duplo™ to build a representation of their home and enact the roles of people within the home.

Verbal methods

Some of the more traditional qualitative research methods which have been employed in research with children and young people involve verbal interactions.

Conversations

In conversational approaches, a topic is introduced and participants invited to comment not only on the topic, but on the view of other participants. Effective conversation is guided and directed by participants, with minimal researcher intervention or questioning (Mayall, 2008). Conversations can occur in small or large groups, among peers as well as children and adults, dependent on the context and situation. Conversation is one of the most common methods used in research with young children – often taking the form of informal interactions within children's regular interactions. For example, it is not uncommon for researchers to have conversations with pre-school children as they play (Figure 6.9) – often with the researcher participating alongside the child (Carr, 2000).

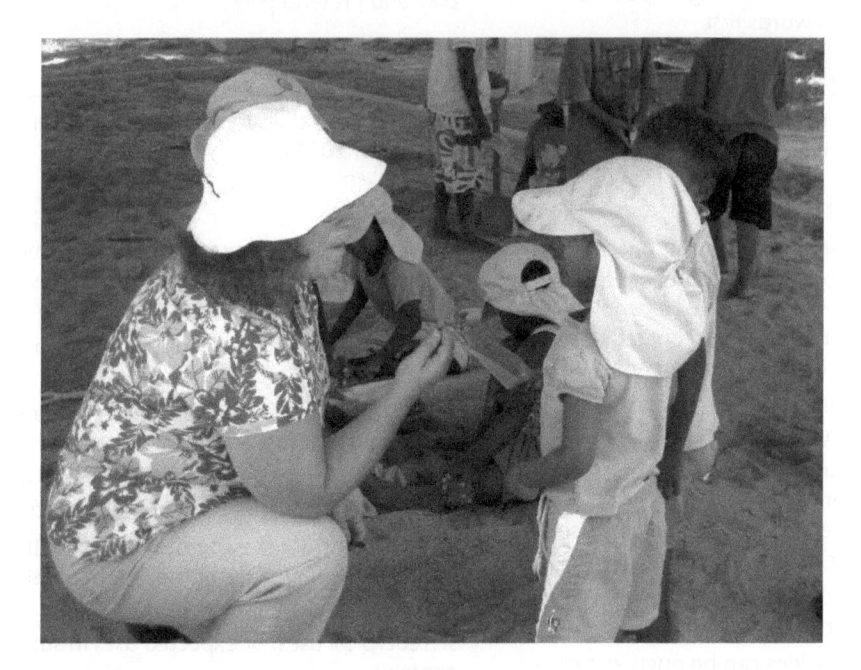

Figure 6.9 Conversations during play

The defining feature of conversations is reciprocity, requiring genuine interaction among participants. While researchers may introduce a topic – possibly in response to a specific focus, such as a book, photograph, shared experience or story – and prompt conversation, the ongoing interaction of participants is critical. Important also is the process of active listening, whereby researchers listen not just to the words that are spoken, but to the many ways in which children and young people express themselves (Rinaldi, 2005). Potential challenges and opportunities associated with conversations are noted in Table 6.7.

Table 6.7 Conversations: Opportunities and challenges

Potential opportunities	*Potential challenges*
• Participants can exert some control over the pace and direction of the conversation • Familiar format for interaction	• Conversation can move away from the topic • Finding a suitable location for conversations and to facilitate recording

Potential opportunities	Potential challenges
• Willingness to engage in conversations with friends	• Conversation requires active listening on the part of the researcher
• Conversations can occur alongside children and young people as they engage in other tasks	• Forming groups that promote interaction for all participants
• Conversations can emphasise children and young people's competence in social interactions	• Transcription of group conversations can be difficult
• Recording of conversation enables revisiting of the data	
• Researchers can be immediately responsive to information – seeking elaboration or providing support	

Examples

Dockett and Perry (2005) report a conversation between a parent and child about the first day of school, and a conversation between three boys who were about to start school.

Carr (2000) reports conversations about learning with four-year-olds as they engaged in construction activity. The activity provided a focus for the conversations and encouraged reciprocal interactions.

Dunphy and Farrell (2011) video-taped the indoor play of children aged four to twelve years in an Irish primary school. Conversations with children as they observed the video were used to encourage reflection and promote positive relationships.

Interviews

Interviews remain a common element of much research with children and young people – either as the primary data source, or as one of a range of methods employed. The many forms of interviews include:

- *Informal interviews*, which can be very much like conversations around a specific topic.
- *Semi-structured interviews*, which use an interview guide to map broad areas to be covered in interviews. Questions or themes can be used in an order that promotes the flow of the interview and the interviewee can add other relevant detail. Questions are often open-ended.
- *Structured interviews*, which use a standard set of questions, asked in an established order. They promote the generation of data that is comparable across participants.
- *Group interviews*, which often involve peers or colleagues.
- *Focus group interviews*, which bring together a number of participants to discuss a specific topic or theme.
- *Narrative interviews*, which invite participants to reflect upon specific events or times in their lives by telling stories about them.

The appropriateness of different styles of interviews will depend on the context, topic being investigated, the preferences of participants, as well as the skill of the interviewer. Some children and young people draw strength and confidence from being interviewed in a group, while others are more comfortable being interviewed alone (Einarsdóttir, 2007); some children may be comfortable being interviewed in the company of a parent or caregiver (Smith et al., 2005); and others may choose to invite a friend to join them. Regardless of the composition of the group, the style of interaction can range from informal to structured (see Table 6.8).

While interviews are most often conducted by adults, there is a growing trend for children and young people themselves to interview others – be they peers, family, friends or researchers. Within the Mosaic approach (Clark and Moss, 2001), child conferencing most often involves adults and children having formal conversations about their environment, but it also includes the potential for children to interview each other. Kellett (2011) argues that, with appropriate training and support, children and young people are not only eminently capable of undertaking a wide range of research, including interviews, but also that in doing so, they ask different questions, reflecting different knowledges, issues and priorities. Similar results are reported by Groundwater-Smith and Mockler (2003) in their project *Learning to Listen: Listening to Learn*, where young people undertook interview training before adopting the role of interviewers.

Focus group interviews have become a popular mode of promoting engagement among participants around a specific topic. Colucci (2007) has outlined a number of strategies that encourage engagement through activity, arguing that such engagement creates conditions that support reflective and unhurried exploration of topics – particularly sensitive topics such as her own explorations of youth suicide. Among the many strategies that have been incorporated into focus group interactions are:

- free listings – where participants commence by making individual lists in response to a particular question, with the lists then being considered by the group;
- choosing among alternatives – where a range of possible solutions to a given issue are presented and the alternatives considered according to various criteria, such as most effective to least effective;
- storytelling – an incomplete vignette or scenario can be offered to participants who then can construct alternative endings;
- projective techniques – using metaphors and analogies as a commencement to a discussion;
- drawings – where participants draw a reaction to a given provocation, thereafter discussing and annotating responses.

Table 6.8 Interviews: opportunities and challenges

Potential opportunities	Potential challenges
• Interviews are familiar social encounters – often seen in the media. Seeking to interview children and young people can generate a sense of being taken seriously	• Participants may try to provide the expected or correct answer to questions
• The use of an interview guide or structured questions promotes the exploration of similar issues across interviews	• The physical and social context of interviews can influence engagement and outcomes
• Where interviews take account of the context and participants involved, they can yield important and rich data	• Discussion can move away from the topic
	• It is possible for participants to respond with minimal information
• *Individual interviews* provide opportunities for in-depth focus on the perspectives of those being interviewed	• *Individual interviews* can be confronting for some children and young people
• Children and young people may value the privacy of individual interviews	• In some contexts, it may not be appropriate to interview children or young people on their own
• *Semi-structured* and *informal* interviews offer the interviewee opportunities to explore other related issues	• *Narrative interviews* can lead to an over-emphasis on individual agency, downplaying the involvement of others or the context
• *Group interviews* can decrease the influence of the interviewer and can be less intimidating than individual interviews	• It can be difficult to obtain informed consent when using open-ended methods such as informal or narrative interviewing
• *Group interviews* recognise the importance of peer culture and the social construction of meaning	• Group interviews need effective management to ensure that all participants have opportunities to contribute
• *Narrative interviews* provide opportunities for participants to share their perspective in some depth	• It is important to attend to the interactions among group members as well as responses to the topic
• *Focus groups* can be an economical and efficient means of generating data	• Members of *focus groups* may not know each other, and may not feel comfortable sharing information with strangers
• Where members of focus groups know each other, they may be comfortable sharing information with friends or colleagues	• Peer pressure and the dominance of some individuals in focus groups can shape the data that emerges

(Continued)

Table 6.8 (Continued)

Examples

Through the *Inventing Adulthoods* project in England and Ireland, Thomson et al. (2002) used narrative interviews to identify critical moments – key moments of change – in the lives of young people, the identity work in which young people engaged around these and the resources available for them during these times.

Group interviews were used by Kuchah and Pinter (2012) to create a mutually negotiated safe space for ten- to eleven-year-old children and adults to discuss notions of good teachers and good teaching in Cameroon.

Kay (2009) described the use of individual interviews to explore the experiences of children and young people living with a parent or carer with HIV. Within the interviews, a range of tools were used to engage with participants, including puppets, drawing and games.

Bagnoli and Clark (2010) have used focus groups to investigate the daily lives, relationships and identities of young people through the *Young Lives and Times* project. Focus groups were used to recruit participants and plan elements of the project, including the design, methods and dissemination.

Birbeck and Drummond (2005) conducted a series of interviews with five- to six-year-old children to investigate perceptions of body image. The interview structure was based on two tasks related to images of body types.

Carr (2000) introduced a picture book about shared experiences in an early childhood setting to interviews with pairs of young children, using the images to guide questions about the activities and her interpretation of these. The picture book was incomplete and promoted open-ended responses. The book provided something to talk about and focused the interviews.

Written methods

In many ways, written methods can parallel the verbal methods described previously: questionnaires can take the form of a written structured interview, and written journals have many similarities with video diaries.

Questionnaires

Both the traditional paper-based questionnaire and the web-based survey are popular methods in research with children and young people (Table 6.9). Questionnaire design and piloting is critical; a well-designed questionnaire can yield a great amount of comparable data in a short period of time. Effective questionnaires often combine a range of types of questions – such as closed questions that require a ticked box or a yes/no response; rating scales; visual response scales; and open-ended questions (Figure 6.10). Written responses may include text and/or symbols. Effective questionnaires tend to be short, with simple instructions.

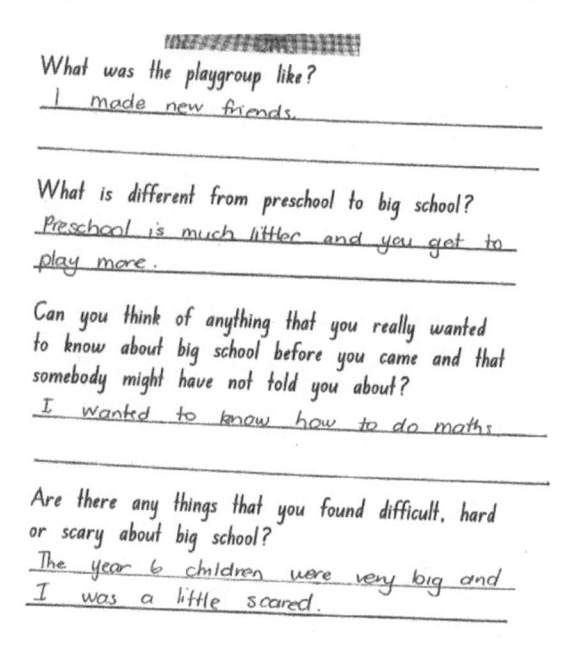

> What was the playgroup like?
> I made new friends.
>
> What is different from preschool to big school?
> Preschool is much littler and you get to play more.
>
> Can you think of anything that you really wanted to know about big school before you came and that somebody might have not told you about?
> I wanted to know how to do maths
>
> Are there any things that you found difficult, hard or scary about big school?
> The year 6 children were very big and I was a little scared.

Figure 6.10 This child's recollections of starting school were recorded in written form

Journals

The written journal has been a staple method in research over many years (Table 6.10). Written journals provide a forum for participants to record events and their reactions to these, over time. Where young children are involved, the process of journal keeping can be a collaborative process. Increasing research attention is being drawn to electronic forms of journal keeping – such as video diaries and blogs. These share many of the same opportunities and challenges as traditional written journals.

Children – sometimes in conjunction with parents – have compiled journals and shared these with researchers as part of ongoing exploration of experiences of starting school (Dockett and Perry, 2005). The journal excerpt in Figure 6.11 notes 'It was scary when I started Kindergarten. I didn't know what to do or anything else. Now I know what to do'. These comments are accompanied by complementary drawings.

Table 6.9 Questionnaires: opportunities and challenges

Potential opportunities	Potential challenges
• Accepts that some participants may prefer to offer anonymous, written information	• Can be tokenistic if used as the only method for seeking the perspectives of children and young people
• Can be used to survey a large number of people	• There is no chance for participants to seek clarification about what is requested, so any explanations need to be clear
• Can generate a lot of data	
• Web-based surveys can be accessed at a time and place of participants' choosing	• Response rates to different types of surveys and formats can be quite low
	• Can be seen as intrusive if there is no apparent reason for some of the questions
• Results from web-based surveys are presented in a form that facilitates analysis	• Requires good literacy skills
	• Can seem like school tasks, with one consequence that completion is not regarded as voluntary
	• It can be difficult to verify the authenticity of the data

Examples

Yeo and Clarke (2005) described a study in which Year 5 Singaporean children designed a questionnaire for children who had just started school. The older children administered it to younger children by reading the questions and recording responses. The older children then analysed the data, grouping responses to identify what younger children were worried about, or liked, at school.

Bondi et al. (2006) conducted a survey with young people aged twelve to nineteen years as part of an evaluation of a youth counselling service in Scotland. The survey was short, to promote a high response rate. Most questions were closed, requiring a tick box response.

Internet and social media

Research using the internet offers potential to extend the use of existing methods and to explore the development of new methods. The internet may also provide access to data that are located on specific sites, such as blogs, chat rooms, Facebook or YouTube. Baker (2013) outlines three ways in which Facebook can contribute to research – as a tool to promote and maintain research interest and communication; as a source of data as participants post information; and as context about participants' lives, experiences and interests. Research utilising the internet, particularly social media sites, recognises the integral role of social media in the lives of children and young people and indeed blurs the traditional sense of the social world, extending it to online, as well as offline, environments.

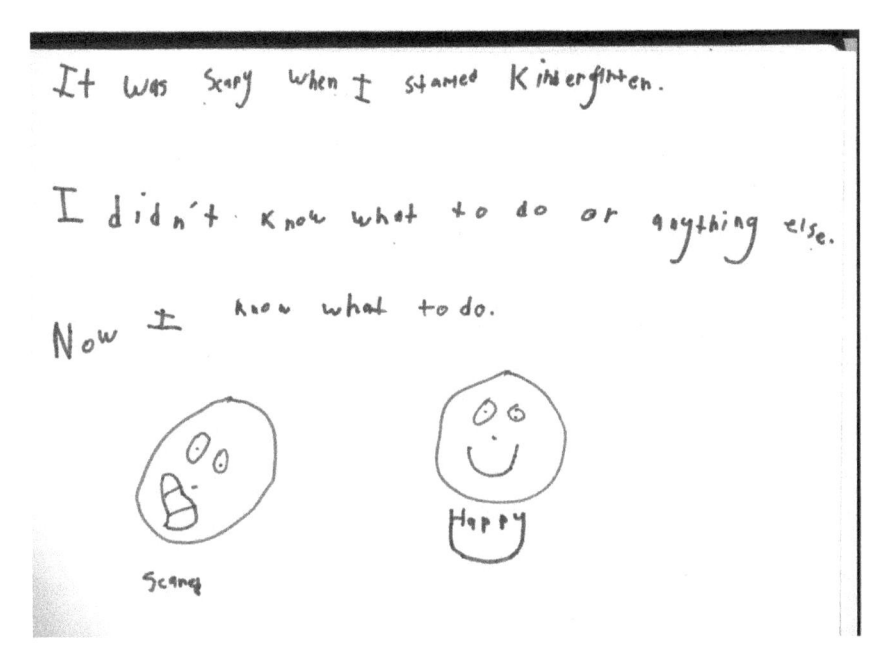

Figure 6.11 One child's starting school journal

Table 6.10 Journals: opportunities and challenges

Potential opportunities	Potential challenges
• Records ongoing interactions, thoughts and experiences • Flexibility of formats • Can include a range of text and visual material • Promotes reflection over time • Records trends and changes • Potential for collaboration	• Can be time-consuming • Entries can be missed over time • Participants may tire of the process • Can be a personal record that participants choose not to share • Undertaking analysis that reflects the nature of data

Example

Young children and their parents compiled journals after visiting a museum. They responded to some general prompts about their visit and added their own comments, reflections and questions (Dockett et al., 2011b).

Blogs have also attained increased prominence in research with children and young people. Part of the appeal of blogs, defined as 'internet communications in which the author writes dated entries that appear in reverse order ... that can link to other webpages and that allow readers to comment' (Snee, 2010: 1), is that the most immediate entries are read first, meaning that readers have access to current topics or issues without having to read all of the background information.

Examples of research utilising the internet and social media, along with an overview of potential opportunities and challenges, are included in Table 6.11.

Table **6.11** Internet and social media: opportunities and challenges

Potential opportunities	Potential challenges
• The internet can provide access to large groups of people with shared interests and/or demographic characteristics • It can promote access to some groups described as 'hard-to-reach' • The scope of internet research is not limited by geography • High levels of access to the internet, particularly among children and young people, can encourage participation in internet research • Participants who are highly mobile can maintain involvement in research that uses the internet • Through the internet, it is possible to bring together virtual communities, facilitating research access to such groups • Can facilitate research on sensitive topics • Can promote anonymity and confidentiality for participants – there is no need for researchers and participants to meet • Anonymity may promote greater levels of self-disclosure and less reliance on socially acceptable responses • Can be cost-effective	• There remain inequalities in access to the internet • The cost of internet access in some contexts can make regular or ongoing use prohibitive. The result is that some groups of children and young people have greater access to the internet than others. As a consequence, there may be bias in the responses generated by internet research • Some participants may respond to internet surveys more than once • There are potential ethical concerns about accessing participants and reporting data. For example, boundaries between public and private are blurred • Negotiating access to specific sites may require negotiations with a range of gatekeepers • There are potential issues about the authenticity and verifiability of data • Who owns and can use the data to be found on websites such as Facebook, blogs and chat rooms? • There is an age restriction on the use of some social media, such as Facebook

Potential opportunities	Potential challenges
• Can promote both synchronous and asynchronous interactions – with instant messaging options promoting real-time interaction, and other options providing time to think and reflect upon responses • Prompts exploration of not only what is shared, but how the information is shared on internet sites	• It may be difficult to consider broad issues of context

Examples

Young people's experiences of bullying, as recorded in an internet community, constituted the data for Osvaldsson's (2011) study. Data was retrieved from an internet notice board accessed by a Swedish youth mental health service. The research was introduced by an announcement on the homepage of the site.

Baker (2013) describes the potential for Facebook to maintain relationships and interest in research with young people, as well as its potential as a source of rich data. Her study of literacy as young people made the transition from school to university identified Facebook as a means to gain in-depth knowledge of the lives of participants from the information they chose to share on the site, and as an important strategy to maintain contact and research involvement over long periods of time.

Mobile phones were used by parents of three-year-old children to send photographs and text messages to the research team in a study of young children's everyday experiences (Plowman and Stevenson, 2012). Over several days, parents contributed to mobile phone diaries of their children's activities at home.

Multiple methods

Many of the methods described in this chapter are used together. The rationale for this is often to provide genuine choices for participants – not only about whether or not they choose to participate, but also the nature of participation. In the following discussion we provide brief overviews of three approaches that serve as organisers for multiple methods – that is, approaches that bring together multiple methods.

Case studies

Cases studies are generated from interactions around a specific topic over time, often utilising a range of methods. Case studies have been constructed to report on the perspectives of children and young people, and on the research processes involved (Table 6.12). As examples, Mallan et al. (2010) report a case study outlining the processes of their research of Australian high school students' everyday use of media and the internet to construct identities and generate social relationships; Osler and Osler (2002) constructed a case study from the second author's experiences of exclusion from school, informed by the Convention on the Rights of the Child (United Nations, 1989), and, from this, argued that schools have a responsibility to respond appropriately to the special education needs of students; and Sumsion et al. (2011) have drawn on several layers of data to generate case studies of the experiences of infants in day care in Australia. In this latter study, the data include video footage, photographs, observation, field notes, document analysis, researcher and parent perspectives of experiences.

Table 6.12 Case studies: opportunities and challenges

Potential opportunities	*Potential challenges*
• Researchers working with children and young people over time can develop strong relationships that offer support and enrich the data generated • Can be flexible and include a range of methods over time • Can be adapted to specific cases or contexts • Offers opportunities to explore events, situations and experiences over time • Can highlight diversity among groups	• Can be regarded as intrusive by participants or by parents/other adults • Participants may become weary of involvement • Informed consent can be difficult when the activities and outcomes are open-ended • Researchers working with children and young people over time can develop strong relationships – this may influence the research and make it hard to exit from the project • Can generate a great deal of data from diverse methods that may be difficult to analyse • Can be resource intensive

Example

Case studies were used by Wade et al. (2006) to explore the resources available to unaccompanied asylum-seeking children in England. In addition to other methods, case studies were constructed to highlight the diversity of children's experiences. Case studies were constructed from semi-structured interviews with children and practitioners whose roles were to support the children.

The Mosaic approach

The Mosaic approach (Clark and Moss, 2001) utilises multiple methods to canvass the views and experiences of young children (Table 6.13). The Mosaic approach provides a framework incorporating a wide range of methods through which children, and those who engage with them, can contribute to a 'composite picture or "mosaic" of children's lives' (Clark, 2010: 117). Methods often include photography, child-led tours and map-making, as well as observation and interviews. The artefacts produced through these methods are not necessarily ends in themselves: rather they provide prompts for conversations which, in turn, lead to reflection, interpretation and further discussion about potential changes as a result of the investigation. Essential elements of the Mosaic approach are genuine choices for children, particularly about participation, and an active role in 'exploring meanings with their peers, researchers and other adults' (Clark, 2010: 117). The approach has three phases. Each involves children and the adults with whom they interact – families, caregivers and educators:

1. children and others generate data;
2. data is reviewed as children and others discuss and interpret it; and
3. children and adults discuss what will happen as a result of the investigation.

Table 6.13 The Mosaic approach: opportunities and challenges

Potential opportunities	*Potential challenges*
• Multiple methods provide choices for children about participation and the form of that participation	• Convincing adults and funding bodies that there is value in exploring the perspectives of very young children
• Acknowledges the importance of children and adults in the construction of the mosaic	• Respecting the views of young children as not only important, but also valid and reliable
• The range of methods accommodates children's preferences and different interaction styles	• Can be regarded as intrusive by participants or by parents/other adults
	• Can be time-consuming and resource intensive
• Does not rely on verbal interaction alone	• Participants may become weary of involvement
• Focus on discussion and interpretation throughout the process	• Informed consent can be difficult when the activities and outcomes are open-ended
	• Researchers working with children and young people over time can develop strong relationships – this may influence the research and make it hard to exit from the project
	• Can generate a great deal of data from diverse methods that may be difficult to analyse

Example

In a study entitled *Spaces to Play*, Clark and Moss (2005), outline multiple ways of incorporating children's perspectives about the development of their outdoor play environment. The range of methods used included observation; photography; book-making; tours; map-making; reviewing photographs and comparing them with those of others; interviews with children, parents and early childhood educators; as well as reviewing, discussing and reflecting on the information gathered with each of these groups. An evaluation phase of the project involved seeking the perspectives of children and educators about the project itself and the processes of participation it afforded. Analysis of the data generated through the project led to an action plan that included making changes to the outdoor space and continuing to involve children in reviewing progress towards these.

Participatory action research

Participatory action research frames research as both investigation and intervention – where, in addition to the research outcomes, participation itself generates new knowledge for those involved. When combined, these elements offer the potential to promote individual and social change (Kemmis and McTaggart, 2005).

Participatory action research occurs in cycles, as participants identify problems or issues, assess these, determine a course of action or investigation, implement this and then assess the investigation or intervention. Multiple methods are used in these processes – often including surveys, focus group interviews, observations, community mapping and photographic tours (Table 6.14).

Table 6.14 Participatory action research: opportunities and challenges

Potential opportunities	Potential challenges
• Is often used in evaluation studies, where it provides opportunities for all stakeholders to have input • Focuses on the collaborative relationships between the researcher and participants • Promotes reflexivity over the various cycles • Provides opportunities for different types and levels of participation • Takes account of the context in which the research occurs	• It can be hard to identify a specific beginning and end to the project • Reliance on existing, or building, relationships. This can require extensive time commitments • The research is linked closely with everyday experiences, so it can be difficult to withdraw • Participation may increase the visibility of children and young people and contribute to greater surveillance • Requires a commitment to promote positive change

Examples

Porter et al. (2010) used a range of methods to investigate and improve children's safety as they negotiated travel in Ghana, Malawi and South Africa. Working with children, they conducted interviews and weighed loads carried to explore the nature and extent of their travel, transportation problems and concerns about safety.

Chen et al. (2010) report the evaluation of after-school programmes undertaken by girls across several cities in the United States. The evaluation identified elements of programmes that were deemed effective and recommended a range of improvements.

Researchers from around the world engaged on the *Growing Up in Cities* project reflect on their experiences using participatory action research with diverse groups of young people in multiple communities. They describe the challenges and opportunities afforded by this approach and the ways in which it can prompt social change and genuine listening to the perspectives of young people (Chawla et al., 2005).

Which method/s?

At the beginning of this chapter, we referred to methods being fit for purpose – that is, relevant and appropriate not only for the research questions being addressed, but also for the participants. One important strategy to determine such fitness is to consult with the children and young people who have either engaged, or will engage, with the methods. Without such consultation, there is the risk that methods – however novel or well-intended – promote tokenistic, rather than genuine, participation. Further, there is the risk that methods are chosen because they are fun, rather than for the depth and quality of data they generate.

Explorations of children and young people's perspectives of research participation have been an integral element of a range of studies (Graham and Fitzgerald, 2010; Hill, 2006; Moore et al., 2008). Mockler and Groundwater-Smith (2011) share one example of a strategy used in their series of projects undertaken with the Coalition of Knowledge Building Schools where, having engaged in focus group interviews, students are invited to complete the following brief survey:

> How did you feel about being in today's focus group discussion? Tick as many of the responses as you would like.
>
> I felt comfortable
>
> It was enjoyable
>
> I didn't get to say much
>
> Some respondents did all the talking
>
> I had a good chance to say what I thought
>
> If I had a chance I'd do this again
>
> Are there any other questions you would have liked to have been asked?

The feedback received both guides future interactions and prompts reflection from researchers and participants.

Choosing methods

Many methods have been used in research with children and young people. Their effectiveness in promoting participation depends largely on the methodology underpinning them – the reasons for their use. This chapter has canvassed a range of methods, highlighting potential opportunities and challenges in their application to research with children and young people. Reflection on these and the multiple ways in which they have been used has prompted our own reflections, leading us to ponder the following questions:

- Is it sufficient to employ a single method in research with children and young people? Does some of the power of these methods come from their complementary use?
- What makes any of these methods participatory? From whose perspectives? What do we each mean by participation?
- How do we navigate ethical issues around participation and the outcomes of that participation? For example, who 'owns' the artefacts generated through these methods? Who can speak to the artefacts, about the artefacts and with the artefacts?
- Mindful of the importance of choice, and children and young people's rights to opt out of research, how easy is it to withdraw from participatory or group methods?
- What strategies help manage the wealth, range and complexity of the data that are constructed?
- What strategies ensure that the products (artefacts) are not considered in isolation – either as the outcomes of the research or as the embodiment of meaning?
- Is there a danger that methods considered to be 'child-friendly' are construed as 'child-like', simplistic or apparently simplistic? Such an approach would ignore the complexity of many of the methods described, as well as the requisite interpretation and analysis.

Key points

- Methods alone do not constitute participatory research with children and young people. Attention needs to be paid to the methodology underpinning their use.
- There is debate about whether or not specific child-friendly methods are required to engage in participatory research with children and young people. This has resulted in moves to promote person-centred research methods, where fitness for purpose is a prime concern.
- Reflexivity is required in order to consider the potential opportunities and challenges offered by various methods.
- Many studies utilise multiple methods in complementary ways.
- In any consideration of methods, it is important to consider the perspectives of the children and young people involved.

References

Bagnoli, A. and Clark, A. (2010) Focus groups with young people: A participatory approach to research planning. *Journal of Youth Studies*, 13(1): 101–19.

Baker, S. (2013) Conceptualising the use of Facebook in ethnographic research: As tool, as data and as context. *Ethnography and Education*, 8(2): 131–45.

Banks, M. (1995) Visual research methods. *Social Research Update No 11*. Guildford: University of Surrey. http://sru.soc.surrey.ac.uk/SRU11/, accessed 13th October, 2013.

Bessell, S. (2009) *Research with children: Thinking about method and methodology*. In Australian Research Alliance for Children and Youth and New South Wales Commission for Children and Young People (Eds) *Involving children and young people in research*, pp. 17–27). www.childhealthresearch.org.au/media/54379/involvingchildrenandyoungpeopleinresearch_1_.pdf, accessed 16th October, 2013.

Birbeck, D. and Drummond, M. (2005) Interviewing, and listening to the voices of, very young children on body image and perceptions of self. *Early Child Development and Care*, 175(6): 579–96.

Bondi, L., Forbat, L., Gallagher, M., Plows, V. and Prior, S. (2006) *Evaluation of the youth counselling service, Airdrie Local Health Care Co-operative*, University of Edinburgh. www.ed.ac.uk/polopoly_fs/1.37873!/fileManager/evaluation.pdf, accessed 16th October, 2013.

Buchwald, D., Schantz-Laursen, B. and Delmar, C. (2009) Video diary data collection in research with children: An alternative method. *International Journal of Qualitative Methods*, 8(1): 12–20.

Carr, M. (2000) Seeking children's perspectives about their learning. In A. Smith, N. Taylor and M. Gollop (Eds) *Children's voices: Research, policy and practice*. Auckland, NZ: Longman, pp. 37–55.

Chalfen, R. and Rich, M. (2004) Applying video research: Patients teaching physicians about asthma through video diaries. *Visual Anthropological Review*, 20(1): 17–30.

Chambers, D.W. (1983) Stereotypic images of the scientist: The Draw a Scientist Test. *Science Education*, 67(2): 255–65.

Chawla, L., Blanchet-Cohen, N., Cosco, N., Driskell, D., Kruger, K., Malone, K., Moore, R. and Percy-Smith, B. (2005) Don't just listen – do something! Lessons learned about governance from the *Growing Up in Cities* project. *Children, Youth & Environments*, 15(2): 53–88.

Chen, P., Weiss, F. and Nicolson, H. (2010) Girls study Girls Inc.: Engaging girls in evaluation through participatory action research. *American Journal of Community Psychology*, 46(1–2): 228–37.

Christensen, P. and James, A. (2008a) *Research with children: Perspectives and practices*. 2nd edition. London: Falmer.

Christensen, P. and James, A. (2008b) Childhood diversity and commonality. In P. Christensen and A. James (Eds) *Research with children: Perspectives and practices*. 2nd edition. London: Falmer, pp. 156–72.

Christensen, P., Mikkelsen, M.R., Nielsen, T.A.S. and Harder, H. (2011) Children, mobility, and space: Using GPS and mobile phone technologies in ethnographic research. *Journal of Mixed Methods Research*, 5(3): 227–46.

Clark, A. (2010) Young children as protagonists and the role of participatory, visual methods in engaging multiple perspectives. *American Journal of Community Psychology*, 46(1–2): 115–23.

Clark, A. (2011) Breaking methodological boundaries? Exploring visual, participatory methods with adults and young children. *European Early Childhood Education Research Journal*, 19(3): 321–30.

Clark, A. and Emmel, N. (2010) Using walking interviews. *Realities Toolkit #13*. http://eprints.ncrm.ac.uk/1323/1/13-toolkit-walking-interviews.pdf, accessed 3rd July, 2014.

Clark, A. and Moss, P. (2001) *Listening to young children: The mosaic approach*. London: National Children's Bureau and Joseph Rowntree Foundation.

Clark, A. and Moss, P. (2005) *Spaces to play: More listening to young children using the Mosaic approach*. London: National Children's Bureau.

Colucci, E. (2007) Focus groups can be fun: The use of activity oriented questions in focus group discussions. *Qualitative Health Research*, 17(10): 1422–33.

Corbin, J. and Strauss, A. (2008) *Basics of qualitative research*. 3rd edition. Thousand Oaks, CA: Sage.

Corsaro, W.A. (2003) *We're friends, right?* Washington, DC: Joseph Henry Press.

Cremin, H., Mason, C. and Busher, H. (2011) Problematising pupil voice using visual methods: Findings from a study of engaged and disaffected pupils in an urban secondary school. *British Educational Research Journal*, 37(4): 585–603.

Dockett, S. and Perry, B. (2005) Researching with children: Insights from the Starting School Research Project. *Early Childhood Development and Care*, 175(6): 507–21.

Dockett, S., Einarsdóttir, J. and Perry, B. (2011a) Balancing methodologies and methods in researching with young children. In D. Harcourt, B. Perry and T. Waller (Eds) *Researching young children's perspectives*. Abingdon, UK: Routledge, pp. 68–81.

Dockett, S., Main, S. and Kelly, L. (2011b) Consulting young children: Experiences from a museum. *Visitor Studies*, 14(1): 13–33.

Dunphy, L. and Farrell, T. (2011) Indoor play provision in the classroom. In D. Harcourt, B. Perry and T. Waller (Eds) *Researching young children's perspectives*. London: Routledge, pp. 128–42.

Einarsdóttir, J. (2005) Playschool in pictures: Children's photographs as a research method. *Early Child Development and Care*, 175(6): 523–41.

Einarsdóttir, J. (2007) Research with children: Methodological and ethical challenges. *European Early Childhood Education Research Journal*, 15(2): 197–211.

Einarsdóttir, J., Dockett, S. and Perry, B. (2009) Making meaning: Children's perspectives expressed through drawings. *Early Child Development and Care*, 179(2): 217–32.

Eldén, S. (2013) Inviting the messy: Drawing methods and 'children's voices'. *Childhood*, 20(1): 66–81.

Emmel, N. (2008) Participatory mapping: An innovative sociological method. *Realities Toolkit #3*. http://eprints.ncrm.ac.uk/540/2/2008-07-toolkit-participatory-map.pdf, accessed 3rd July, 2014.

Graham, A. and Fitzgerald, R. (2010) Progressing children's participation: Exploring the potential of a dialogical turn. *Childhood*, 17(3): 343-59.

Groundwater-Smith, S., Ewing, R. and Le Cornu, R. (2011) *Teaching: Challenges and dilemmas*. 4th edition. Melbourne: Cengage Learning Australia.

Groundwater-Smith, S. and Mockler, N. (2003) *Learning to listen: Listening to learn*. Sydney: Centre for Practitioner Research, University of Sydney and MLC School.

Herssens, J. and Heylighen, A. (2012) Blind photographers: A quest into the spatial experiences of blind children. *Children Youth and Environments*, 22(1): 99-124.

Hickey, A. and Phillips, L. (2013) New kids on the block: Young people, the city and public pedagogies. *Global Studies of Childhood*, 3(2): 115-28.

Hill, M. (2006) Children's voices on ways of having a voice: Children's and young people's perspectives in methods used in research and consultation. *Childhood*, 13(1): 69-89.

Holm, G. (2008) Visual research methods: Where are we and where are we going? In S.N. Hesse-Biber and P. Leavy (Eds) *Handbook of emergent methods*. New York: Guilford Press, pp. 325-41.

Hwang, S.K. (2013) Home movies in participatory research: Children as movie makers. *International Journal of Social Research Methodology*, 16(5): 445-56.

Jesuvadian, M.K. and Wright, S. (2011) Doll tales: Foregrounding children's voices in research. *Early Child Development and Care*, 181(3): 277-85.

Kay, H. (2009) Listening to children and young people affected by parental HIV. In E.K. Tisdall, J.M. Davis and M. Gallagher (Eds) *Researching with children and young people*. London: Sage, pp. 40-7.

Kellett, M. (2011) Empowering children and young people as researchers: Overcoming barriers and building capacity. *Child Indicators Research*, 4(2): 205-19.

Kemmis, S. and McTaggart, R. (2005) Participatory action research. Communicative action and the public sphere. In N.K. Denzin and Y.S. Lincoln (Eds) *Handbook of qualitative research*. 3rd edition. Thousand Oaks, CA: Sage, pp. 559-603.

Kuchah, K. and Pinter, A. (2012) 'Was this an interview?' Breaking the power barrier in adult-child interviews in an African context. *Issues in Educational Research*, 22(3): 283-97.

MacArthur, J., Sharp, S., Kelly, B. and Gaffney, M. (2007) Disabled children negotiating school life: Difference and teaching practice. *International Journal of Children's Rights*, 15: 99-120.

Mallan, K.M., Singh, P. and Giardina, N. (2010) The challenge of participatory research with 'tech-savvy' youth. *Journal of Youth Studies*, 13(2): 255-72.

Mayall, B. (2008) Conversations with children: Working with generational issues. In P. Christensen and A. James (Eds) *Research with children: Perspectives and practices*. 2nd edition. Abingdon, UK: Routledge, pp. 109-24.

Mockler, N. and Groundwater-Smith, S. (2011) Weaving a web of professional practice: The Coalition of Knowledge Building Schools. In B. Lingard, P. Thomson and T. Wrigley (Eds) *Changing schools: Alternative models*. London: Routledge, pp. 294–322.

Moore, T., McArthur, M. and Noble-Carr, D. (2008) Little voices and big ideas: Lessons learned from children about research. *International Journal of Qualitative Methods*, 7(2): 77–91.

Muir, S. (2008) Participant produced video: Giving participants camcorders as a social research method. *Realities Toolkit #4*. http://eprints.ncrm.ac.uk/541/1/2008-07-toolkit-camcorders.pdf, accessed 3rd July, 2014.

Noyes, A. (2004) Video diary: A method for exploring learning dispositions. *Cambridge Journal of Education*, 34(2): 193–209.

Osler, A. and Osler, C. (2002) Inclusion, exclusion and children's rights: A case study of a student with Asperger syndrome. *Emotional and Behavioural Difficulties*, 7(1): 35–54.

Osvaldsson, K. (2011) Bullying in context: Stories of bullying on an internet discussion board. *Children & Society*, 25: 317–27.

Pimlott-Wilson, H. (2012) Visualising children's participation in research: Lego, Duplo, rainbows and clouds and moodboards. *International Journal of Social Research Methodology*, 15(2): 135–48.

Plowman, L. and Stevenson, O. (2012) Using mobile phone diaries to explore children's everyday lives. *Childhood*, 19(4): 539–53.

Porter, G., Hampshire, K., Bourdillon, M., Robson, E., Munthali, A., Abane, A. and Mashiri, M. (2010) Children as research collaborators: Issues and reflections from a mobility study in sub-Saharan Africa. *American Journal of Community Psychology*, 46(1–2): 215–27.

Punch, S. (2002) Research with children: The same or different from research with adults? *Childhood*, 9(3): 321–41.

Reed, A. and Hill, A. (2010) 'Don't keep it to yourself!': Digital storytelling with South African youth. *Seminar.net – International Journal of Media, Technology and Lifelong Learning*, 6(2): 268–78.

Richman, A. (2007) The outsider lurking online: Adults researching youth cybercultures. In A. Best (Ed.) *Representing youth: Methodological issues in critical youth studies*. New York: New York University Press, pp. 181–202.

Rinaldi, C. (2005) *In dialogue with Reggio Emilia: Listening, researching and learning*. London: Routledge.

Sewell, K. (2011) Researching sensitive issues: A critical appraisal of 'draw-and-write' as a data collection technique in eliciting children's perceptions. *International Journal of Research & Method in Education*, 34(2): 175–91.

Smith, A., Duncan, J. and Marshall, K. (2005) Children's perspectives on their learning: Exploring methods. *Early Child Development and Care*, 175(6): 473–87.

Snee, H. (2010) Using blog analysis. *Realities Toolkit #10*. http://eprints.ncrm. ac.uk/1321/2/10-toolkit-blog-analysis.pdf, accessed 3rd July, 2014.

Sumsion, J., Harrison, L., Press, F., McLeod, S., Goodfellow, J. and Bradley, B. (2011) Researching infants' experiences of early childhood education and care. In D. Harcourt, B. Perry and T. Waller (Eds) *Researching young children's perspectives*. London: Routledge, pp. 113–27.

Thomson, R., Holland, J., Henderson, S., McGrellis, S. and Sharpe, S. (2002) Critical moments: Choice, chance and opportunity in young people's narratives of transition. *Sociology*, 36(2): 335–54.

United Nations (1989) Convention on the rights of the child. New York. www.unicef.org/crc, accessed 17th October, 2013.

Wade, J., Mitchell, F. and Baylis, G. (2006) *Unaccompanied asylum seeking children: The response of social work services*. London: British Association for Adoption and Fostering.

Waite, S., Boyask, R. and Lawson, H. (2010) Aligning person-centred methods and young people's conceptualisations of diversity. *International Journal of Research and Methods in Education*, 33(1): 69–83.

Weber, S. and Mitchell, C. (1995) *'That's funny, you don't look like a teacher'. Interrogating images and identity in popular culture*. London: Falmer Press.

White, J., Rockel, J. and Toso, M. (2007) Reflecting on a research project on play through sociocultural eyes: 'Eureka' moments. *Journal of Australian Research in Early Childhood Education*, 14(2): 47–60.

Winter, K. (2010) Ascertaining the perspectives of young children in care: Case studies in the use of reality boxes. *Children & Society*, 26(5), 368–80.

Yeo, L.S. and Clarke, C. (2005) Starting school: A Singapore story told by children. *Australian Journal of Early Childhood*, 30(3): 1–8.

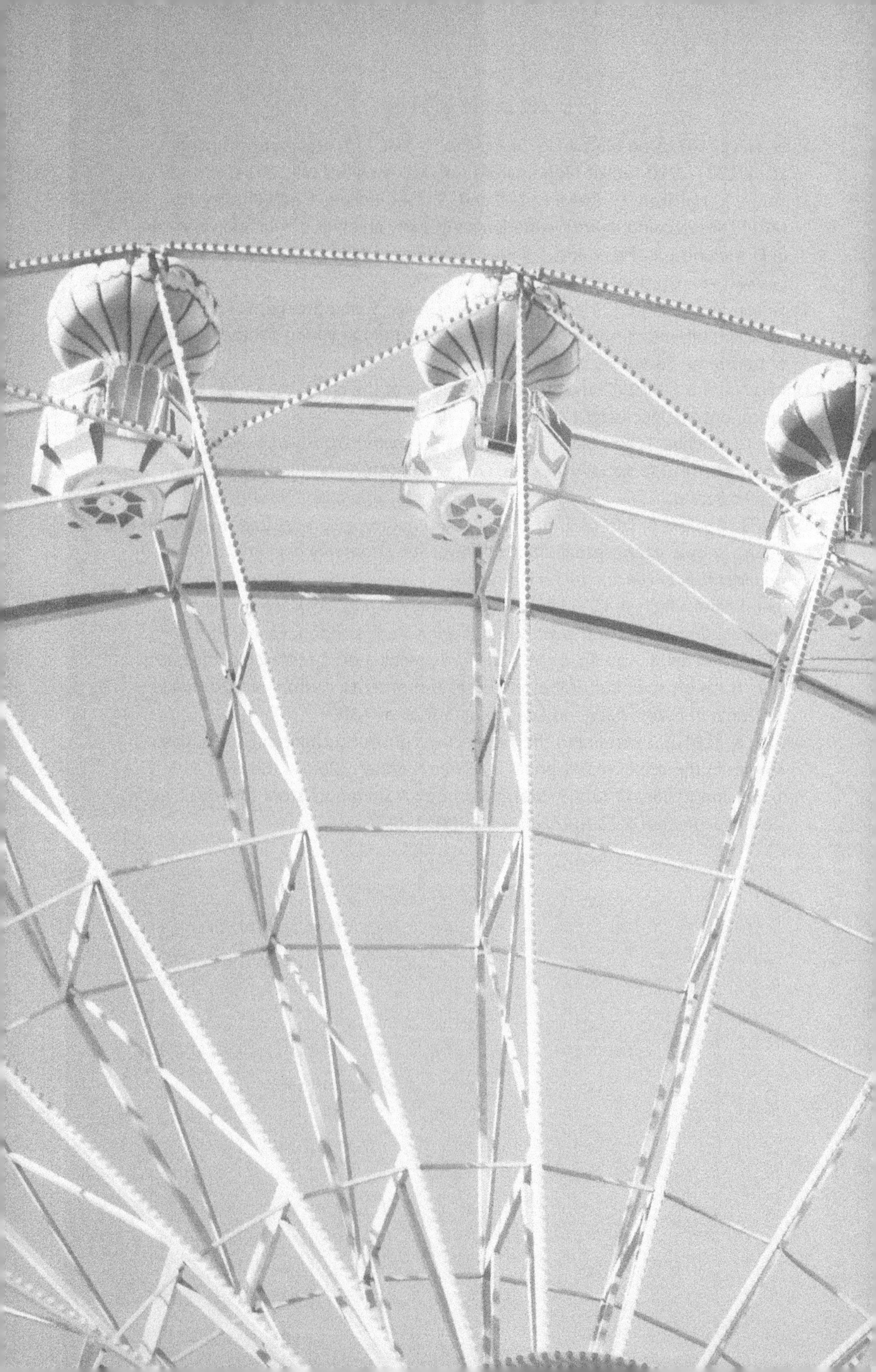

SEVEN

ISSUES OF IMPACT AND SUSTAINABILITY IN THE CONTEXT OF PARTICIPATORY DESIGN AND CONSTRUCTION

This chapter is concerned with matters in relation to the impact and sustainability of projects that take participatory research with children and young people beyond the ephemeral and transitory. While undoubtedly short term 'one-off' projects may have some merit in disturbing settled ideas and practices, it is unlikely that they will have a long-term effect. In this chapter we are concerned with examining the ways in which participatory research projects with children and young people can inform the planning and design of policies and practices that hitherto have been difficult to maintain over time (Alderson, 2012). Often groups will form and re-form in varying and different configurations with the scope and reach of projects being limited to addressing immediate concerns. We argue that there is a need to build connections that are meaningful and serve positive social consequences as opposed to short-term and possibly self-interested purposes. For this reason we have chosen to look specifically at projects that vary from the political ecology that is focused upon in Chapter 5 and instead use, both literally and metaphorically, projects that are concerned with ecological issues as understood in the built and natural environment.

Thus, this chapter will address:

- Broad issues related to impact and sustainability as related to participatory research with children and young people.
- The argument that by exploring specific cases that move from consultation to actualisation we can better understand and critique Hart's ladder of participation and its relation to the impact and sustainability of a range of projects.
- The limitations and benefits of engaging with children and young people in designing and constructing features of the built and natural environment as a series of specific examples.

CASE STUDY 7.1

Imagine this. A nun, in a hard hat, with her arms around the shoulders of an eight-year-old child, assisting in guiding a pneumatic drill into the dreary asphalt of a school playground. In 1978 a small primary school in Sydney's inner west undertook a year-long project in conjunction with the Faculty of Architecture, and the Department of Education at the University of Sydney to re-design and re-build its school playground, supported by funding from the Disadvantaged Schools Program.[1] Every child in the school, from Kindergarten to Year 6 was

---

[1] The Australian Disadvantaged Schools Program commenced in the 1970s and concluded in 1997. It was the longest-running Australian equity programme, focusing on socio-economic disadvantage, schools practices and management. For a full account of the program and its genesis see Ayres (2003).

placed in one of three multi-age teams. With the support of architecture and teacher education students, they worked for one day a week to map their school playground and identify those features that they liked and disliked, and developed three alternative models for a re-imagined space. After much discussion, one model was selected, the materials purchased and over the ensuing months the playground was built with all children and their teachers participating. The scenario at the commencement of this portrayal was filmed and documented as 'I Like to Slide Down Slippery Dips' with the film now archived in the Faculty of Architecture at the University.

The children had observed, during the first phase of the project, how they wished for: smaller, intimate spaces where they could hide and congregate in secrecy; equipment that they could climb and swing from; a sandpit; gardens; shade; and colourful walls. Over the course of the year all of these desires were achieved. The school students' sense of being able to influence environmental changes was so enhanced that two years later, when the local council proposed altering the nearby park, the students investigated the plans, surveyed the park and participated in its regeneration. Such was the power of their input that they were recognised with an environmental award by the state's largest daily newspaper. Twenty-five years later the playground no longer exists, the suburb has been gentrified and occupational health and safety standards are enforced.

So, why begin a chapter on impact and sustainability, in the context of participatory design and construction, with this particular case study? Undeniably, the project had an impact upon all who had participated, including parents and local authorities. The project continued to be sustained over a number of years with teacher education students working with the children on a variety of small-scale projects including film making and gardening. Throughout this chapter, we draw upon projects of this kind to illustrate our arguments. Engaging and partnering with children and young people to support improvements in the built and natural environments allows us to scale up the arguments for participatory inquiry and action; while at the same time addressing some of the current obstacles and barriers that act as impediments to developing child-friendly places and spaces in the community.

Why sustainability matters

In their discussion of sustainability with respect to practitioner inquiry in education, Groundwater-Smith et al. (2013: 76) argue that four concepts are at work when projects are to be sustainable: *depth, length, breadth* and *relations*. In the case of the first of these, and in the context of this book, we believe that when engaging with children and young people to investigate and work on features of the environment, or other factors in their lives, the challenge is to go beyond the ephemeral and strive for a project that has authentic resonance for them and has the capacity to strengthen the community of which they are a part. This cannot be achieved following some kind of hasty consultation, but takes time and effort so that the length of projects is critical. As Fielding (2004: 296) has observed:

> Too much contemporary student voice work invites failure and disillusion, either because its methodologies and contextual circumstances reinforce subjugation, or because its valorization pays too little attention to the extent to which young people are already incorporated by the practices of what is cool or customary.

As well, sustainable projects will need to have a public face that allows them to be adopted and adapted by others – thus having breadth. Finally, the interactive nature of the enterprise brings with it the need for the development of sound communication and the building of positive relationships between all who take part. As Graham and Fitzgerald (2010: 356) have concluded:

> We have suggested that a participatory approach that seeks to facilitate the recognition of children entails much more than 'listening to their voices', but, instead, points to the potential of a dialogic approach. Such an approach to participation is based in relationships, that is, oriented towards children's self-understanding and individual agency, as well as to the self-understanding of the adults involved. We have posited that it is only in engaging in such an approach that 'change' grounded in respect is possible.

We also need to consider and take account of a dimension that signals that the work has a sound moral purpose. Smith (2010) makes the case for the participation of children and young people in a sustainable manner as one that is a matter of citizenship within a rights framework, as discussed throughout this book. She points to the need to avoid the 'one-off' project and those cases where there are insufficient resources to undertake the work successfully. Citing many positive examples from a number of studies undertaken across the world, she concludes that children and young people do have the capacity to strengthen their communities and render them safer, more humane and more responsive. However, as Sinclair (2004: 106) has observed, children and young people's participation often 'takes place at the margins of many organisations rather than being part and parcel of the ways in which the agency goes about its everyday business in respect of matters relating to children.'

Although not easily found, we can identify examples of ways in which organisations have demonstrated a sustained commitment to nurturing young people in ongoing engagement in projects that concern them. As one example, Roger Holdsworth, from the state of Victoria in Australia, has published a bi-monthly resource entitled *Connect* that documents student participation approaches and initiatives. The publication supports reflective practices and has developed and shared resources since 1979 – an enviable record. Each issue includes examples, from Australia and overseas, with contributors being both adults and young people themselves. Since moving to an electronic form access is via an e-mail list, r.holdsworth@unimelb.edu.au, with no subscription costs.

In another vein, in New South Wales, the Coalition of Knowledge Building Schools that has functioned for over ten years (Mockler and Groundwater-Smith, 2011; Needham, 2011) can claim to have sustained participative research by young people. A hybrid group of schools and cultural institutions, the Coalition has as a central element of its platform of practice the work and engagement of children and young people as enquirers with a capacity to undertake research into aspects of learning inside and outside schools.

CASE STUDY 7.2

Saint Angelo College (name anonymised) is a Kindergarten to Year 12 non-government school in New South Wales. It is a member of the Coalition of Knowledge Building Schools. Under the auspices of a government initiative known as Building the Education Revolution (BER) it was funded to create a new flexible learning environment that was envisaged to attend to the 21st Century digital revolution and to be connected to the children's range of experiences. A unit was developed that would embody the equivalent of four classroom spaces.

The decision was taken to develop the new space across stages 1 and 2, i.e. Years 2 and 3 (chronological years, six to eight). At the time, groupings in the junior school were arranged in clusters: K/1, Foundation and Discovery; 2/3 Inquiry and Investigation; 4/5 Apprenticeship and Competence. Each cluster takes a view of the learners and their dispositions for learning at the appropriate level.

The new building was completed in 2010 and moved into at the end of that year. Given that its design was considered to vary radically from the 'egg-crate' classroom arrangements, now so typical of school design, it was seen that all would be learning under new conditions, teachers and children alike, and that the community should also be well-informed of the innovative building and its impact on student learning. After three years implementation a review was conducted. This case study looks only at the ways in which students were able to participate in the review and have their perspectives taken account of.

All young people in Years 2 and 3 were invited to prepare drawings in relation to their learning in the flexible space, what assisted them and what difficulties they might encounter.

(Continued)

(Continued)

Teachers of Years 4 and 5 were then asked to select fifteen students from each year who were sufficiently skilled to take notes in a timely manner. The students, in turn interviewed Years 2 and 3 respectively in pairs. They were advised that their role was one of being 'research assistants' for the flexible learning space review. Each year group was briefed regarding the task and given half an hour to undertake their interviews that were based upon the Year 2/3 students' visual representations of what was seen to help learning in the flexible space. The Years 4/5 students then re-convened to discuss their findings and share the matters that surprised them.

Each pair explained what they had gathered and how they had annotated the drawings. The following themes emerged as matters that facilitated learning, motivation and engagement in the flexible space:

- The relationship with peers for learning and social purposes;
- The relationship with teachers;
- The physical design of the space, both indoors and outdoors;
- Accessibility and range of resources, including technical resources; and
- Having fun.

The students valued highly their opportunities to engage with their peers in a variety of ways that were not only social/emotional, but also cognitive. Students perceived that the space provided opportunities to share learning both within given groups and across the grade.

> We are all a big community and we can work with new people (Year 2).
>
> I can communicate and cooperate a lot better with other people (Year 3).
>
> You can make a better connection with people (Year 3).
>
> You can teach other kids and learn from others, you can help when people don't know something that we know, we can teach them (Year 3).

Only one student noted her dislike of the flexible learning space.

> I don't like the open learning space because there is way too much background noise. I prefer being in a closed learning space because being able to see my friends distracts me and causes me to talk and my friends and I don't get any work done. This is not for everything. Just some things (Year 3).

The students acting as 'research assistants' were not only surprised by the willingness of their interviewees to discuss their drawings and what they might mean, but also by how the process made them feel that they were part of an exciting project that mattered to their school.

Engaging young people in this way contributed to a meaningful portrayal of the operation of the new learning space, it also enabled those who were recording the events to develop skills that could be employed again at a later point. Indeed, the Years 4/5 students were clamouring to undertake further inquiries about the school's functions and practices.

Relating impact and sustainability

So, what comes first, impact or sustainability? We shall argue that each is inextricably linked with the other. A project that engages children and young people as participants may have impact in the short term, but not be sustainable. We shall be returning to Hart's ladder of participation (Figure 7.1) as a framework for discussing the ways in which sustainability, in particular, can be maintained

The Ladder of Participation

8. Child-initiated shared decisions with adults
7. Child-initiated and directed
6. Adult-initiated shared decisions with children
5. Consulted and informed
4. Assigned but informed
3. Tokenism
2. Decoration
1. Manipulation

Degrees of participation

Non-participation

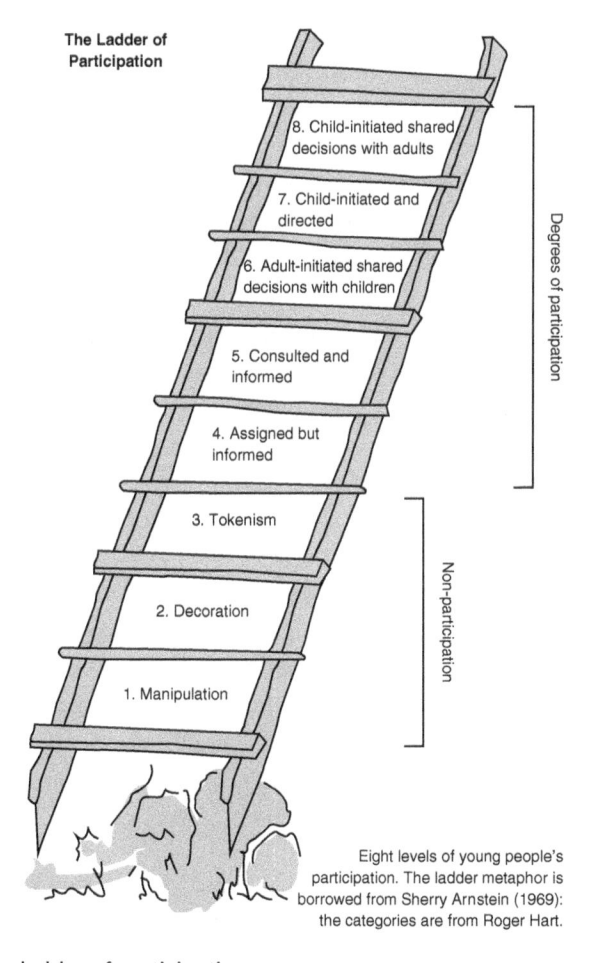

Eight levels of young people's participation. The ladder metaphor is borrowed from Sherry Arnstein (1969): the categories are from Roger Hart.

Figure 7.1 The ladder of participation

(Hart, 1992). Hart's ladder has been cited over the past twenty years and itself can be seen as an example of having an impact and remaining relevant, albeit with many new insights being developed.

Clearly, we shall not be focusing here upon the first three steps of non-participation: manipulation, decoration and tokenism. Neither shall we consider the step of being assigned but informed, but will be turning our attention to those remaining steps: consulted and informed; adult-initiated shared decisions with children; child-initiated and -directed; and child-initiated shared decisions with adults. Furthermore, we shall be concerned with the shift from participation in planning to the actualisation of plans and designs.

When we consider sustainability in terms of participative inquiry and action with children and young people, especially in relation to their engagement with the built and natural environment and how it might be changed, we need to be well-attuned to the various and significant challenges. Who has the power? How is that power exercised? What are the social and political conditions that may act as impediments? We need to understand the potential differences in the ways children and adults view the world, as well as the potential similarities in worldviews. On the one hand, it is important to recognise, as Day with Midbjer (2007: 3) have noted, that 'adult experiences centre on how we use places, we need to know what they are *for*. For children it's more about what the places "say", how they meet and *experience* them.'. On the other hand, it is important to remind ourselves of that neither adults nor children are homogeneous groups.

Elsewhere in this book we have spoken to issues in relation to power and control; here we think it apposite to turn specifically to the work of Alcoff (1991/1992) when she writes of the problems that are associated with those who believe that they have the power and authority to speak *for* others; but equally she asks whether speaking for others can be misconstrued as 'arrogant, vain, unethical, and politically illegitimate' (6). She juxtaposes the 'violence' that may be done by speaking for others, against the harm that can be caused by avoiding responsibility and accountability by retreating from giving an account on behalf of others. Thus, within a specific problematic, associated with children and young people and their adult mentors, there is a need to recognise that each is caught up in a complex web where neither is free of the other. What we argue for here is that the desired condition is that which ensures that all who participate have an ability to 'move over' to enable others to be heard and understood, taking cognisance of the different positions that they occupy, their interests and experiences, for as Alcoff writes:

> It is not *always* the case that when others unlike me speak for me I have ended up worse off, or that when we speak for others they end up worse off. (1991/1992: 29)

In effect, when considering representation in relation to sustainability we need to have a concern that we speak together. This is not merely a matter of replacing 'I' with 'we', but also taking account of how a phenomenon is represented, who is doing the speaking at the time and who is listening.

Across the world, with the imprimatur of UNICEF, a number of projects have emerged that have as their aim the development of child-friendly environments that seek to consult and engage children and young people. Karen Malone (2001) as the Asia Pacific Director of the 'Growing Up in Cities' project has long argued for local government and other authorities with connections to children and young people to actively engage with them in re-considering a range of provisions. It is this engagement to which we now turn.

Child-consulted and -informed projects

In considering the independence and social competence of children and young people Tranter and Pawson (2001) examined access to the local environment in four areas in Christchurch, New Zealand, with a particular view to identifying those impediments that would hamper their ability to more freely move about with less adult supervision. They were able to enumerate a number of features that acted as deterrents to children and young people being able to negotiate their way through the built environment. In particular, they cited the increased traffic on the roads, the perceptions of 'stranger danger' and the possibility of injury, accident or misadventure. While this project involved initial consultation with young people, it did not move beyond this to share the results of the consultation or to explore potential solutions.

Similarly, using a photo-voice method, Karlsson (2007) engaged with students from five schools in the Durban/eThekwini local government area in South Africa to take photos of their journey between school and home. The students shared their photos, and the researcher analysed these in order to construct inter-textual readings of the photographs that allowed her to identify recurring elements and attribute meaning to them. She concluded that social class largely shaped children's experience of the post-apartheid city. She argued that children from poor families experienced the city within confined and limited horizons, while children from wealthier families experienced the city in larger and more bountiful ways. In this case, while the children were participative in gathering the data, they were not contributors to its interpretation – leaving open the question of whether they would have arrived at similar conclusions.

In the literature it is possible to find a number of such examples of young people being consulted regarding their perceptions. Lehman-Frisch et al. (2012) for example, asked young people in a Parisian district to create drawings of their neighbourhood and to explain these to the researchers. They recognised that to undertake this task required a number of competencies such as memory, imagination and an understanding of scale, as well as confidence in using the medium of drawing. They were able to elicit a number of perspectives that the children had of their neighbourhood, its parks, libraries, markets and schools, as well, of course, of where their own homes fitted into the picture. Not only did the children explain their drawings they also contributed further information such as the sounds that they heard and their sensitivity to the neighbourhood's smells and the people that they might meet. They were able to establish that girls had less spatial freedom than boys and thus less knowledge of what the neighbourhood had to offer. They concluded 'the neighbourhood is made up of what they (the children) see, of what they do, what they feel and the people they meet' (Lehman-Frisch et al., 2012: 33). While this study revealed a great deal of information about children's perspectives of their neighbourhood, it did not extend to exploring with children and young people the ways in which the neighbourhood could contribute more effectively to their enjoyment of it.

In another case, Ramezani and Said (2013) explored what children took to be places with which they had a 'place friendship' in one of Iran's macro-cities. Following chance encounters with young people (aged six to fourteen), field interviews were conducted along a route in a public space. Once a child (or group of children) using the space was noticed, the interview was commenced by the researchers introducing themselves. In order to identity child-friendly places from the children's point of view, children were asked to nominate the places they most preferred under each of the dimensions identified by Chatterjee (2005) as places which they cared for and respected; could have meaningful exchanges within; could learn from; could have some control over; could provide secret places; and would allow for freedom of expression. The objective of the study was to understand which places were assessed by children as ones that they regarded as friendly. Each child was asked to nominate only one place under each dimension. It was hoped that with data on child-friendly places, that involved those children who actively use a variety of places in a given neighbourhood, useful information could be generated based upon children's preferences. The data demonstrated that natural elements, functional opportunities and potential affordances of the environment, both social and physical, and proximity to home were the attributes of places nominated as child-friendly. Size was also important, in that larger sites could provide the children with different settings that could be used for different activities with some freedom from outside controls and interference. What was noteworthy about the study, aside from its findings, was the direct approach to the children themselves, rather than through a number of gatekeepers. This serves as a reminder of the contribution of context to research.

It could well be argued that a major impediment to children and young people being more fully participative in developing ways in which they might exercise their right to creative and active access to their local built environments, is the current over-protective milieu that fosters fear and induces parents to 'bubble-wrap' their offspring (Malone, 2007). In 2008, a New York columnist created a media storm when she described her decision to allow her nine-year-old son to ride the subway alone. Following a television series, that tested over-protective parents' perceptions of risk and the intensification of parenting practices, Skenazy (2009) published her book *Free Range Kids* that argues for children's right to make choices and understand the consequences as part of their development – a skill set often ignored in today's over-management of children and young people, and which is not acknowledged by risk-averse organisations the world over.

Kytta, in writing of young people's perceptions of what works for them, argued that what is important is the development of skills that will contribute to greater independence and enjoyment of the environment:

> For instance, in countries like Finland, where children's independence and the acquisition of basic environmental skills are highly appreciated, learning to perceive environmental dangers may be regarded as an essential skill for every child. In order for the children to become 'streetwise', they cannot be overly protected. (2003: 85)

And yet, designers of public spaces continue to allow adult conceptualisations of what they should be, and how they might be actualised, to dominate. This is a serious impediment to the sustainability of initiatives that fully engage children and young people. Despite their role as key stakeholders, traditionally they have not been involved in planning because they are seen to be lacking in responsibility, experience, interest, legitimacy and power.

Adult-initiated shared decisions with children

The investment in children and young people to promote their having a greater voice not only in inquiries undertaken by adults, but also in becoming the means by which the inquiry is undertaken, is a further step in the ladder proposed by Hart. If subsequent initiatives are to not only have short-term impact, but also be sustainable, then the design of the inquiry itself is enhanced by the input of these key stakeholders. Laughlin and Johnson (2011: 440), in their examination of young people's views of public and semi-public spaces in a Toronto suburb that has been subject to gentrification, employed a number of strategies to maximise engagement. They were mindful that they needed to avoid surveys, often designed with no recourse to the informants, and that required relatively high literacy skills. In order to develop interesting activities, an issue discussed in Chapter 6, they conducted preliminary discussions with two different groups of young people at a local youth organisation and evolved two group activity sessions. The first of these involved discussions centred on photographs taken in the community by the participants with a focus upon what public space meant for them; the second session involved creating a form of artwork that would display their perceptions about these spaces that might not be easily captured by a camera. Analysis, with the participants, demonstrated that the lines between public and semi-public spaces were less clearly defined than had otherwise been imagined. Public spaces involved three criteria: they were easily accessible; provided a sense of belonging; and allowed young people to find, and be with, friends. Sometimes, their enjoyment of such spaces was marred by unpleasant smells and the hazards of garbage and litter. Semi-public spaces could include local shops where they were made to feel welcome and depended upon a notion of belonging rather than ownership. While designers had considered various qualities, such as the island-like nature of the community, its lack of permeability and through traffic, these were the very attributes that were regarded as assets and highly valued by the participants.

In Chapter 4 we discussed the need to take things slowly and carefully. It is important to take practical and unspectacular steps that can make a difference in generating hope in children and young people. As Laughlin and Johnson (2011: 453) conclude, 'without these steps, public housing revitalization plans are at risk of treating young people as absent presences, where changes are made with a view to the future rather than the now'. These studies remind us that engagement with children and young people takes time.

Child-initiated and -directed – facilitating sustainability when engaging with children and young people

At the beginning of this chapter we argued that engaging and partnering with young people to support improvements in the built environments allows us to scale up the arguments for participatory inquiry and action, while at the same time addressing some of the current obstacles and barriers that act as impediments to developing child-friendly places and spaces in the community. Clearly, it is also important to examine those conditions that will facilitate the greater sustainability of projects.

In their resource, *Built 4 Kids,* the New South Wales Commission for Children and Young People (2009) outlined the major benefits of involving children in developing features of the built environment where they might take the initiative and included:

- Grounding adult understanding and decision-making in the reality of children's and young people's experience.
- Removing the need for assumptions by adults about who children and young people are, what they need and what they want.
- Recognising children's right to participate in community development processes as citizens of their community.
- Recognising the value of children and young people's contribution to community development.
- Recognising that the knowledge and experience of children and young people of their environments differs from that of adults.

The resource is replete with advice and a number of case studies.

Many initiatives that place children and young people at the centre of urban renewal have come about as a result of UNESCO's 'Growing Up in Cities' programme. Salvadori tells of one such project undertaken in Oak Park, California, where the children of the Mexican and Cambodian residents came together to reconceptualise possibilities for their local environment. She quoted from a local housing cooperative regarding the restrictions placed on children and young people:

> Children should not be allowed to play in the building corridors. This can disturb others in the building. Also, children can be injured in the hallways, since they are not appropriate for playing. No children can play or climb the trees because they can get hurt. This is strictly prohibited. The parents of any children found playing in the trees will receive a termination of tenancy letter.
>
> No children can ride their bikes in or around the corridors of the parking lot. Furthermore, no children at all are allowed to play in the parking lot. Also, no children can play with any hard balls anywhere in the apartment. No one is allowed to socialise in the parking lot. (2001: 88)

Undeterred, she embarked on the project that engaged the local children and young people in a participatory process where they would design renovations of the community's common spaces. She showed them many examples of public places and playgrounds that were not encased in concrete, where flowers and trees grew freely and fences were few. In this case, not only did the children and young people re-design the site, but they also became active in reinvigorating it. Their own initiatives overtook those of the adults. Initially they proposed that the courtyard be divided into smaller 'niche' subspaces that would serve different purposes: a sandpit; a roller blading ramp; benches with shady trees; and a basketball court. They also proposed a mural for the car park. As a third project they proposed the establishment of a kitchen garden that could serve the whole community. It was in relation to this third project that they became pro-active.

A small group physically tore down a fence that separated out the wasteland that could become the garden. After some debate the community backed them and the garden became a reality.

As well as UNESCO's initiatives, a second and related programme of Child Friendly Cities has evolved under the auspices of UNICEF, outlining the following:

> The child-friendly cities framework refers to communities committed to fulfilling children's rights to:
>
> Influence decisions about their city
>
> Express their opinion on the city they want
>
> Participate in family, community and social life
>
> Receive basic services such as health care and education
>
> Drink safe water and have access to proper sanitation
>
> Be protected from exploitation, violence and abuse
>
> Walk safely in the streets on their own
>
> Meet friends and play
>
> Have green spaces for plants and animals
>
> Live in an unpolluted environment
>
> Participate in cultural and social events
>
> Be an equal citizen of their city with access to every service, regardless of ethnic origin, religion, income, gender or disability. (UNICEF, 2004: 3)

A long-time advocate for children and young people's participation in planning and development in terms of the urban built and natural environment, Malone (2011) undertook an ambitious project in the small New South Wales town of Dapto where she and her team consulted with children from Kindergarten (the first year of school) and Year 5 in a local school from the very outset of the innovation. A number of both qualitative and quantitative tools were employed including visual, verbal and textual methods that allowed for the range of abilities and competencies of the participating students. Their brief was to document the nature of available places and spaces that appealed to them in their local community. Following broad consultation a smaller reference group was formed to undertake three activities: to analyse the data in order to construct a children's report that would make design recommendations; a 'dreaming play space' that would recommend key elements for a playground site; and, the design and development of a walkable adventure pathway between the old and newer neighbourhoods. In the preface to the final report one of the reference group children wrote:

Our Dapto dreaming report is about the things we like about our neighbourhood and the things we think could be changed to make it even better. It's about making sure adults listen and value us and include our dreams in their designs for our place. The report is organised around the eight things children told us help make this neighbourhood child friendly. These eight themes are discussed on each page of our report alongside the information provided by the children of Dapto. (Malone, 2011: 33)

There are several other examples of the ways in which UNICEF's programme, Child Friendly Cities, have been taken up by communities. Wilks (2010) has reported on a number of such projects undertaken in Italy and the UK. For example, schools in Cremona, Italy, developed what were known as 'Piccolo Guides' whereby the students collected historical information about the town and developed a tourist guide. They used these to escort their parents around the town and opened their eyes afresh to what the town had to offer. 'The Piccolo Guides are now very popular because children are very creative at making games and seeing things in a city that adults do not normally notice' (Wilks, 2010: 32).

This, and many similar examples, reveal that child-friendly city programmes can demonstrate that it is possible to involve children and young people in authentic, significant ways that allow them to have a voice in their own future and that of their communities. Through their participation they develop confidence and skills to identify and analyse the places, spaces, resources and issues of their communities. But this is not one-way traffic, for the process is such that rich and powerful information can be generated that will inform local governments and various other authorities of the perceptions of children and young people regarding their needs. Such information is a central element of creating and maintaining vibrant communities.

Child-initiated shared decisions with adults

That children and young people are the citizens of the future, as well as the present (Kjorholt, 2002), is indisputable. The spaces and structures that they help to create may have a lasting effect not only on themselves but also the generations that are to come. Even so, it is difficult to find substantial examples of where they have entered into authentic collaborative relationships with adults and where they took the initiative. Even Hart (1992) struggled to identify projects of this kind. In Chapter 2 we reported upon Lolichen's (2009) observations of the ways in which young people in India took the initiative in curbing alcoholism in their community, but such instances are rare especially in relation to investigations into the built and natural environment.

Grugel (2013: 19) has observed that while the Convention on the Rights of the Child is one of the most widely ratified of the UN rights charters:

> Nevertheless, there remains a disjuncture between the expansion in rights based advocacy for children and their visibility in development discourses, on the one hand, and their continuing vulnerability, on the other. Children are winning rights in theory; but this is not yet translated into real, meaningful and sustained improvements in terms of children's well-being and status.

We acknowledge that her discussion is in the context of the world's most vulnerable children; however, it is something of a disappointment to find that relatively little has been recorded of children and young people initiating projects that would make a difference to their inhabitation of their environment. Certainly we now find a number of modest, but well-conducted projects published by the Open University's Children's Research Centre that provide us with evidence, that given the motivation, children and young people can take the initiative. An example is an eleven-year-old boy's investigation of the impact of young drivers on road safety (Rodden, 2013). The study was not only competent in its design, scope and breadth, but also demonstrated considerable care and responsibility in garnering informed consent from all of his participants.

Examining projects for impact and sustainability is critical to the ongoing evolution of participative research with children and young people. The studies reviewed in this chapter give us insight into the ways in which Hart's ladder of participation can give us an indication of the depth, length, breadth and relations as they apply to participation that have been experienced (Groundwater-Smith et al., 2013). By working through the final four levels we have been enabled to see that, while there are many ongoing efforts to promote young people's involvement in design and actualisation, there is still some distance to travel.

As well, we need to consider, in terms of sustainability and impact, not only participation but also the capacity to influence decision-making. Kirby et al. (2003), discuss decision-making in both formal and informal contexts; they argue that the first of these tends to go from the top down, where children and young people are invited to participate and contribute to decisions, while the latter works from the ground up, through concerns, questions and ideas that are generated by them. Formal activities may have a regularity about them, while some informal encounters may be serendipitous. Nonetheless, they argue that children and young people's perspectives should be respected and acted upon. Quoting a voluntary sector organisation they claim, 'children have a right to be INVOLVED ALL the time, not just when it is convenient for adults, or as a tick box to say "yes, we have consulted with under fives"' (Kirby et al., 2003: 64). It is worth noting that in their extensive study there was no reference to sustainability and that there was recognition that little research has been conducted into the impact of participation. Given that projects that do work closely with children and young people to take account of their perspectives are likely to generate new ways of seeing the enterprise under consideration, it is somewhat disappointing that we have so little evidence of this kind, although some instances that take account of action will be outlined in our concluding chapter.

If authentic participative research into matters that concern children and young people is to be further developed, sustained and rendered impactful, it will be important that there is a determination for it to thrive rather than merely survive.

Key points

- Sustainability needs to be considered in terms of the depth, length, breadth and relationships as they apply to participation (Groundwater-Smith et al., 2013) that are embedded in any one project.
- Authentic participatory projects have a sound moral purpose and have a capacity to change and strengthen local communities and beyond.
- Hart's ladder of participation sees the first three 'rungs' as limited, but we can think of them as precursors that may lead to later, more sustainable engagement. Being consulted may not lead to participation in considering conclusions and solutions but may be thought of as a first step.
- A major impediment to children and young people participating in projects that take them into the community is the nature of a more risk-averse society that is over-protective and thus acts to inhibit greater involvement.
- Greater participation by children and young people brings significant benefits to projects in terms of impact and sustainability, as it brings with it better-informed decision-making owing to an enhancement of the range of perspectives beyond those of adults.

References

Alcoff, L. (1991/1992) The problem of speaking for others. *Cultural Critique*, 20 (Winter): 5–32.

Alderson, P. (2012) Rights-respecting research: A commentary on 'the right to be properly researched: Research with children in a messy, real world'. *Children's Geographies*, 10(2): 233–9.

Arnstein, S. (1969) A ladder of citizen participation. *Journal of American Planning Association,* 35(4): 216–24

Ayres, R. (2003) Government policies and processes for the support of the education of disadvantaged students in Australian Schools. Paper presented at the joint AARE/NZARE Annual Conference, University of Auckland, Auckland, NZ.

Chatterjee, S. (2005) Children's friendship with place: A conceptual inquiry. *Children, Youth and Environments,* 15(1): 1–26.

Day, C. with Midbjer, A. (2007) *Environment and children.* Oxford: Architectural Press, Elsevier.

Fielding, M. (2004) Transformative approaches to student voice: Theoretical underpinnings, recalcitrant realities. *British Educational Research Journal,* 30(2): 295–311.

Graham, A. and Fitzgerald, R. (2010) Progressing children's participation: Exploring the potential of the dialogical turn. *Childhood,* 17(3): 343–59.

Grugel, J. (2013) Children's rights and children's welfare after the Convention on the Rights of the Child. *Progress in Development Studies,* 13(1): 19–30.

Groundwater-Smith, S., Mitchell, J., Mockler, N., Ponte, P. and Ronnerman, K. (2013) *Facilitating practitioner research.* London: Routledge.

Hart, R. (1992) Children's participation: From tokenism to citizenship. *International Development Centre.* Florence: UNICEF.

Karlsson, J. (2007) On the way to school: Children in the post-apartheid city. In J. Fiedler and C. Posch (Eds) *Yes they can! Children researching their lives.* Austria: Schneider Verlag Hohengehren GmbH, pp. 154–64.

Kirby, P., Lanyon, C., Cronin, K. and Sinclair, R. (2003) *Building a culture of participation: Involving children and young people in policy, service planning, delivery and evaluation.* Nottingham: DfES Publications. http://dera.ioe.ac.uk/17522/1/Handbook%20-%20Building%20a%20Culture%20of%20Participation.pdf, accessed 28th August, 2013.

Kjorholt, A. (2002) Small is powerful: Discourses on children and participation in Norway. *Childhood,* 9(1): 63–82.

Kytta, M. (2003) *Children in outdoor contexts: Affordances and independent mobility in the assessment of environmental child friendliness.* Dissertation for the Degree of Doctor of Philosophy. Centre for Urban and Regional Studies. Helsinki University of Technology.

Laughlin, D. and Johnson, L. (2011) Defining and exploring public space: Perspectives of young people from Regent Park, Toronto. *Children's Geographies,* 9(3–4): 439–56.

Lehman-Frisch, S., Authier, J. and Dufaux, F. (2012) 'Draw me your neighbourhood': A gentrified Paris neighbourhood through its children's eyes. *Children's Geographies,* 10(1): 17–34.

Lolichen, P. (2009) Rights-based participation: Children as research protagonists and partners in mainstream governance. In J. Fiedler and C. Posch (Eds) *Yes they can! Children researching their lives.* Austria: Schneider Verlag Hohengehren GmbH, pp. 135–43.

Malone, K. (2001) Children, youth and sustainable cities. *Local Environment: The International Journal of Justice and Sustainability,* 6(1): 5–12.

Malone, K. (2007) The bubble-wrap generation: Children growing up in walled gardens. *Environmental Education Research,* 13(4): 513–27.

Malone, K. (2011) *Designing and dreaming a child friendly neighbourhood for Brooks Reach, Dapto*. Bankstown, NSW: University of Western Sydney.

Mockler, N. and Groundwater-Smith, S. (2011) Weaving a web of professional practice: The Coalition of Knowledge Building Schools. In B. Lingard, P. Thomson and T. Wrigley (Eds) *Changing schools: alternative models*. London: Routledge, pp. 294–322.

Needham, K. (2011) Professional learning in an across school network. In N. Mockler and J. Sachs (Eds) *Rethinking educational practice through reflective inquiry*. Rotterdam: Springer, pp. 197–212.

New South Wales Commission for Children and Young People (2009) Built 4 Kids. www.architectureinsights.com.au/education/built4kids, accessed 8th July, 2014.

Ramezani, S. and Said, I. (2013) Children's nomination of friendly places in an urban neighbourhood in Shiraz, Iran. *Children's Geographies*, 11(1): 7–27.

Rodden, A. (2013) A research project about young drivers. www.open.ac.uk/researchprojects/childrens-research-centre/files/crc-pr/file/ecms/web-content/Alasdair-Rodden.pdf, accessed 14th November, 2013.

Salvadori, I. (2001) 'Remove a fence, invite chaos': Children as active agents of change. *Local Environment: The International Journal of Justice and Sustainability*, 6(1): 87–91.

Sinclair, R. (2004) Participation in practice: Making it meaningful, effective and sustainable. *Children & Society*, 18(2): 106–18.

Skenazy, L. (2009) *Free range kids: Giving our children the freedom we had without going nuts with worry*. New York: John Wiley and Sons.

Smith, A. (2010) Children as citizens and partners in strengthening communities. *American Journal of Orthopsychiatry*, 80(1): 103–8.

Tranter, P. and Pawson, E. (2001) Children's access to local environments: A case-study of Christchurch, New Zealand. *Local Environment: The International Journal of Justice and Sustainability*, 6(1): 27–48.

UNICEF (2004) *Building child-friendly cities: A framework for action*. Innocenti Research Centre. www.childfriendlycities.org, accessed 12th November, 2013.

Wilks, J. (2010) Child-friendly cities: A place for active citizenship in geographical and environmental education. *International Research in Geographical and Environmental Education*, 19(1): 25–38.

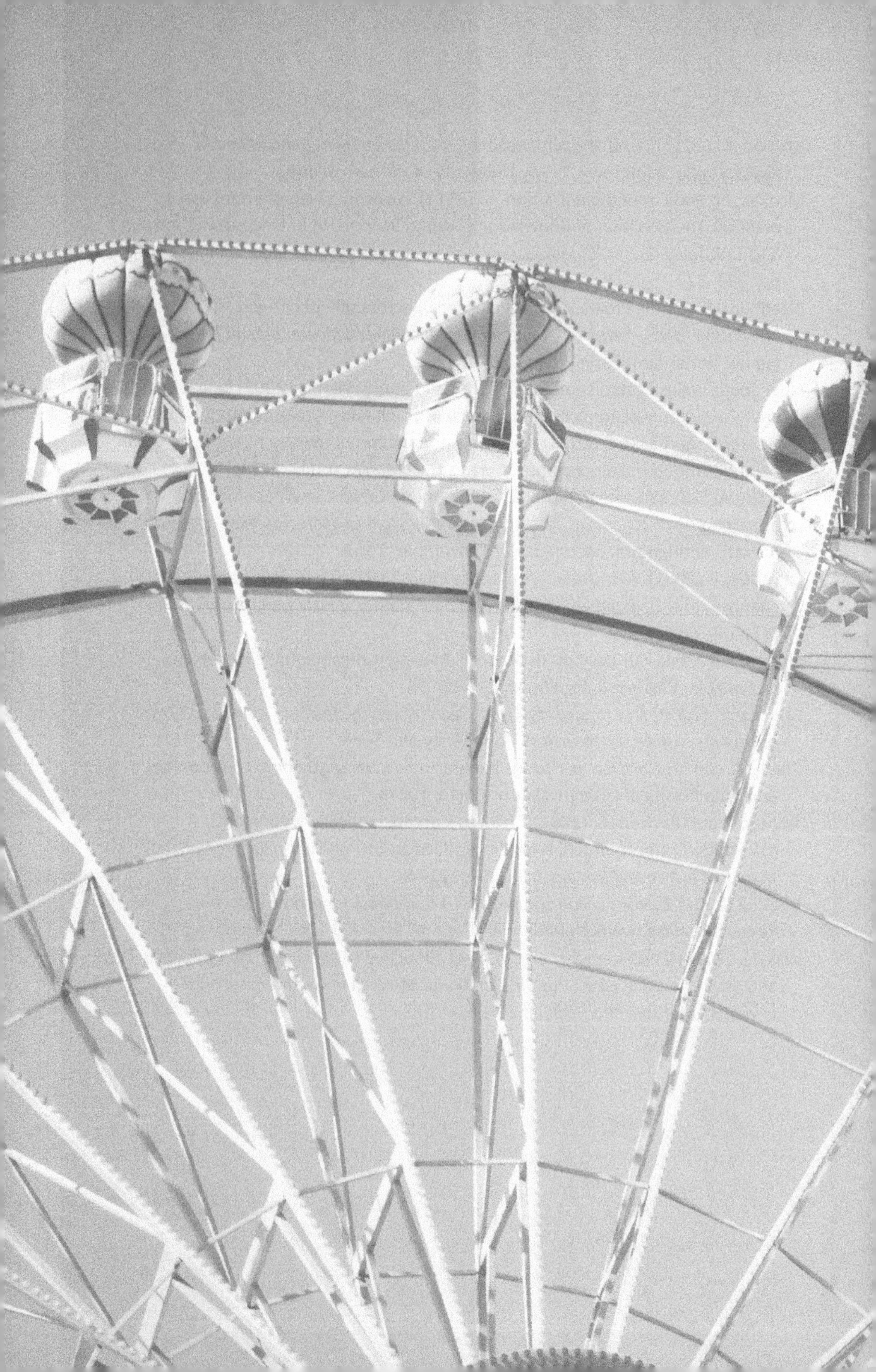

EIGHT
PUBLICATION AND DISSEMINATION

This chapter discusses a range of forms and means of disseminating the findings, insights and products of research with children and young people and examines who participates in these processes. Considering some different approaches taken and issues encountered, the chapter draws attention to the ethical and political nature of decisions concerning children and young people's participation in publication and dissemination and recommends careful consideration of how children and young people can and should be involved.

It addresses:

- Who may speak and to whom.
- 'Speak-outs' and performance/theatre.
- Arts exhibitions.
- Online or hard copy reports in the form of youth brochures, magazines, comics or posters.
- Consequences of dissemination and publication, both positive and negative.

Who may speak and to whom

Publication and dissemination are mainly concerned with communicating the results or findings of research. Who may speak and to whom are important questions for publication and dissemination of research with children and young people that aims to 'give voice' to their experience and perspectives on issues. How these questions are answered depends on the position of the researcher/s, the context and aims of specific projects, and intended audiences and impacts, giving rise to multiple layers of dissemination activity. For academic and practitioner researchers, dissemination is an integral part and often the final phase of a research project in terms of reporting their findings back to participants and the early childhood service, school, community organisation or funding body. Dissemination also typically includes, especially for university researchers, a separate set of activities such as scholarly publication and related presentations in conferences and seminars.

The question of *participatory* publication and dissemination has been given relatively limited attention. Some researchers do publish and disseminate research *with* participants or young co-researchers within and beyond the host organisation. However, research with children and young people has mainly focused on the negotiation of research questions, project designs, methodologies and modes of participating in the inquiry at the level of data generation. While children and young people are increasingly involved in analysis, this is not always the case and the normative expectation of the adult researcher's responsibility for final analysis and dissemination prevails. For academic researchers, this model of knowledge work is an amalgam of: methodological standpoint, including the researcher's position on the uses of knowledge; the researcher's defined position and institutional expectations that researchers will conduct multiple projects over a research career and meet institutional research 'output targets'; priorities within time-limited project funding; and community expectations accompanying the expert status of the academic researcher. Early childhood services, schools and community agencies may justifiably expect that in addition to the benefits to children and young people from the experience of participating in and perhaps reporting back on the project, that the researcher's expertise should result in analysis and findings that will be valuable to the organisation or to their field – of education, youth work, health and so on. Researchers' own self-positioning in terms of roles and responsibilities in participatory research also emphasises that ultimately it is our responsibility and privilege to situate young people's perspectives and agendas for change within a broader context and to make the links between the findings, practice and policy, drawing on our 'tools of trade' including epistemological and substantive knowledge in the field (Veale, 2005).

Yet these positionings raise questions about whose voices are heard, who are listening and, consequently, the extent to which the power of voice is actually shared with children and young people. Limiting dissemination to research reports and academic journal articles has been critiqued as 'passive' forms of dissemination (van Blerk and Ansell, 2007; Tisdall, 2009) as they reach a limited audience (Alderson and Morrow, 2011), and as stand-alone research products may mainly accrue benefits to the researcher (Lykes et al., 2011). Moreover, while academic publication is crucial to progressing children and young people's participatory rights, it would clearly be unjust if benefits only accrued to researchers and other adults (te Riele, 2013). Extending the reach of knowledge and insights derived from research with children and young people, and their participation in processes of dissemination, challenges us to think in terms of active engagement in a range of forums and actions, and with different stakeholders. The more powerful position and critical, authoritative voice (Haw, 2008) of adults/researchers is, then, vital to enabling the views of children and young people to be expressed in decision-making forums and acted upon. The challenges for researchers include 'how to honour different "voices" alongside each other' and 'to produce a range of research outputs that meet the needs of participants and researchers' (Haw, 2008: 204; 206).

Although approaches to involving children and young people in publication and dissemination have been limited, a number of trends may be pushing the boundaries of what dissemination means and the forms it may take. First, the scholarship and practice of participatory research has been a source of innovative methods that, in tandem with the broader developments of child and youth 'friendly' modes of participation, especially in education and the community sector, may extend into dissemination as the social and political meanings of voice and participation are elaborated. Second, the familiarity of multi-media technologies as means of children and young people's expressive participation in society (and in research) proffers new modes of research dissemination. Third, as Tisdall (2009) suggests, the trend toward 'evidence-based' policy and practice has produced greater demand for children and young people's participation and increased pressure on researchers to produce knowledge of 'what works'. Relatedly, the performance of researchers is increasingly measured in terms of their promotion of knowledge transfer or translation to fields of practice, raising expectations that dissemination moves beyond passive modes. However, the meaning of these demands as top-down accountabilities, the selection of policy-based evidence (France and Utting, 2005), and rhetorical support for participation where being seen to consult, overrides authentic interest in children's, young people's and intergenerational perspectives and their work for social justice, is very different from participatory work from the ground up. For example, participatory action research and community-based participatory research (with a focus on community development) share a commitment to the research being empowering for the communities in which it is conducted. The research questions derive from identification of children and young people's and/or broader community concerns, and local action is always integral to the project, as a representation or expression of knowledge developed (Cammarota and Fine, 2008; Minkler, 2012). The question of dissemination then is in the first instance directed toward community learning from the co-production of knowledge and developing strategies for community and social change as a consequence of dialogue with the data (Reason and Bradbury, 2008). In these ways, participation aims to be transformative in both process and 'outcomes', particularly for marginalised children and young people and their communities (Nixon et al., 2012; White, 1996). Moreover, the processes of publication and dissemination in these participatory approaches to research may involve many more people than the researcher (or research team) and the project participants, as the findings and insights are owned by a community and the uses of the research are negotiated within the community.

Decisions about dissemination are, then, highly contextual issues and may relate to the nature of the project, who is involved and the particular orientation of participatory methodology. Additionally, the questions of who speaks to whom involve ethical as well as political decisions; and these two orientations may at times present significant dilemmas. For example, some researchers argue for children and young people's right to present their findings to practitioners and policy-makers, while also recognising that coming to the table would in all likelihood breach the anonymity that has been assured when consent and assent were obtained. Others have questioned the benefit to children and young people in light of past experience when authorities have censored what may be presented publicly, or appeared to listen but failed to act on children and young people's advice. There are also questions of who owns the research in terms of intellectual property rights of researchers, children and young people as co-researchers and participants, and sometimes organisations and funding bodies, and who then controls what is done with the data and findings. As discussed in Chapter 3, the ethical process of informed consent is multi-layered and can be significant to publication and dissemination, applying to young contributors of ideas and artefacts as well as to parents and to the management or directors of the service partner. Questions of representation are always ethically and politically significant in the translation of data into text and knowledge mobilisation; and are particularly consequential if our aim is to not reinforce deficit discourses yet at the same time to faithfully document the views and lived experience of children and young people in marginal, disadvantaged and vulnerable circumstances, especially in the context of growing social inequities that tend to disproportionately affect children and young people (Fine and Ruglis, 2009).

In this chapter we discuss some of the difficulties and debates about developing participatory approaches to publication and dissemination that have been the subject of researcher reflections, along with a range of creative practice examples. In the following discussion we recognise that varied kinds of research and multiple 'outcomes', including academic research findings, 'products' such as artworks, books, videos and social actions, often in combination as dissemination strategies, may all contribute in complementary ways to disseminating knowledge and cultural understandings, influencing professional practices and policies, and improving conditions for the participation in education, community and civic life of all children and young people.

'Speak-outs' and performance/theatre

Speak-outs and performance/theatre are participatory methods for communicating children and young people's perspectives and may be especially powerful ways of reporting on and engaging others with the findings of research. 'Speak-outs' are historically associated with the women's and civil rights movements of the 1960s–1970s, and in contemporary times with community development research, including speak-outs specifically for community engagement that include children and young people articulating their views of community issues and in planning for local change (Sarkissian et al., 2009). UNICEF, children's commissions and non-government organisations, particularly those involved in majority-world development studies and campaigns, also utilise children and young people's speak-outs as forums that are part of action research cycles. They may be both part of the feedback process in which children respond to draft reports based on consultations with them (NSW Commission for Children and Young People, 2006) and means of dissemination, where children and young people who have taken part in research present their views in the action phase of action research. As speak-outs are often one part of a set of dissemination strategies, we also use the term here to refer to ways that children and young people communicate findings to particular communities, in conference presentations and in giving feedback on participation in these activities. For example, the Foundation for Women's Health Research and Development in the UK conducts programmes of research, training and young women's speak-outs on sexual and reproductive health of African Diaspora women and girls. Young women have been participants and co-researchers, and are supported through training to present their views at conferences, community forums and in documentaries and campaigns (Forward, 2013).

While a plethora of similar forums are emerging online, the value of speak-outs – and participatory theatre – lies in the face-to-face encounter. The benefits of the live interaction are not only that children and young people may report the findings in their own way and to a listening audience. Speak-outs and participatory theatre provoke responses through the immediacy of contact and enable performers and audience to 'actively engage in dialogue' (van Blerk and Ansell, 2007: 321) about the findings. This may be especially consequential where the focal issues are institutional and system processes and the audience comprises those in positions of power to effect change (Dentith et al., 2012). Webster and Broadhead (2011: 213) underline the significance of a captive audience of powerful people: 'Consultants have nowhere to hide when a young person is standing before them', articulating the truth of their lives and perhaps also speaking back with advice on the consultation process.

Drama, role-play, music, dance and other forms of expressive performance have been valuable means of co-inquiry in participatory research and are emerging as modes of research dissemination. Performing arts are recognised as effective means for children and young people to communicate their research results and may express dimensions of experience, emotion and insight not so readily conveyed by words alone. Drawing on traditions of activist theatre in majority-world contexts, such as Boal's theatre of the oppressed (Boal, 1985; Guhathakurta, 2008), children and young people have been actively involved in documenting the life conditions of poor communities and their suggestions for change at local and policy level (Tisdall, 2013). For example, van Blerk and Ansell (2007) researched with children and young people on their experience of migration due to the effects of the HIV/AIDS pandemic occurring in southern Africa. The researchers devised a multi-layered dissemination strategy that included children and young people developing dramatic performances for a peer audience, to raise awareness in ways that may result in better support systems for the young migrants. The dramas were also video-taped and, alongside community participants' contributions in video and poster format, were used in forums with practitioners and policy-makers to prompt discussion and develop strategic responses. The researchers had intended to arrange for children and young people's participation in these forums, though resources did not allow for that. Nonetheless, they observed that the video did enable children and young people's voices to be heard and incorporated into the policy dialogue.

Children and young people's feedback on sharing their projects with an audience suggests a number of benefits, including being listened to and taken seriously; developing specific skills such as public speaking or in multi-media; understanding of participatory processes and how social or institutional systems work; and confidence that they will continue to take and make opportunities to participate in future (Kränzl-Nagl and Zartler, 2009; Levac, 2013).

Speak-outs and participatory theatre in which children and young people voice their concerns to peers, professionals, community members and sometimes directly to public service decision-makers (especially when research is commissioned by a government department), also have their weaknesses and challenges. It may be intimidating for children and young people to present to public audiences, and there is the risk that children and young people's research presentations may be regarded as curiosities or infotainment rather than as rigorous contributions (Tisdall, 2013). The risk may be heightened where dissemination involves creative performance, as children's work as co-researchers and co-designers may be of less interest than the production itself as a 'showcase' of talents (Gattenhof, 2008). While speak-outs are typically co-presentations in groups, there is also the risk that they may be heard as a collection of individual stories. It is important that presentations reflect the diversity of voice of the research participant group, yet equally and perhaps more crucial to ensure that the collective issues and perspectives are carried by the representative voices and are not limited to personal stories (van Blerk and Ansell, 2007). Additionally, as Haw (2008: 203) has suggested, involving children and young people in dissemination should not solely be concerned with supporting them to articulate their 'voice', but also 'directed at getting adults and professionals to listen and respond'.

The Polling For Justice (PFJ) project (Stoudt et al., 2012) (see Chapter 5 for an overview) provides one exemplar of participatory theatre that illustrates how performance may move beyond tokenism and support young people's critical voice whilst also deliberately challenging the idea of passive audiences. Conference presentations of the results utilise performance methodologies in ways that elude what is often tacitly or overtly a disconnect between embodied knowledge of lived experience and the formality and 'distancing' of academic representation.

Playback theatre was incorporated as a method of data analysis, bringing to life (again) the survey statistics. For example, this included 'developing a human sculpture, a brief monologue or a short scene that re-enacted our understanding/interpretation of each piece of data' (Fox and Fine, 2013: 330). These embodied vignettes have been a feature of the numerous presentations by young people at local and international conferences and serve to provoke 'collective accountability' (Fox and Fine, 2013: 330). The 'performance' of the survey results builds layers of understanding and accountability as the audience is invited to respond to the young people's presentations and, in turn, the young people respond to the audience contributions through affective tableau. The aim is to unsettle audiences, build political solidarity amongst those who may see themselves as 'witnesses and bystanders' (Stoudt et al., 2012: 187) and invite the audience to think about ideas for action.

Arts exhibitions

Visual arts-based methodologies have been analysed as accessible and inclusive research approaches, in part because the media such as drawing, painting and photography are often part of children's everyday life from an early age (Prosser and Burke, 2008), and children of diverse abilities, languages and communicative competencies may find their expertise more readily expressed than in words (Johnson, 2008). While children and young people's artworks are included in research reports, books and academic articles, there has been little attention to how exhibitions of the culminating work may constitute forms of research dissemination.

Arts exhibitions may be an apt way for children and young people to present their insights and responses to issues within their early childhood service, school or community context. For example, ten photo-voice projects discussed by Wang (2006) addressed a broad range of health issues of concern to young people and their communities, including violence, sexual health, community health and HIV, with varied intended audiences, including school personnel, education boards, law officers, community and faith leaders, and policy-makers. Merging creative processes, methodological and ethical inquiry, and activism, the projects enabled marginalised young people to discuss the change strategies they developed with key decision-makers. One project involved adults and several policy-makers in the action research alongside young people. Wang (2006) analyses the intergenerational approach as entailing a shift in power. As health officials moved out of their comfort zones to participate as contributors to adult–youth shared expertise, they saw the community and issues differently. The critical consciousness-raising through dialogue on different perspectives created not only openings for making local issue-specific changes and programmes, but new relationships that may in the longer-term be important to formalising spaces for young voices and the consideration of diverse groups in policy decisions.

The important messages conveyed through drawings, paintings and photographs may cause adults to think differently about the categories we put children and young people into as well as taken-for-granted assumptions about spaces, relationships and activities. For example, some young people with chronic illnesses who participated in visual storytelling were very intent on representing themselves as 'as just normal kids' with preoccupations other than their health (Drew et al., 2010). In the 'Seeing beyond violence' project, children and young people's images of what they valued in their lives captured their spheres of non-violence and spoke back to adults about the violence of their environments in Nicaragua, Colombia, India and Thailand (Egg et al., 2004). The children's exhibitions invited a different way of looking and thinking about violence that constitutes an opening for the social imaginary based in extremely difficult conditions yet seeking to carve out a space for children and young people's rights and influence.

Public art is a means of reaching a wider audience and has been an effective way of communicating young people's social critiques. The 'Fed Up Honeys', a group of 16–22-year-old young women who were involved in researching the stereotypes of urban young women of colour (Cahill, 2004), created a sticker campaign aiming to counter the negative and partial portrayals of young women that they had analysed, and to inspire other young women to 'go against the grain' (Cahill et al., 2008: 115). The six stickers parodied advertisements that objectify and misrepresent women and were designed to provoke questions and action but also to speak back to dominant discourses associated with the gentrification of their neighbourhoods. The stickers were put up all around their neighbourhoods in the lower east side and other parts of the city of New York. Naming six key stereotypes, each sticker challenges the assumptions or beliefs that 'Young Urban Womyn of Color are ...': 'Likely to become teen moms'; 'In abusive relationships'; 'Promiscuous'; 'Lazy and on welfare'; 'Burden to society'; 'Uneducated' (Cahill et al., 2008: 114; see also www.fed-up-honeys.org). Such images are intended to serve pedagogical purposes, communicating to viewers across differences in age, race, class and gender, compelling viewers to engage and query the statements and representations from their social position. In the longer-term, dissemination of the research has taken several additional forms, including the development of two websites, reports and several journal articles and book chapters.

The public display of children and young people's artworks has also been the subject of ethical debates. In arts-based research the issues of privacy, confidentiality and anonymity are complex and if the artworks 'go public', the ethical issues are heightened. Researchers have dealt with these issues in different ways, including presenting all artworks unsigned, altering images to protect anonymity and engaging children and young people in ethical discussion on the selection of images for exhibition (Vaughn et al., 2008). However, dilemmas remain. Wood and Kidman (2013) query whether de-identifying images may be disempowering for the young researchers and perhaps require re-negotiation of informed consent. Moreover, setting ethical boundaries on content may limit the analytic capacity and potential impact of the research project as a whole. The rigour of ethics committees on these issues is important to maintaining the confidentiality of participants, yet it also delimits the scope for exhibitions. Responsibility for what is done with the products of research may then need to be negotiated with the children and young people, their parents and the host organisation.

Arts-based dissemination may be a means of democratising research (Chalfen, 2011). However, researchers have taken different positions on the potential for art to convey children and young people's viewpoints and challenging the worldviews of those who engage with the artworks. Again, 'audiencing' is a key issue (Rose, 2007). On the one hand, there is a view that images can 'speak for themselves' and, on the other hand, that production, presentation and viewing are always processes of representation and interpretation of visual material (Pink, 2001). The context of publication and dissemination is also important to situating the images as research. Drew et al. (2010) argue that including young people's images in conference presentations provides an opportunity to proffer findings that are open to dialogue rather than the researchers' interpretation being conclusive, and that conference participants may analyse the work for themselves. However, this approach may not be appropriate outside the context of the academic conference of experienced researchers. In school-based exhibitions, conversations or commentaries accompanying the artworks may be important to ensuring that the viewing of visual representations of research moves beyond celebratory tendencies of responses to children and young people's exhibitions of their work (Chalfen, 2011). In photo-voice research projects, elaborating the significance of the visual content and 'participation' has relied on discussion with the children or young people to explore their meanings, intentions and insights (Liebenberg, 2009). The reflexive analytic work of the project enables children and young people to learn from the process and to deepen their critical appreciation of the substantive issues. This engagement may also serve to prepare them to present their work and to adopt the pedagogic role of explaining the artwork in terms of the messages from the research. In the project Johnson (2008) recounts, the children's artworks were part of their presentation to the school council, and their priorities for improved amenities were funded the following year.

Online or hard copy reports in the form of youth brochures, magazines, comics or posters

The increasing use of technologies in everyday life has provided openings and opportunities for many children and young people to more fully participate in civic life. It is unsurprising, then, that many researchers are incorporating these media as methods of research. The products of research include children and young people's videos, blogs, podcasts and zines as well as websites that document whole projects. One view of the prevalence of online information and activism is that children and young people – and adults – may be less inclined to read written reports in other forms. However, pocket pamphlets, information cards and comics may be popular and accessible forms of hard copy research dissemination. For example, Streetwize comics are popular forms of accessible information produced by Streetwize Communications between 1984 and 2007 and distributed Australia-wide. The research process included broad-scale consultations and focus groups with young people in urban and rural areas and had a particular focus on Indigenous and marginalised groups. The issues addressed in the comics are diverse and include legal rights, racism, reconciliation, mental health, safe sex, housing, sexual harassment, graffiti and drug use (Gale and Bolzan, 2004).

The appropriateness and effectiveness of online or other modes of reporting primarily relates to the purposes of dissemination. Many research projects undertaken in early childhood services and schools aim to inform the immediate community, and the reach of online documentation may hold little relevance in these situations. Dockett and Perry's (2003) research with children on starting school included children photographing aspects of the school that were important to them. Selections of photos and accompanying children's text were made into books that highlighted a broad range of issues, from rules and rooms to people and play areas, and were used for further classroom discussion, while the young researchers shared their knowledge and experience with pre-schoolers in school orientation sessions.

All of these different modes of disseminating research products and findings may have an important place in speaking to diverse purposes and audiences, though again the importance of dealing with the ethics and politics of utilising particular media is emphasised in researchers' reflections on practice. Beals' (2012) discussion of a digital storytelling project with young people in Aotearoa/New Zealand provides some helpful insights into issues of confidentiality associated with the production of videos and posting them online. Confidentiality may be addressed in the research process, for example by only choosing images available in the creative commons, exploring the use of symbolic images rather than images of people, and establishing websites that build in restricted access and that can be monitored and moderated. Promoting youth voice does not literally require participants' voices to be heard. In Beals' project anonymity was a particularly sensitive issue as stories were told of 'vulnerability, abuse, bullying and discrimination' (Beals, 2012: 40). Working in teams to develop collective stories, using a mix of written texts, music and voiceovers (that were not one young person's narration of an individual story) enabled 'individual stories [to] be carried within this shared framework' (Beals, 2012: 39). Finding creative ways of negotiating ethical dilemmas may, in fact, enrich the content and insights expressed in digital narratives of the research inquiry. For example, the Wall of Hands project of the YAHAnet through the Participatory Cultures Lab at McGill University included hundreds of photos of young people's hands, inscribed with messages about youth rights in relation to HIV and AIDS (MacEntee et al., 2011; participatorycultureslab.com).

While the online forms of dissemination may have the particular advantage of reaching wide audiences and thereby, to varying extents, pushing the boundaries of children and young people's participation in local and global arenas of public life, whether their voices and findings reach those in positions to effect institutional, legal and systemic change remains open to question. As Walsh (2011: 115) argues, over-emphasis on the benefits of access and interaction may not be indicative of actual effectiveness in contributing to social and political change but be incorporated into the 'rhetoric of digital participation'. Key issues, then, for researchers are how we conceptualise the new spaces of online participation, how we negotiate the openings for democratisation within institutional and social spheres of hierarchically distributed power, and how online dissemination of research with children and young people may recognise and shift the processes of managed performance of voice and participation (Harris, 2004: esp. 125–50; Thomson and Holdsworth, 2010).

Whether reporting through online forums or in hard copy, collaborative approaches to dissemination may be significant in addressing these aims. A Canadian participatory action-research-based health project on developing 'youth-friendly' health services (Amsden and Van Wynsberghe, 2005) illustrates the need to enhance the participatory dimensions of dissemination. Young people had co-designed the project, conducted a survey of clinics and compiled the findings and recommendations into a formal report and a zine (hard copy booklet) that incorporated photos and symbolic images to capture the young people's lived and emotional experience of health clinics. Subsequently they presented their research at a local research conference on child and youth health. Reflecting on the project, Amsden and Van Wynsberghe suggest that while young people participated in significant ways in the dissemination processes, there was a limit to the time they could dedicate, and as their lives moved on, their involvement drew to a conclusion before further strategies could be implemented, including their presentations to health service providers. In retrospect, the researchers believed that the impact of the project would have been greater had they been less preoccupied with assuring participation within the project, and had extended the notion of participation to include the health service providers to bring their perspectives into dialogue with the young people's and to work collaboratively on putting into action the results. Such collaboration can be very effective in extending the reach of research impacts, as documented in the sequential reports to and by Wodonga Council on children and young people's views of their city (Charles Sturt University, n.d.; City of Wodonga, 2010) (discussed in Chapter 9).

Monographs, journal articles and more traditional research reports remain important forms of research dissemination for different audiences. Some research reports deliberately provide minimal analysis of children and young people's views in order to underline the diversity of views and/or issues identified by young participants. These may be complemented by more traditional academic publications in which the researcher brings their interpretive expertise to situate the findings in context and speak to particular purposes such as the implications for policy, practice and future research. Some researchers attempt to bridge these approaches. Anarfi et al.'s (2005) report on a multi-site project undertaken in India, Bangladesh, Ghana and Burkina Faso, with child migrants aimed to 'imaginatively engage policy-makers, and others working in relevant fields with the lives and experiences of independent child migrants' and to address the gap between 'how children see their own experiences of migration and the way that child migrants are often represented' (Anarfi et al., 2005: 2). The report consists of a brief introduction, sixteen children and young people's one to two page narratives of their stories, each followed by a half to one page commentary that highlights themes of the stories as part of the larger collection of stories gathered in the project, a brief conclusion, and further details of the project and related academic publications contained in the appendix. The research with children and young people was part of a larger programme of research over a seven-year period and involved dialogue with practitioners and policy-makers toward change in policy approaches to migration and development.

Whether children and young people should participate as co-authors, consultants on written reports and articles and/or produce their own is not solely a decision for the adult researcher. As already noted, the time required, life demands and other interests of children and young people may mean they are not especially interested in participating in this aspect of the research. For example, McHugh and Kowalski (2009) intended to involve their participants – Aboriginal young women in a Canadian secondary school – in writing the final research report. However, the young women had other priorities. They were passionate about the project on body image up to the point of writing it up. The academic researchers then confronted a dilemma in respecting the wishes of the young women whilst also respecting the importance of Indigenous people's control of their knowledge and implementation of their project initiatives. In this instance, the conventional researcher-participant roles in dissemination prevailed. They took their text back to the young women to discuss whether they had captured and appropriately represented the young women's perspectives.

Many participatory projects have published collections of children and young people's poetry, short stories, articles and social commentary that were both part of the research process and products of the research (Fine et al., 2004). In these approaches there is a deliberative synergy of critical inquiry and critical literacy. This was the case in a series of Summer Research Seminars for urban high school students, their teachers and parents, at the University of California (Morrell, 2004). The project team adopted a critical pedagogy that recognised the significance of students' literacy development, as personal liberation, preparation for university and as political praxis in their research on popular culture and communities. All of the young people were encouraged to write for public audiences, to document their political learning and as an act for social justice. Some students wrote for online journals, or their school newspapers; others wrote and presented their research to politicians and community organisations. The participatory research of these teams shows that contributing to research dissemination may flow on from a focus on writing throughout a project, and that writing for dissemination is a valued form of political education. Indeed, student-led projects documenting literacy development may speak to the political inequities of changing urban landscapes and imperatives related to their effects on urban youth (Kinloch, 2010).

Consequences of dissemination and publication, both positive and negative

There are no easy answers to the ethical and political dilemmas associated with participatory publication and dissemination. Such dilemmas underline the significant responsibility of adult researchers in negotiating children and young people's right to participate, to be heard and to benefit, taking account of the specific purposes and contexts of publication and dissemination. As Walsh et al. (2013) suggest, there is also an important advocacy role for researchers who aim to ensure that the frank and balanced representation of marginalised young people's agency and constraints on them is appreciated by the users of the research, especially policy-makers. This is especially the case because the consequences of decisions taken on children and young people's participation in disseminating research and its reception cannot always be anticipated.

The advantages of media attention to new research findings need to be weighed against the ethical issues already discussed that are critical in this context. Children and young people's contribution to the research may itself garner media interest (Heath et al., 2009), though the presence of children and young people at media conferences may tend to better serve the interests of the media than those of the participants and researchers. Researchers and practitioners working with particularly vulnerable groups have erred on the side of protection, whilst finding appropriate ways for children and young people to be involved in decisions about dissemination rather than direct involvement in presentation or publication. For example, Kay et al. (2003) researched with children affected by parental HIV illness. They worked with great care and reflexivity and created safe spaces and processes, but were acutely conscious of the social stigma attached to HIV and the need to ensure that children and their parents were not exposed to re-stigmatisation through their participation in the project. This was especially pertinent in relation to media attention to the research. Television reportage of research with or about children and young people often includes visuals or brief commentary by participants; and in general there are formal ethical procedures to be followed by the media companies, researchers, host organisations and parents, in such cases where children could be subject to ostracism or vilification based on public ignorance or misinformation. However, these researchers drew a clear line on children's participation. Of course, one of the aims of the research was to contribute to public education on the issue to shift the conditions of fear that silenced children and families affected by HIV. Children's *right* to talk about their experience was at the forefront of the researchers' processes but they were very clear about the boundaries in dissemination of the findings.

Arts-based researchers have sometimes found creative ways to deal with the ethical demands of anonymity and confidentiality of images published on and offline or in exhibitions without the process being too restrictive of young people's desired ways to represent their perspectives (Wood and Kidman, 2013). In online postings of videos, for instance, web access to the material can be restricted (Prosser and Burke, 2008) which may expand the scope of the visual content; though in this case, by definition the breadth of dissemination is also limited. There remains, however, the question of to what extent the researcher should be concerned with what young participants may do with their images or videos when a project has concluded, especially as posting such work online is now part of the everyday culture for young people. To some extent, these issues may be addressed by differentiating productions made for the research project and additional productions undertaken in tandem or subsequently. In this case, though, ownership and issues of intellectual property need to be worked out. In some contexts such as photo exhibitions that were only for the children's families and host organisations, including young people's names in exhibition programmes may be negotiated through differentiated responsibilities of the researchers and service management without compromising ethical protocols, and accord appropriate respect to their creative and intellectual ownership of the work (Egg et al., 2004).

While researchers are in many cases pushing the boundaries of children and young people's participation in research into the realm of publication and dissemination, the question of who will listen and how they will act on the research persists. Tisdall (2013) cautions that decision-makers in services and policy arenas may be more interested in how the research can be used to enhance service delivery, rather than effecting structural change necessary for equitable participation in civic life. Beals and Wood (2012) describe the regulatory responses to young people's online posting of their activism that was a corollary of their research. There was little support for their protest concerning minimum wage. Instead they incurred an onslaught of rebuke and ridicule from the media, bloggers, politicians and their teachers. In some contexts, speaking out may be very risky for children and young people, and their consciousness of how they are being regulated and positioned by others may be cause for their refusal or wariness to participate in the mobilisation of their knowledge.

Researchers have nonetheless recounted the benefits of and to children and young people of participating in publication and dissemination. In Flicker's (2008) research with socially excluded young people living with HIV, they had the opportunity to speak, and be listened and responded to in a forum with service providers, in order to share the findings and plan responses at the level of advocacy, programmes and policy change, which were subsequently implemented. For the young people, being listened to and seeing their work result in concrete change was most significant, as they had rarely been asked their views and had previously felt disempowered by numerous professionals making decisions about them and for them. The project provided the young people a renewed sense of purpose and meaningful contribution, particularly as the forum galvanised a collaborative network of young people, service providers and researchers who subsequently worked to progress the change agenda over a two-year period. Alongside this collaborative work, young people created and distributed four zines and assisted with the production of community newsletters and conference presentations. When children and young people's projects elicit community interest and recognition, the longer-term consequences may be significant shifts in how the participants are viewed (Kränzl-Nagl and Zartler, 2009) and potentially greater 'participatory capital' (Wood, 2013) accrued to children and young people in that community.

While participation in research can be empowering for children and young people, their limited participation in dissemination presents a challenge for participatory research.

Involving children and young people in publication and dissemination is complex work and requires significant investments of time and funds. It may not always be feasible or desirable, given some of the ethical tensions highlighted. Yet children and young people may still take an active role in shaping publications and dissemination by providing feedback on a project report written by the researcher (or team of researchers), suggesting who should receive the final report, which findings they believe should be emphasised, their ideas for useful 'products' that incorporate the findings and what kind of action they would like to see resulting from the presentation of findings (Qiang, 2006). Harris (2004: 188) succinctly sums up the challenge of negotiating the opportunities and constraints of diverse contexts:

> The issue of youth voice – who it belongs to, where it is expressed, who is listening, what is said in its name, and so on – is highly complex. So too is silence. An acknowledgment of this complexity must become part of our conversations about how to construct research projects and policy for, with, and by youth.

In practice, multiple forms of dissemination, appropriate to purposes and audiences may be a way of working with these tensions. The different forms and means of publication and dissemination may differently position young voices through 'in-house' or localised re/presentation and action, as contributions to change at the institutional, systemic or regional level – and possibly all of these over the longer-term. These approaches may include researchers, young participants and the professionals in partner organisations all taking the lead in different modes of dissemination to their respective peer audiences, and the engagement of these groups, separately and together, with other stakeholders, including relevant decision-makers, advocates and community activists, aiming to ensure that the benefits of research are equitably distributed and the results are put into action (Flicker, 2008; Minkler, 2012).

Key points

- In considering publication and dissemination we need to be alert to the ethical and political nature of the context.
- Who may speak out is often governed by the position taken by the academic researcher or sponsoring agency.
- The medium for speaking out, public, academic, semi-private, has an impact upon the manner in which issues may be discussed in different forums.
- Ownership of research involving children and young people may be contested. There are attendant costs and benefits to negotiating ownership of the whole and/or the part.

References

Alderson, P. and Morrow, V. (2011) *The ethics of research with children and young people: A practical handbook*. 2nd edition. London: Sage.

Amsden, J. and Van Wynsberghe, R. (2005) Community mapping as a research tool with youth. *Action Research*, 3(4): 357–81.

Anarfi, J., Gent, S., Hashim, I., Iversen, V., Khair, S., Kwankye, S., Tagoe, C.A., Thorsen, D. and Whitehead, A. (2005) *Voices of child migrants: 'A better understanding of how life is'*. University of Sussex: Development Research Centre on Migration, Globalisation and Poverty. www.migrationdrc.org, accessed 13th November, 2013.

Beals, F. (2012) Moving beyond the academic doors. Addressing ethical issues in NGO youth research. *Youth Studies Australia*, 31(3): 35–42.

Beals, F. and Wood, B. (2012) Negotiating agency: Local youth activism in Aotearoa/New Zealand. In K. Brison and S. Dewey (Eds) *Super girls, gangstas, freeters, and xenomaniacs: Gender and modernity in global youth cultures*. New York: Syracuse University Press, pp. 193–210.

Boal, A. (1985) Theatre of the Oppressed. New York: Theatre Communications Group.

Cahill, C., Rios-Moore, I. and Threatts, T. (2008) Different eyes/open eyes: Community-based participatory action research. In J. Cammarota and M. Fine (Eds) *Revolutionizing education: Youth participatory action research in motion*. New York: Routledge, pp. 89–124.

Cahill, C. (2004) Defying gravity. Raising consciousness through collective research. *Children's Geographies*, 2(2): 273–86.

Cammarota, J. and Fine, M. (Eds) (2008) *Revolutionizing education: Youth participatory action research in motion*. New York: Routledge.

Chalfen, R. (2011) Differentiating practices of participatory visual media production. In E. Margolis and L. Pauwels (Eds) *The Sage handbook of visual research methods*. London: Sage, pp. 186–201.

Charles Sturt University (n.d.) *Children and young people's views of Wodonga*. Wodonga: CSU/Wodonga City Council, Victoria.

Dentith, A., Measor, L. and O'Malley, M. (2012) The research imagination amid dilemmas of engaging young people in critical participatory work. *Forum: Qualitative Social Research*, 13: Art. 17.

Dockett, S. and Perry, B. (2003) Children's views and children's voices in starting school. *Australian Journal of Early Childhood*, 28(1): 12–17.

Drew, S., Duncan, R. and Sawyer, S. (2010) Visual storytelling: A beneficial but challenging method for health research with young people. *Qualitative Health Research*, 20(12): 1677–88.

Egg, P., Schratz-Hadwich, B., Trubwasser, G. and Walker, R. (2004) *Seeing beyond violence. Children as researchers*. SOS-Kinderdorf/Hermann Gmeiner Akademie. www.earlyyears.org.au/__data/assets/pdf_file/0011/49718/SEEING_BEYOND_VIOLENCE.pdf, accessed 17th November, 2013.

Fine, M., Roberts, R. and Torre, M., with Bloom, J., Burns, A., Chajet, L., Guishard, M. and Payne, Y. (2004) *Echoes of Brown: Youth documenting and performing the legacy of Brown v. Board of Education.* New York: The Graduate Center, City University of New York.

Fine, M. and Ruglis, J. (2009) Circuits and consequences of dispossession: The racialized realignment of the public sphere for U.S. youth. *Transforming Anthropology,* 17(1): 20–33.

Flicker, S. (2008) Who benefits from community-based participatory research? A case study of the Positive Youth Project. *Health Education & Behavior,* 35(1) 70–86.

Forward (2013) *Forward: Safeguarding rights and dignity. Programmes.* forwarduk.org.uk, accessed 10th November, 2013.

Fox, M. and Fine, M. (2013) Accountable to whom? A critical science counter-story about a city that stopped caring for its young. *Children & Society,* 27(4): 321–35.

France, A. and Utting, D. (2005) The paradigm of risk and protection focused prevention and its impact on services for children and young people. *Children & Society,* 19(2): 77–90.

Gale, F. and Bolzan, N. (2004) The graffiti's on the wall. In R. Leonard (Ed.) *A fair go: Some issues of social justice in Australia.* Altona: Common Ground Publishing, pp. 55–72.

Gattenhof, S. (2008) In the mouth of the imagination: Positioning children as co-researchers and co-artists to create a professional children's theatre production. Paper presented at gener8 – Drama Australia National Conference, 9–11 May, Adelaide.

Guhathakurta, M. (2008) Theatre in participatory action research: Experiences from Bangladesh. In P. Reason and H. Bradbury (Eds) *The Sage handbook of action research: Participative inquiry and practice.* 2nd edition. London: Sage, pp. 510–22.

Harris, A. (2004) *Future girl. Young women in the twenty-first century.* New York: Routledge.

Haw, K. (2008) 'Voice' and video: Seen, heard and listened to? In P. Thomson (Ed) *Doing visual research with children and young people.* London: Routledge, pp. 192–207.

Heath, S., Brooks, R., Cleaver, C. and Ireland, E. (2009) *Researching young people's lives.* London: Sage.

Johnson, K. (2008) Teaching children to use visual research methods. In P. Thomson (Ed.) *Doing visual research with children and young people.* Abingdon: Routledge, pp. 77–94.

Kay, H., Cree, V., Tisdall, K. and Wallace, J. (2003) At the edge: Negotiating boundaries in research with children and young people. *Forum: Qualitative Social Research,* 4(2): Art. 33, May.

Kinloch, V. (2010) *Harlem on our minds: Place, race, and the literacies of urban youth.* New York: Teachers College Press.

Kränzl-Nagl, R. and Zartler, U. (2009) Children's participation in school and community. European perspectives. In B. Percy-Smith and N.Thomas (Eds) *A handbook of children and young people's participation: Perspectives from theory and practice.* London: Routledge, pp. 164–73.

Levac, L. (2013) 'Is this for real?' Participatory research, intersectionality, and the development of leader and collective efficacy with young mothers. *Action Research,* published online 11 November, DOI: 10.1177/1476750313508327.

Liebenberg, L. (2009) Visual methods when working with youth across cultures. In L. Liebenberg and M. Ungar (Eds) *Researching resilience*. Toronto: University of Toronto Press, pp. 129–52.

Lykes, M.B., Hershberg, R. and Brabeck, K. (2011) Methodological challenges in participatory action research with undocumented Central American migrants. *Journal for Social Action in Counseling and Psychology*, 3(2): 22–35.

MacEntee, K., Labacher, L. and Murray, J. (2011) Girls use digital photography to speak out about sexuality and HIV. *Girlhood Studies*, 4(1): 156–67.

McHugh, T. and Kowalski, K. (2009) Lessons learned: Participatory action research with young Aboriginal women. *Pimatisiwin: A Journal of Aboriginal and Indigenous Community Health*, 7(1): 117–31.

Minkler, M. (2012) *Community organizing and community building for health and welfare*. 3rd edition. New Brunswick, NJ: Rutgers University Press.

Morrell, E. (2004) *Becoming critical researchers: Literacy and empowerment for urban youth*. New York: Peter Lang Publishing.

Nixon, S., Casale, M., Flicker, S. and Rogan, M. (2012) Applying the principles of knowledge translation and exchange to inform dissemination of HIV survey results to adolescent participants in South Africa. *Health Promotion International*, 28 (2): 233–43.

NSW Commission for Children and Young People (2006) *Participation: Sharing our journey*. Surry Hills: NSW Commission for Children and Young People.

Pink, S. (2001) *Doing visual ethnography: Images, media and representation in research*. London: Sage.

Prosser, J. and Burke, C. (2008) Image-based educational research: Childlike perspectives. In J.G. Knowles and A. Cole (Eds) *Handbook of the arts in qualitative research: Perspectives, methodologies, examples, and issues*. Los Angeles: Sage, pp. 407–21.

Qiang, C. (Ed.) (2006) *Listen, secrets! Issues and research by children affected by HIV/AIDS in Xinjiang and Yunnan, China*. Beijing: Save the Children.

Reason, P. and Bradbury, H. (2008) *The Sage handbook of action research: Participative inquiry and practice*. 2nd edition. London: Sage.

Rose, G. (2007) *Visual methodologies: An introduction to the interpretation of visual materials*. 2nd edition. London: Sage.

Sarkissian, W. and Bunjamin-Mau, K.S., with Cook, A., Walsh, K. and Vajda, S. (2009) *Speak out: The step-by-step guide to speakouts and community workshops*. London: Earthscan.

Stoudt, B., Fox, M. and Fine, M. (2012) Contesting privilege with critical participatory action research. *Journal of Social Issues*, 68(1): 178–93.

te Riele, K. (2013) Formal frameworks as resources for ethical youth research. In K. te Riele and R. Brooks (Eds) *Negotiating ethical challenges in youth research*. New York: Routledge, pp. 3–15.

Thomson, P. and Holdsworth, R. (2010) Theorizing change in the educational 'field': Re-readings of 'student participation' projects. *International Journal of Leadership in Education: Theory and Practice*, 6(4): 371–91.

Tisdall, E.K. (2009) Dissemination – or engagement? In E. K. Tisdall, J. Davis and M. Gallagher, *Researching with children and young people: Research design, methods and analysis*. London: Sage, pp. 194–221.

Tisdall, E.K. (2013) The transformation of participation? Exploring the potential of 'transformative participation' for theory and practice around children and young people's participation. *Global Studies of Childhood*, 3(2): 183–93.

van Blerk, L. and Ansell, N. (2007) Participatory feedback and dissemination with and for children: Reflections from research with young migrants in Southern Africa. *Children's Geographies*, 5(3): 313–24.

Vaughn, L., Rojas-Guyler, L. and Howell, B. (2008) 'Picturing' health. A photovoice pilot of Latina girls' perceptions of health. *Family & Community Health*, 31(4): 305–16.

Veale, A. (2005) Creative methodologies in participatory research with children. In S. Greene and D. Hogan (Eds) *Researching children's experience: Approaches and methods*. London: Sage, pp. 253–73.

Walsh, L. (2011) Emergent forms and tools of change-making. In L. Walsh and R. Black, *In their own hands: Can young people change Australia?* Melbourne: ACER Press, pp. 107–25.

Walsh, L., Black, R. and Berman, N. (2013) Walking the talk. Youth research in hard times. In K. te Riele and R. Brooks (Eds) *Negotiating ethical challenges in youth research*. New York: Routledge, pp. 43–54.

Wang, C. (2006) Youth participation in photovoice as a strategy for community change. *Journal of Community Practice*, 14(1): 147–61.

Webster, L. and Broadhead, P. (2011) Their life, their choice: Ethical challenges for supporting children and young people in the self-management of Type 1 diabetes. In A. Campbell and P. Broadhead (Eds) *Working with children and young people: Ethical debates and practices across disciplines and continents*. Oxford: Peter Lang, pp. 197–214.

White, S. (1996) Depoliticising development: The uses and abuses of participation. *Development in Practice*, 6(1): 6–15.

Wodonga City Council (2010) *Building a child-friendly city: Report to children and young people from Wodonga Council*. December. Wodonga: Wodonga City Council.

Wood, B. (2013) Participatory capital: Bourdieu and citizenship education in diverse school communities. *British Journal of Sociology of Education*, DOI:10.1080/01425 692.2013.777209, 1–20.

Wood, B. and Kidman, J. (2013) Negotiating the ethical borders of visual research with young people. In K. te Riele and R. Brooks (Eds) *Negotiating ethical challenges in youth research*. New York: Routledge, pp. 149–62.

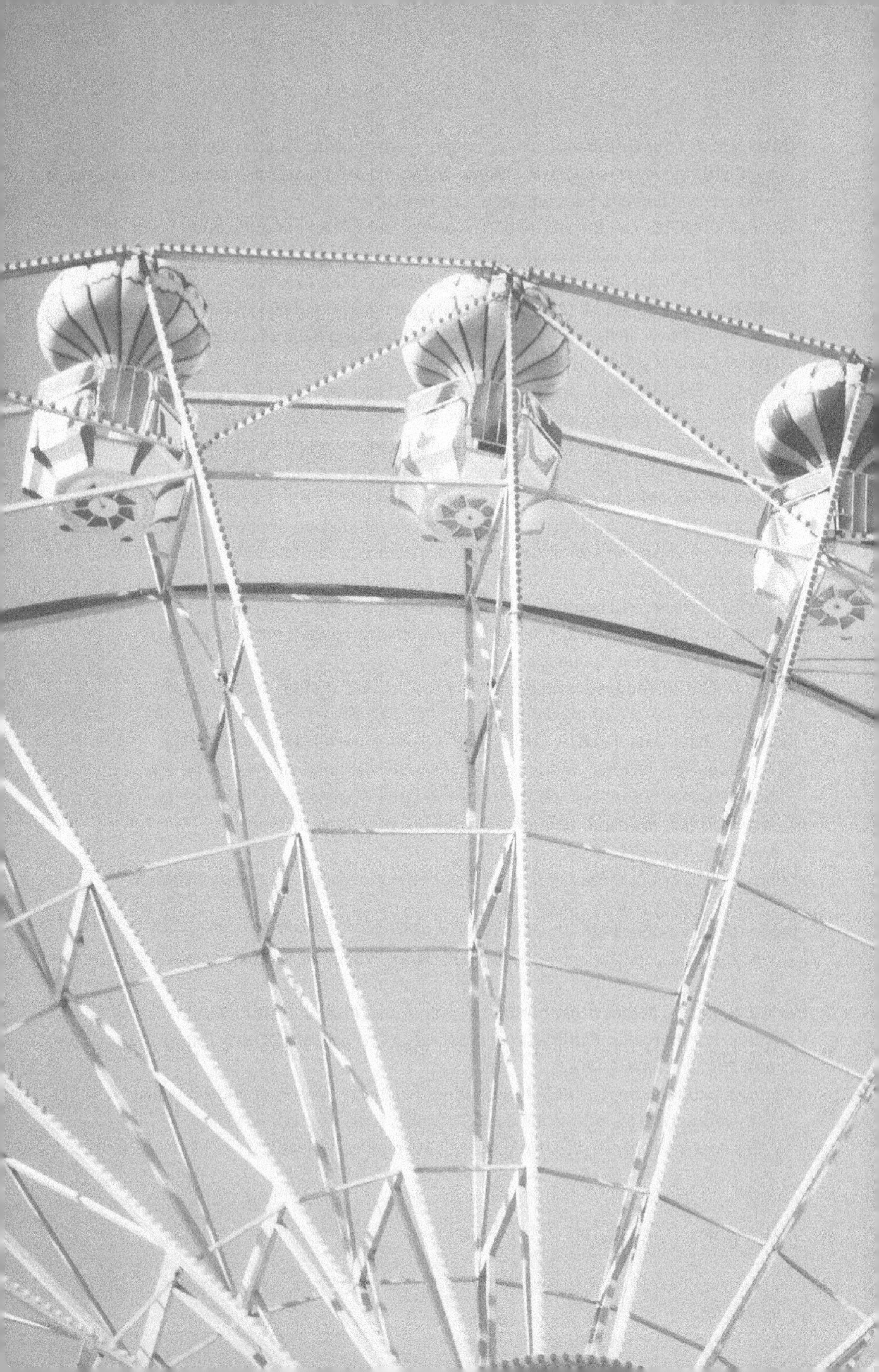

NINE
ACTION AND PARTICIPATION

This concluding chapter seeks to draw together the major themes with which the book has been concerned within a discussion of 'action'. It is clear that engaging in participative inquiry with children and young people is a complex, multi-faceted enterprise, in social contexts that are forever shifting and dynamic. Our concern throughout has been to simultaneously draw attention to these challenges, while also offering examples of ways in which researchers have sought to address them in their interactions with children and young people. The principal project for the book has been to consider how one might be inclusive, ethical, innovative and responsive when working with children and young people in a range of arenas. Importantly, in this final chapter we propose an orientation to action that will support broad, communitarian values.

We accept that it is impossible to distil the many actions undertaken in the name of participative research with children and young people under one rubric. Some children and young people will be among the most marginalised in our society (see Chapter 5); others will be those who already have significant amounts of participatory capital (Wood, 2013), that will enable them to more readily achieve their social and cultural goals. Some will have degrees of social and cognitive competence that will be manifest in their participation; others will struggle.

This chapter addresses the following matters:

- Action as a set of practical intentions.
- Action and activism – three case studies.
- Action and subversion.
- Addressing the problems of practice.

Action as a set of practical intentions

'Action', in the context of this book, is taken to mean a practical intention to follow through the kinds of participative inquiries that have been portrayed throughout the preceding chapters. The purpose of action, in this sense, is to improve the situation that has been under scrutiny, whether it be to change classroom practices, build community facilities, engage in health planning, examine juvenile justice provisions, or challenge attitudes to children and young people's rights to contribute to the well-being of themselves and others. It can take the form of social action, political action or physical action. Action, in this sense, is an outcome of research that may initially have as its purpose the creation of knowledge, but takes the next essential step of using that knowledge in ethical and productive ways. In the best of circumstances it is collaborative action, involving not only those who participated in the inquiry, but also those who may have sponsored or commissioned it, as well as the audience for the research. How the research is received, and any impetus to action, depends largely on who has access to the outcomes – the audience – and how they react, understand and interpret the research (Gubrium and Harper, 2013).

However, taking action should not be taken as an easy task. Griffiths (2009: 90) has observed how difficult it is to engage with others across conditions where there are real differences in perspectives and backgrounds, resulting in a 'paucity' of reports of action that illustrate such collaboration. Collaborative action is often tricky, requiring compromises and risks. Successful collaborative action depends not only on agreement about at least some perspectives on, and understandings of, a situation, but also about what to do to improve it.

Who is listening and is able to act? Who may be hostile and seek to create barriers? It is critical to reflect upon matters associated with diversity as it relates to the capacity to engage in participative inquiry and to subsequently act. Children and young people, themselves, are acutely aware of variations in the ways in which their peers may engage in, and understand, a particular project. Hill (2006) argues that they will hold a diversity of views about methods and approaches and ultimately the interpretation of results leading to action; while Spyrou (2011: 151) reminds us that there is complexity that lies behind the voices of children and young people whose worlds are 'messy, multi-layered and non-normative' in character. While there are variations between social markers such as class, ethnicity, gender, race and geographic location, which themselves intersect, there are also variations within these groups.

It has been observed, in earlier chapters, that authentic participation that will enable actions to be taken requires dialogue, or what Percy-Smith (2006) refers to as a 'social learning' model of participation. This model recognises the necessity for spaces that allow all parties, adults and young people, to come together in dialogue, reflection and social learning within a given community in ways that support development and local decision-making. Kirby et al. (2003) believe that it takes time and resources to build such a culture of participation. They advocate for an open process that avoids the kind of quasi-participation that they have identified as tokenistic, where the actions have already been decided and the consultation is little more than ticking a box. They argue that integral to meaningful participation, in relation to action and feedback, is the kind of planning that ensures ongoing interactions that will advise of ways in which the views of children and young people are being taken forward, or identify what the current barriers might be and how they may be overcome.

For example, one of the least powerful groups in our society is that of children and young people who are in care. A Northern Ireland Group – Voice of Young People in Care (VOYPIC) provides a medium through which they can at least make themselves heard – an action in itself. In the autumn of 2012, the

Department of Health, Social Services and Public Safety in Northern Ireland set up a group to review minimum standards for children's homes. VOYPIC ran workshops with children and young people living in children's homes, as well as a survey on their website so that other children, young people and adults interested in children's homes could express and share their views. They heard from 21 children's homes and received responses from over 50 young people living in those homes. These were collated into the following recommendations:

- Make a good, clear plan for the future of children's homes in Northern Ireland. Include children and young people in the plans and ideas.
- Create homely environments with access to the internet to promote learning and educational achievement.
- Create comfortable, personal and private spaces to increase the sense of stability and permanence for young people.
- Adopt a proportionate and effective response to risk-taking behaviour. Promote a sense of safety and fairness through effective rules and discipline.
- Involve young people in aspects of planning and preparing mealtimes to promote a sense of home and support the transition to independence.
- Manage greater accessibility to common rooms such as kitchens and consider older members of the household having their own house key.
- Support and promote essential life skills such as budgeting, money management, shopping and cooking.
- Promote and support young people to stay in touch with family and friends; participate in local activities; and get involved in their local community. (VOYPIC, 2013: 7)

While these may not sound radical or very different from those strategic policy initiatives that may have been developed by bureaucrats, they are grounded in the experiences of the participants and reflect an effort to engage with the agency of those living in children's homes.

In contrast to this cohort of young people, there are other provisions that encourage the voicing of issues through quasi-political forums. In Australia, for example, the YMCA (n.d.) manages Youth Parliament programmes in every Australian state and territory (with the exception of the Australian Capital Territory). The programmes cater for 16–25-year-olds and are designed for them to become politically engaged and to feel enabled to influence the political process. Youth Parliaments are seen to be run by young people, for young people. They mirror parliamentary procedure and debate a range of topics ranging from migrant support and cultural awareness to rural development, mental health and youth homelessness. The action is in the engagement in a process of dialogue, rather than the accomplishment of actual social change. The motivation and involvement of the participants can be seen to be mediated through their capacity for what Wood (2013: 2) has named participative capital, that is 'the combined and interrelated social, economic and cultural capital related to the logic, network and practices of citizenship participation within a social field'.

In most of the preceding chapters we have been conscious of acknowledging and promoting the agency of those who participate, whether as young children considering the facilities available to them in their environments, or as citizens about to take up their voting rights. Although we have cited a number of instances that stand outside schools and classrooms, we are also well aware that it is in these particular institutional settings that the majority of our children and young people function, other than in their families. In writing of participative inquiry by students in schools, Thomson and Gunter (2007: 331) argued that student agency could be considered from the students' standpoint if it:

- Addresses issues of importance to students and is thus in their collective interests;
- Works with students' subjugated knowledge about the ways in which the school works;
- Allows marginalised perspectives and voices to come centre stage;
- Uses students' subjectivities and experiences to develop approaches, tools, representations and validities;
- Interrupts the power relations in schools, including, but not confined to those which are age-related; and
- Is geared to make a difference.

We have argued throughout the book that all of this work is in one form or another 'political', for it rests upon power, its manifestation and distribution. Who has been selected to participate? Who become advocates for the project and its outcomes? As the NSW Commission for Children and Young People has indicated, there are often information gaps because children and young people, as the consequential stakeholders (a term that we have used to indicate that they bear the consequences of the decisions that are often made on their behalf with little or no consultation), and those responsible for developing policy have little to say to each other. In a study undertaken with the University of Western Sydney in NSW, Australia, the Commission sought advice from children and young people regarding the meaning of the term 'well-being' (Fattore et al., 2007). They found that important components of well-being were: a sense of agency, whereby the children and young people perceived that they have the power and capacity to take independent action; feeling safe and secure, so that they could fully engage in life, not only in the community, but also in the wider world; and, a positive sense of self, being valued and respected by others. In its own report of the study, The New South Wales Commission for Children and Young People and the Social Justice and Social Change Research Centre (2007: 16) pointed out that policy and research agendas should become more sensitive to what children say, rather than being constrained by current research and policy agendas that rely on adult perspectives. They concluded:

These findings suggest that some aspects of children's experience have not been sufficiently considered in policy, for example agency, social responsibility and sense of self. Consequently, our current policy frameworks may not deliver to children the well-being outcomes they value. Further, our policies and actions may have had unintended consequences because some key components of children's well-being have been regarded as policy irrelevant or unimportant. They also suggest that children's well-being requires a coordinated effort involving families, government and the broader community and that policies need to reflect this holistic nature of well-being.

Action and activism – three case studies

Here we offer three case studies that illustrate the ways in which participative research with children and young people has resulted in actions beyond recommendations. We cite them not as exemplary studies, but ones that can demonstrate that, through their engagement, the children and young people who participated had an impact that resulted in action. In this chapter we are arguing the case for children and young people to be what Fleming (2011: 210) refers to as 'research activists' whereby they become 'builders' not 'borrowers'.

CASE STUDY 9.1

FARES FAIR

Fleming cites, among others, the case where research undertaken with children and young people has led to actions that have an impact upon their lives and well-being. She refers to the ways in which concessionary fares were secured across the north of England city of Durham as a result of young people's research through their contribution to the Children's 'Fares Fair' project. This case is reproduced in detail because it embodies the very real complexity of dialogue, negotiation and the distribution of power when it comes to action (Cairns, 2001: 355–6).

When it became clear from initial work that transport was an issue all around the county, the different research teams were invited to get together and think about this further. Having helped to identify the problem, they were keen to help create some solutions.

The group, consisting of sixteen young people from a variety of backgrounds and with a variety of abilities, thought that the process should be straightforward. If all of the key decision-makers could be got together, the young people could explain the issues, and through a process of dialogue, some new answers would be found.

A group of transport professionals was duly assembled, from the local authority and the commercial bus companies. For a variety of reasons, however, the hoped for dialogue never took place. In part, this was because the adults were not prepared to enter into discussions with children on the basis of there being some equality. Rather than listen, they saw the meeting as an opportunity to explain why things were as they were. The adults paraded their expertise. This had the effect of throwing the young people off balance. They found themselves unable to assert their case in the face of the apparently robust defence of the status quo presented by the adults.

The group withdrew, but rather than accept that there was no change to be had, the group determined to continue to pursue their case. Their experience had taught them that knowledge can be a source of power, so they decided to acquire knowledge. Over the next ten months or so, this group of sixteen young people aged between fourteen and sixteen, set out to find out as much as they could about public transport. They visited other local authorities and even went to look at arrangements on the continent.

Finally, they produced their report, 'Fares Fair' in which they argued that the transport system was environmentally unsustainable because it encouraged dependence upon the private car, and socially unjust in that it favoured children from better-off families. Some areas of County Durham have the highest rates in the country of families who don't own cars. Furthermore, they produced evidence to show that children and young people in other parts of the country, and perhaps more significantly, in other parts of the region, enjoyed better opportunities for cheaper transport than children and young people in Durham.

Armed with their report, the group met again with the transport professionals. However, this time the atmosphere was completely different, and the adults present listened carefully and with respect as the young people presented their case.

As a consequence, in May 2000, 17,000 young people in Durham became eligible for a new travel card (named appropriately enough, the 'Investing in Children Card') which allows them to travel for a reduced fare. The scheme was designed by a group consisting of local authority staff, the bus companies and *the young people themselves* – genuine participation.

This case of action cuts across Marker's (2009: 30) concern that too often there is a gap, a chasm even, between 'the truth that gets told and the truth that gets sold'.

CASE STUDY 9.2

IMPACT OF CONSULTATION UPON AN EXHIBITION HELD AT THE AUSTRALIAN MUSEUM, SYDNEY

A consultation was conducted with young people, recruited from the Coalition of Knowledge Building Schools (Mockler and Groundwater-Smith, 2011, see Chapter 6) to test the waters regarding a proposed temporary exhibition in relation to Birds of Paradise. Temporary exhibitions at the Australian Museum are generally of long duration and it was emphasised how important it is that they should be of wide

(Continued)

(Continued)

interest to the community including young people and their families. The exhibition was to feature both the birds themselves, their physical appearances and mating rituals, and the ways in which they have been a significant part of cultural activities in Papua New Guinea through ceremonial headdresses and dance. Thus it was to be a marriage between natural science and human practice.

For the purposes of this exercise two schools were approached. One was an independent girls school, the other a metropolitan boys school with students whose backgrounds were mainly Middle Eastern and Pacific Islander. Altogether, nineteen students attended the workshop. They were drawn from Years 6–8 and aged twelve to fourteen years. Their respective schools were visited prior to the event and teachers were briefed on the design of the day and images of Birds of Paradise were made available. In the case of the boys school it was also possible to speak briefly with the boys themselves. These processes were used to provide advanced organisers for the students who were asked to reflect upon something 'amazing' that they had experienced – the rationale being that the birds themselves were exotic and arresting in their appearance.

In this preliminary meeting the Head of Audience Research explained that exhibitions took anything from six months to two years to plan. Teams were made up of a range of people functioning in different roles. Many of the Birds of Paradise team were going to be present during the day to hear what students had to say. She pointed out that in the past audience research was seen as an evaluative function at the end of an exhibition, but that now the focus was far more on collecting information prior to the mounting of the exhibition itself.

After visiting the bird collection students were asked to reflect upon what was special and unique about Birds of Paradise. They had been provided with a rare opportunity to touch the skins and to see close up the specific features of the different specimens. Some students found it quite difficult to deal with the preserved nature of the birds, 'looking at dead birds can be frightening and realistic', but others were fascinated by stories of where and when they were collected. In their booklets[1] they recorded:

- They look so exotic;
- They are colourful and fascinating;
- How they use their colourful feathers to attract and scare away other birds;
- The texture of the plumage;
- The uniqueness and diversity of the birds;
- How different they are from other birds;

---

[1] A convention for the range of consultations that the Museum has undertaken with schools has been to provide students with personalised notebooks with digital photographs of each student on the cover. These are collected at the end of the day(s) and used as a form of data.

- The ways in which the 'flags' are used to attract females;
- Their dances 'their colours, dance and natural habits, such as showing off their amazing feathers etc. for the females. Their feathers, plumes and wires are incredible';
- Their rarity (only Australia and New Guinea); and
- The contrasts between the males and females.

Part of the day took the students through existing exhibitions and they were provided with opportunities to comment on their characteristics and how these might be applied when planning for the Birds of Paradise exhibition. Among the many observations it was noted that little attention had been given to people who had language backgrounds other than English and to what their needs might be – even a few welcoming signs in other languages would help. Students spoke openly to a camera, set up for this purpose, and their perspectives and thoughts were documented as part of the audience research enterprise.

The young people were consulted regarding promoting the exhibition and creating slogans that would attract attention. A favourite was 'Fancy fellas and choosy chicks!'. The day was a full one. The feedback from the two schools was that the students believed themselves to be respected and they in turn, greatly enjoyed the opportunities that were afforded to them.

The encounter was an ongoing one. The students were invited back to the Museum to view the exhibition and the ways in which their ideas had been incorporated. One year older, and one year taller, the young people who had been at the earlier encounter met once again in the Museum reception area. Without delay they were directed to the exhibition area to browse and to comment. Observing them, it was clear that they were greatly enjoying the humour of the exhibition and the ways in which it connected to contemporary life. They responded to the provocations on the signs that surrounded them, such as 'Are we more alike than you think?' – it was possible to overhear some girls having such a conversation, as one observed 'well, yes and no, we like to dress up and show off, but it's the girls not the boys who do it'. Another sign read 'Can you imagine living up in the mountains? What advantages and dangers would you have to deal with?'. Some imagined the terror of being lost in dense jungle.

Students generally distinguished between those text panels that provided technical information about the birds and their habitats, the rites of sexual selection, and matters of evolution; and those that made the cultural connections with respect to rituals both historic and contemporary with relation to dance and dress.

They spent time on the touch screen, exploring the great array of birds and their characteristics. It took a little time for them to unravel the mystery of a misted showcase, and felt that it required more explanation so that visitors were clear that it was not a malfunction but a way of dealing with the display of so many dead skins. As noted on the earlier visit, this had been a matter of some concern to them. Students had expressed a belief that visitors would find a display of so many unmounted skins, offputting, alienating even. The Museum's

(Continued)

(Continued)

response was to display them under a glass cover that only allowed the viewer to see one exhibit at a time.

The students welcomed the spacious nature of the exhibition 'It's great in here, it's not too crowded', as well as the colour and variety. They were bewitched by their own presence in the form of the video that recorded their previous visit, much of it being greeted by gales of laughter. One boy was most interested in a large colourful monograph. It was hard for him to imagine that the book was created before photography and commented, 'it must be worth a lot'. He wondered whether there could be some kind of page-turning mechanism.

There was interest in the notion of 'Risky business and sexual selection' and the concepts of iridescence and fluorescence. A small group of boys speculated on Men as Birds and Birds as Men and wondered about who copied whom.

Students had suggested, during the consultation that it would be great fun to be able to dress up 'in fancy clothes' as if they too were Birds of Paradise. They were delighted to find that the Museum had provided a corner for just that purpose.

Students then assembled with Museum staff to discuss their experiences. As a background, staff who were responsible for curating the exhibition and its design, discussed the many challenges that they had faced. Students were able to respond by indicating what had surprised them and what excited them about the exhibition.

Clearly the colourful and dynamic nature of the exhibition appealed to the young people. They believed it fulfilled more than a 'showcasing' function, rather it demonstrated the diversity and specialisation of the species. They were able to make the links between the natural science and cultural adaptations. They also were pleased to see the ways in which the Museum had solved the problem of displaying a showcase of 'dead birds' – they thought the misty effect very powerful and put in a plea, during the subsequent conversation, for the exhibit to remain as it is, but with a well-displayed explanation regarding the purpose of its design.

The students were also delighted and surprised by the extent to which they believed that the Museum had heard their concerns and responded to them. They saw themselves as advocates for the exhibition and would certainly encourage others to visit.

In sum, as one student put it: 'I think overall the exhibition was very interesting and I could see our ideas incorporated in it. It was something more people should know about as before I came I didn't even know the birds existed. The videos were good and I never got tired of listening to them'.

Three years later it was decided to re-visit a number of the students in their two schools and ask them to recall their experience. By now they were in their final year of schooling. They were shown a short PowerPoint presentation made from photos taken during the two days of consultation. They remembered their visit with affection and indicated that it was a rare experience.

Some features stood out for them: 'That glass case was really cool, they were listening to us'. As one boy remarked, 'That glass made them look as if they were frozen in time'.

They commented on the opportunity to be called back and see how the Australian Museum had responded to their ideas. 'We were really privileged to have this experience'.

They were also reflective about their own changed perspectives as they had gone through several more years of schooling. One girl commented:

> It wasn't something that is seen every day, it's not a common topic for us, but it connects to the world around us, with global warming I wonder if the birds are now endangered, it helps us to keep in mind what happens and how important it is to keep species alive.

This was a common theme among the boys as well,

> it made us think about conservation and that people should stop killing things just because they want to look special. It's like today people are killing animals just so that they can have a wonderful fur coat.

Finally, the students were asked about the value of such consultation, were they, perhaps, just being used by the Museum for its own purposes? They were unanimous in disputing this. They saw the experience as being mutually beneficial, 'It was not just one-sided', said one. 'We had new experiences and the whole things gave us so much to think about', said another. Finally, 'It was so exciting, it made us feel as if we were part of history'.

CASE STUDY 9.3

CHILDREN'S PERSPECTIVES OF THEIR LOCAL COMMUNITIES

Wodonga, a city in northern Victoria, NSW, has a strong history of consulting children and young people in their community, including seeking young children's advice about playground development and design and holding a range of youth summits to seek input into council decisions and priorities. While the consultation had proven insightful, during 2009 it was decided to broaden the avenues for children and young people to contribute their views about their community, what they liked and ways to improve it. Researchers from the council and local university invited all schools and prior-to-school services in the local area to join the project. Approximately 350 children and young people, aged two to seventeen years, and their teachers, accepted the invitation and began to plan ways in which they could share their views about what was important in their community.

(Continued)

(Continued)

Through the project, children and young people – with their teachers – undertook walking and bus tours of their community, mapped, drew, painted, photographed, constructed images of and talked about, their community. Some created video diaries; others written diaries or posters. Throughout the processes of data generation, they made decisions about which data they wished to share with the project and how this was to be done. They discussed issues of participation and withdrawal, copyright, privacy and confidentiality, as well as the potential outputs and actions they wished to see as a result of their endeavours. They then discussed issues of fairness and representation when some, but not all, of those who participated were invited to share their findings at a Children and Young People's Summit. Each of the projects undertaken by the children and young people was represented at the summit, in ways that they had decided were appropriate. The summit was attended by members of the local council and other community leaders, as well as some members of the public, children and young people. During the day, each group of children and young people described what they had done, why it was important and indicated what they would like to see in their community. The audience listened and a panel of community leaders responded to each presentation. Some young people were interviewed by local media.

At the end of the day, children and young people indicated that their views had been presented, listened to and respected. As a means of checking that the intended messages had been heard, the adult researchers created posters which identified issues raised and the suggested responses (see Figure 9.1). The key messages identified were:

- Safety and security;
- Parks and open spaces;
- Fun activities;
- Shops and the main street.

The posters were presented to the council in the form of a report. The council then prepared their own report to children and young people in response to these (see Figure 9.2).

Both the summit and these reports brought the views of children and young people to the attention of the council and broader community and contributed to a discernible change in attitude. Indeed, a number of councillors became advocates, promoting greater involvement and recognition for children and young people in ongoing council processes. As a result of the summit and ongoing interactions, the views of children and young people were shared and discussed in council forums. Eighteen months after the summit, Wodonga Council formally adopted a Child-Friendly City Framework and a Child- and Family-Friendly City Policy. While these took some time, they commit the council to ongoing interaction with children and young people and the accountable reporting of this. The Wodonga Council vision for children now states:

ACTION AND PARTICIPATION

Our children have a voice within our community and we actively seek to hear it. We embrace what our children can add to the future of our city and also celebrate the growth and achievements that they experience every day [...]

Our children are not just part of our city's future; they are an important and valued part of today. (City of Wodonga, 2012)

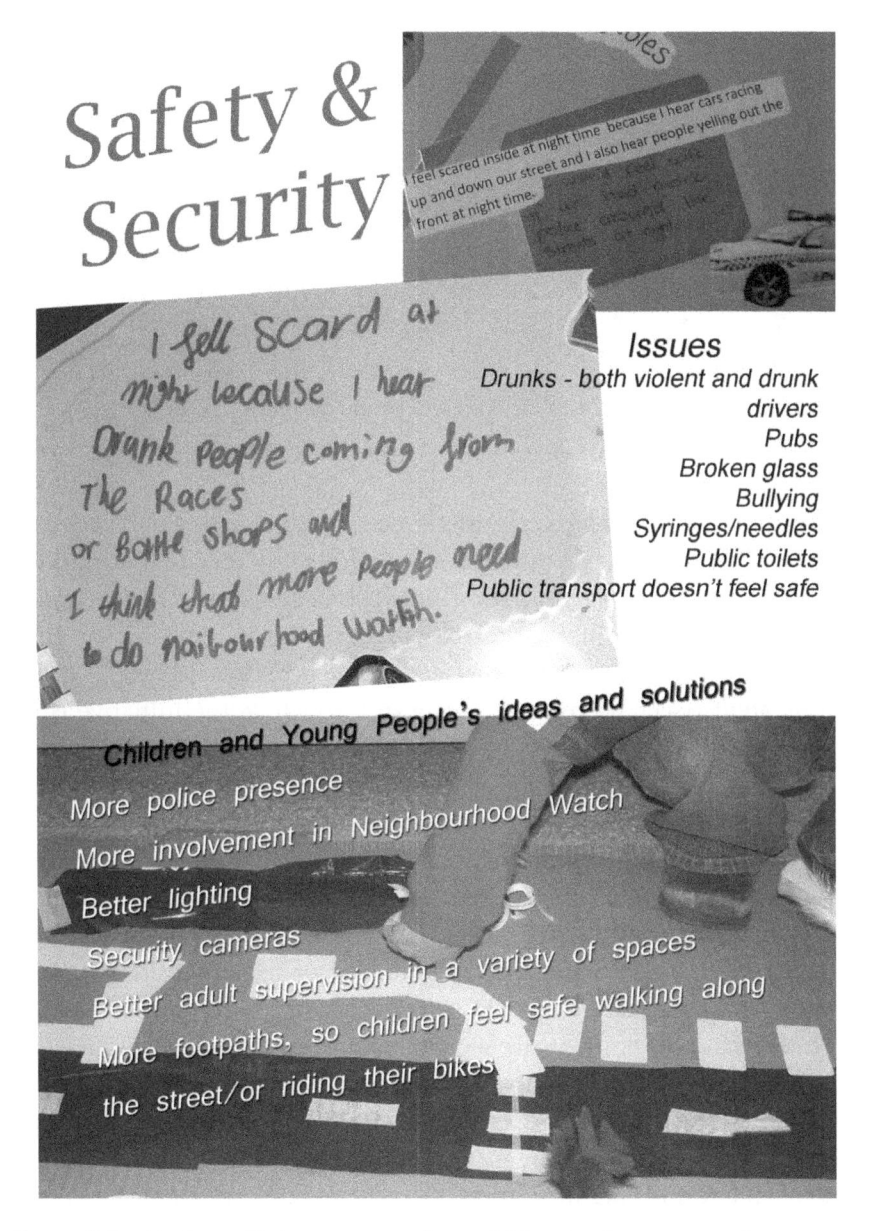

Safety & Security

I feel scared inside at night time because I hear cars racing up and down our street and I also hear people yelling out the front at night time.

I fell scard at night because I hear drunk people coming from the races or bottle shops and I think that more people need to do naibourhood warth.

Issues
Drunks - both violent and drunk drivers
Pubs
Broken glass
Bullying
Syringes/needles
Public toilets
Public transport doesn't feel safe

Children and Young People's ideas and solutions
More police presence.
More involvement in Neighbourhood Watch
Better lighting
Security cameras
Better adult supervision in a variety of spaces
More footpaths, so children feel safe walking along the street/or riding their bikes

Figure 9.1 Posters with key messages from children and young people

(Continued)

(Continued)

CITY OF WODONGA Early Years

Report to children and young people from Wodonga Council in response to the information received from the Building a Child-Friendly City Summit

Figure 9.2 Council report to children and young people

It is clear that these cases are very different examples of action and activism. As reported in Chapter 2 the New South Wales Commission for Children and Young People (2008) proposed that initiating and acting upon projects or programmes progresses from: adult-initiated projects with the decision-making shared with young people; through to those that are initiated by young people and supported by adults (seen as youth-led activism); to where the initiative is taken by young people and the decision-making is shared between young people and adults. Clearly, in the cases reported here they were adult-initiated projects in that the City of Durham, the Australian Museum and Wodonga Council were looking to their young 'consultants' for advice. In the former case the young people's persistence paid off once they backed up their proposition with data that they had collected. Taking the second case, regarding the mounting of a large and complex exhibition, this was, in and of itself, a risky proposition. Ordinarily, audience research would be conducted once the exhibition was in place. In this case the students were given opportunities not only to advise the Museum about the ways in which they might engage with their visitors, but also were enabled to point out matters that might be troublesome. While the students were not able to solve the problem of displaying unmounted dead birds they were able to indicate how unpalatable such a display might be. In effect, they influenced the actions undertaken by the Museum. Even three years later, in a retrospective discussion they saw mutual benefits in having the experience of being consulted. In the third case, showcasing the views of children and young people and bringing these to the public view prompted recognition that they not only knew their community, but had clear commitments to improving it. While the mechanics of council processes took time and were somewhat removed in time from the project and the summit, the action of embedding respect for children and young people's views within policy is regarded as significant in prompting sustained change.

Action and subversion

As we established at the beginning of this chapter, and indeed throughout this book, dealing with change to well-established practices is not an easy path to tread. Too often the maxim, 'if it ain't broke, why fix it' is an excuse to maintain matters as they have been managed over time. Disrupting conventional thinking takes courage. It also needs to be acknowledged that some of the conservatism can arise from the children and young people themselves. Some may find the prospect of change promotes anxiety and would prefer that things remain as they are.

Rudduck and Fielding (2006: 226) among other matters, point to the differences between younger and older students in schools who may be involved in one form of participative inquiry or another. They suggest that younger students may be concerned about whether their teachers judge them as being 'rude' if they make negative comments, while older students are concerned about retaliation. Under these circumstances it would not be surprising to find that they will veer towards responses that do not challenge the conventional practices of their classrooms.

It is also important to acknowledge that among the children and young people there are power differentials. There are those who are silent and those who are silenced. Some will be more confident and outspoken, others uncertain and believing that their views will be unwelcome. There will be the achievers and those who experience challenges. We observed in Chapter 5 that context and power relations in terms of political ecology and participant heterogeneity are complex, with covert gatekeeping acting to muffle some voices while valorising others. Often these matters are considered to be problems associated with the differences between adults, children and young people, but it should also be acknowledged that they can arise within specific groups and contribute to the many problems of practice.

Addressing the problems of practice

This chapter has sought to remind us of the centrality of action if participative research with children and young people is to transcend token forms of engagement where it is merely a matter of ticking off ready-made plans. It is clear that cultural and organisational change will be accomplished when there are supportive structures and a willingness to authentically attend to what has been said, why it has been said, and how it has been discovered. Practical action requires a resistance to what Czerniawski and Kidd (2011: 430) refer to as 'the gravitational pull' of that conservatism that we referred to above, that misunderstands and fails to acknowledge children and young people as active and informed researchers.

It has not been our intention, in this book, to produce either paralysis or meltdown in the minds of those designing projects that engage children and young people as participants in inquiry. We would hope, however, that our readers have been sufficiently unsettled that they will try out new ideas and engage in new alliances as they seek to improve and develop the lifeworlds of those around them.

Key points

- Action in terms of the participation of children and young people in sustained inquiry is seen as having a practical thrust driven by a sense of moral purpose.
- Children and young people require a sense of agency if they are to be enabled to fully engage in investigating provisions and services that affect them.
- Disrupting conventional thinking around action and change requires reciprocal trust among and between those who participate.
- Action must be undergirded by supportive structures and a willingness on the part of all to risk new and untested ideas as a means of moving forward.

References

Cairns, L. (2001) Investing in children: Learning how to promote the rights of all children. *Children & Society*, 15: 347–60.

City of Wodonga (2012) *Early years directory.* www.wodonga.vic.gov.au/.../COW__EarlyYearsDirectory_FINAL.pdf, Accessed 9th July, 2014.

Czerniawski, G. and Kidd, W. (2011) From blackboard to whiteboard, to 'Smart Board' – Where are we heading? In G. Czerniawski and W. Kidd (Eds) *The student voice handbook*. Bingley, UK: Emerald Publishing, pp. 429–34.

Fattore, T., Mason, J. and Watson, E. (2007) Children's conceptualisations of their well-being. *Social Indicators Research*, 80: 5–29.

Fleming, J. (2011) Young people's involvement in research. Still a long way to go? *Qualitative Social Work*, 10(2): 207–23.

Griffiths, M. (2009) Action research for/as/mindful of social justice. In S. Noffke and B. Somekh (Eds) *The Sage handbook of educational action research*. London: Sage, pp. 85–98.

Gubrium, A. and Harper, K. (2013) *Participatory visual and digital methods*. Walnut Creek, CA: Left Coast Press.

Hill, M. (2006) Children's voices on ways of having a voice. *Childhood*, 13(1): 69–89.

Kirby, P., Lanyon, C. and Cronin, K. (2003) *Building a culture of participation*. London: National Children's Bureau.

Marker, M. (2009) Indigenous voice, community and epistemic violence. In A. Jackson and L. Mazzei (Eds) *Voice in qualitative inquiry: Challenging conventional, interpretive and critical conceptions in qualitative research*. London: Routledge, pp. 27–43.

Mockler, N. and Groundwater-Smith, S. (2011) Weaving a web of professional practice: The Coalition of Knowledge Building Schools. In B. Lingard, P. Thomson and T. Wrigley (Eds) *Changing schools: Alternative models*. London: Routledge, pp. 294–322.

New South Wales Commission for Children and Young People (2008) www.youthcoalition.net/.../documents/Making%20the%20working%20w. Accessed 9 July, 2014.

New South Wales Commission for Children and Young People and the Social Justice and Social Change Research Centre (2007) *Overview of children's understandings of well-being*. www.kids.nsw.gov.au/uploads/documents/ATC_wellbeing.pdf, accessed 14th October, 2013.

Percy-Smith, B. (2006) From consultation to social learning in community participation with young people. *Children, Youth and Environments*, 16(2): 153–79.

Rudduck, J. and Fielding, M. (2006) Student voice and the perils of popularity. *Educational Review*, 58(2): 219–31.

Spyrou, S. (2011) The limits of children's voices: From authenticity to critical, reflexive representation. *Childhood*, 18(2): 151–65.

Thomson, P. and Gunter, H. (2007) The methodology of students-as-researchers: Valuing and using experience and expertise to develop method. *Discourse*, 28(3): 327–42.

VOYPIC (2013) *It's not a unit, it's my home. Newsletter – Special edition*. www.voypic.org/publications/newsletters, accessed 16th October, 2013.

Wood, B. (2013) Participatory capital: Bourdieu and citizenship education in diverse school communities, *British Journal of Sociology of Education*, DOI: 10.1080/01425692.2013.777209.

YMCA (n.d.) *Youth parliaments*. www.ymca.org.au/youthparliament/Pages/default.aspx/, accessed 9th November, 2013.

INDEX

Note: Figures and Tables are indicated by page numbers in bold.

access
  children with disabilities 87
  children in school 78–9
  and constraints on cooperation 81–2
  'contact zones' 84, 85
  cooperation of children 82–3, 84
  creating spaces 86–7
  establishing partnerships 85
  to institutions
    cooperation 81–2, 83–4
    duty of care 80
    resistance 83–4
  'interrupted spaces' 86
  marginalised children 79, 82, 83, 86
  marginalised communities 85
  negotiations for 84–6
  and 'ownership' of research 78
  'ownership' of space 82
  pressure for participation 80–1
  resistance of children 60, 83, 84, 85, 87
  and risk management 79–80
  strengthening relationships 84–5
  vetoed or limited participation 81–2
  vulnerable children 79–80, 83
  see also gatekeepers
action
  and activism 186–95
    case studies
      Children's Perspectives Of Their Locan Communities 191–4
      Consultation Upon An Exhibition At The Australian Museum 187–91
      Fares Fair project 186–7
  as a set of practical intentions 182–6
  and subversion 195
adult insistence on children participating 43
adult-child relationship
  balance of power 11–12, 22, 25–6, 59–61, 86
  manipulating outcomes 21–2
Africa
  children's mobility 61
  research on migration and HIV/AIDS 164–5
age as concept 27, 45

agency
  in research and inquiry 25–8
  sense of 11–12, 27, 185, 186
Ahsan, M. 80
Alcoff, L. 146
Amsden, J. and Van Wynsberghe, R. 170
Anarfi, J. et al 171
anonymity
  arts exhibitions 167–8
  and pseudonyms 50
  and research reporting 50–1
  and sensitive issues 170
  visual data 50–1, 173
Anzac memorial **109**
appraisal of participatory research 91
arts exhibitions
  and anonymity 167–8
  challenging worldviews 168
  changing attitudes and beliefs 166–7
  democratising research 168
  ethics 167–8, 173–4
  ownership of images 173–4
  posting images online 173
  see also visual/arts-based methods
assent and dissent 44–8, **46**
  by children 40, 80, 82
  by parents 45
  and competence of children 47
  in context of relationships 47
  and gatekeepers 49
  and perceived obligation to adults 47
  pressure to participate 80–1
  reasons 46–7
  withdrawal of consent 43
  see also access; consent
Atkins, L. 92
Aubrey, C. and Dahl, S. 12
Australia
  Aboriginal community consultations 58
  Australian Museum 64
    Birds of Paradise exhibition 187–91
  Children's Commissioners 7–8
  Children's Guardians 7, 7n1

Australia *cont.*
   Coalition of Knowledge Building Schools 143–4
      case study 143–4
   Disadvantaged Schools Program 140, 140n1
   elements sought by children in research (Graham and Fitzgerald) 67
   Human Rights Commissioner 4
   journal *Connect* 142–3
   kindergarten consultation: child-friendly spaces 152–3
   New South Wales Commission for Children and Young People 33, 150, 185
   Built 4 Kids 150–1
   rebuilding school playground 140–1
   research on infants in day care 128
   research on use of internet to generate social relationships 127–8
   return of abducted children 25–6
   rights of children 7–8
   Student Action Teams 92
   study of homelessness (Moore) 47
   University of Western Sydney 185
   Wodonga: children's perspectives of their local communities 191–4
   YMCA: Youth Parliament programmes 184
Axford, N. 12

Baker, S. 124, 127
Ball, S. 77
Bangladesh 80
Beals, F. 169, 170
Beals, F. and Wood, B. 174
beneficence 48
Bessell, S. 102
Birbeck, D. and Drummond, M. 122
blogs 126
BMX track **109**
Boal's theatre of the oppressed 164
Bolzan, N. and Gale, F. 86
Bondi, L. et al 124
Bottrell, D. 3
Bronfenbrenner, U. 77
built environment
   child friendly cities 152, 192–3
   children's experiences of 147–8
   designing and developing child-friendly spaces 152–3
   developing a tourist guide 153
   involving children in planning 150–1, 152
   public spaces 32, 149, 150
   renovating open spaces 32, 151–2
   restrictions on children 32, 151
   safety 32, 149
   semi-public spaces 150
Burkett, I. 92

Cahill, C. 39, 40
California 151
Calvert, G. 4
Canada
   Children's Commissioner 8–9
   views of public and semi-public spaces 149
   'youth friendly' health services 170
Carr, M. 48, 119, 122
case studies 127–**8**
categorizing children 77
Centre for Children and Young People 59
Chalfen, R. and Rich, M. 113
change and improvement
   for whom? 32
Chawla, L. et al 130
Chen, P. et al 130
child conferencing 120
Child Friendly Cities 152, 153
child initiated research 154
child-consulted projects 147–9
child-friendly places 147, 148, 152, 192–3
childhood: definition 4, 5
children as active agents 25–8
   case study 25–6
children in care 183–4
children as stakeholders 13, 13n2
children's access to local environment (Christchurch, N.Z.) 147
Children's Act 2004 7
Children's Commissioners 7
children's homes: recommendations 184
Children's Research Centre 57
Christens, B. and Speer, P.W. 21
Christensen, P. et al 115
Christensen, P. and James 107
Christensen, P. and Prout, A. 51
citizenship 142
Clark, A. 12, 115
Clark, A. and Moss, P. 128, 129
class differences 85
Coalition of Knowledge Building Schools 2, 131
codes of ethics 44
collaboration of adults and children **65**
collaborative action 182–3
collage **116**
collective praxis 39, 40
Colucci, E. 120
Committee on Rights of the Child in its General Comment 7 (2005) 5
community
   children's perspectives: case study 191–4
   discussions with 58–9, 85
community building through dialogue 85, 142
community development projects 92

community-based research 162
competence of children 40, 43, 44
　and assent to participation 47
　and diversity 45
　and methods 103
Concerned for Working Children 22
confidentiality 50–1, 169–70, 173
　and 'limited confidentiality' 51
　and questioning by adults 51
Connect 143
Connected Lives project 114
consent 26, 28, 40, 45
　and access to information 47–8
　of children 43
　and participatory dissemination 163
　and reporting data 51
　see also assent and dissent
Constructing an 'ideal' school **116**
construction 115, **116**, **117**
consultation 12, 28, **64**, 152, 194
contexts 42, 76–8
　and access 84
　and 'ownership' of research 78
　political ecology 77–8
　of researchers 78
conversations 117–**19**, **118**
　opportunities and challenges **118–19**
Conversations during play **118**
Cooke, B. and Kothari, U. 21, 59
cooperation
　of children 82–3
　of institutions 81–2, 83–4
　of marginalised children 83
Corsaro, W.A. 104
Cossar, J. et al 4, 7
County Durham transport 186–7
Cremin, H. et al 110
cyberbullying 57
Czerniawski and Kidd 196

Dapto, New South Wales 152
Day, C. and Midbjer, A. 146
decision-making 154
Denith, A. et al 81
developmental psychology 27
dialogue 40, 142, 183, 184
　and power 40
difficulties in engaging with
　　children 10–11
digital storytelling 169
disabled children 79, 110, 111
disadvantaged children 8
　see also marginalised children
diversity among children 45, 77, 183
Dockett, S. 2–3
Dockett, S. et al 46–7, 50, 102–3
Dockett, S. and Perry, B. 119

drama 164–5
drawing **105**, **106–7**, 147–8
　opportunities and challenges **106–7**
Drawing on the sand **105**
Drew, S. et al 168
Dunphy, L. and Farrell, T. 119

early childhood: definition 5
Edwards, R. and Mauther, M. 44, 61
Einarsdóttir, J. 110
empowerment 89–90, 146, 162
Ennew, J. and Plateau, D.P. 23
epistemology 20
Ethical Research Involving Children
　(ERIC) 44
ethics 38–52
　assent and dissent 44–8, **46**
　consultations with community 58, 59
　dilemmas **43–4**
　　questions for consideration 44
　in display of children's art 167–8
　ethical principles 42–3
　ethical symmetry 39–40
　institutional ethics committees 40–1
　and participatory dissemination 172,
　　173–4
　and researchable questions 58
　risk and benefit 48–9
　stance based on strengths 42
　trust and respect 49–51
Ethics Charter (Graham et al) 42–3
ethnography 105, 114
exclusion from school 83

Facebook 125
Fares Fair project 186–7
'fast' research 91
'Fed Up Honeys' 167
feedback from children 131, 175
Fielding, M. 11, 31, 142
Finland 149
Fleming, J. 186
focus groups 102, 119, 120, 121, 122, 131
　case study 23–4
forms of participation 0
Foucault, M. 59–60
Fox, R. 83, 90
France, A. 86
France, A. et al 77
free education, right to 4
freedom of expression 4
funding 58, 91

Gallagher, M. 60, 83, 84
gatekeepers 78–81
　blocking research 49
　exerting pressure to participate 80–1

INDEX

gatekeepers *cont.*
   facilitating research 49
   influencing research questions 81
   marginalised children 79
Gorman, S. 41
Graham, A. et al 42–3, 44
Graham, A. and Fitzgerald, R. 49, 67, 142
grants 91
Groundwater-Smith, S. 2
Groundwater-Smith, S. et al 106, 141
Groundwater-Smith, S. and Mockler, N. 13n2, 120
group interviews 119
   see also focus groups
Growing Up in Cities project 130, 147, 151
Grugel, J. 154

Habermas, J. 40
'hanging out' places 32
Harder, M. et al 28
Harris, A. 175
Hart, R.A. 14, 32, 62, 145–6, 153
Hatzopoulos, P. and Clancey, G. 32
Herssens, J. and Heylighen, A. 110, 111
Hickey, A. and Philips, L. 115
Hickey, S. and Mohan, G. 21
Hill, M. 183
Hill, M. et al 12
HIV illness in parents 173
Holdsworth, R. 142–3
Holland, S. et al 61
homelessness 8, 47, 79, 83, 86, 184
Howard, S. et al 10
Hwang, S.K. 113
hypothesis-driven research 40–1

inclusive approach for learners (case study) 29–31
India 22, 27, 153
individual ethical judgements 41–3
informal interviews 119
information
   access to 47–8, 67
   children as source 27
   and confidentiality 51
   key to effective participation 22
   potentially harmful 43
   right to receive and impart 4
   sharing 42, 50, 127
initiation of programmes by young people 33
Institute of Child Protection 59
institutional ethics 40–1
internet research 124, 125–7
   opportunities and challenges **126–7**
interviews 119–22, **121**
   focus groups 102, 119, 120, 121, 122, 131
   forms of 119–20

interviews *cont.*
   Mosaic approach 120
   opportunities and challenges **121–2**
   peer interviewing 88, 120
   switching interviewer-interviewee roles 88
   walking interviews 114
involvement, children's right to 154
Italy: child-friendly cities 153

James, A. 62
James, A. et al 27
Johnson, K. 168
journals (research method) 123, 124, **125**
   opportunities and challenges **125**

Kay, H. et al 173
Kellett, M. 57, 120
Kirby, P. et al 154, 183
Kytta, M. 149

ladder of participation (Hart) 32–3, 62, 145–6, 154
Lansdown, G. 12, 13, 45, 62
Laughlin, D. and Johnson, L. 149
Lehman-Frisch, S. et al 147–8
levels of participation (Shier) 10
Linklater, A. 40
listening 62, 118
locations for research 86–7
Lolichen, P. 22, 27, 153
Looking at crocodiles **64**

MacArthur, J. et al 104
McCarry, M. 66–7
McHugh and Kowalski 171
Mallan, K.M. et al 127, 152
Malone, K. 147
mapping **114–15**
marginalised children
   access 79, 82, 83, 86
   and empowerment 89–90
   in participatory dissemination 172
Marker, M. 187
media interest 173
methodology 20–1
   and methods 20, 102
   rights-based 22
   valuing multiple perspectives 21
methods
   child-centred 103
   children's perspectives 131
   choosing 131–2
   internet 124, 125–7
   and methodology 20, 102
   multiple 127–31
   observation 104–5
   range of 102

methods *cont.*
  reflection on 103, 132
  verbal 117–22
  visual/arts-based 105–17
  written 123–4, 125
migration 164, 171
Milbourne, L. 10, 84
Millei, Z. and Gallagher, J. 27
Mockler, N. and Groundwater-Smith, S. 131
Mooney-Somers, J. and Maher, L. 85
Moore, T. et al 47, 51
moral purpose 142
Mosaic approach 128–30, **129**
multiple methods 127–31

narrative interviews 119
New Zealand
  children's access to local environment 147
  Children's Commission 8
  Christchurch: access to local environment 147
  community consultations 58–9
  digital storytelling 169
  Treaty of Waitangi 51
Nolas, M. 82
Northern Ireland 183
Norway: Obudsman for Children 6–7
Nygreen, K. et al 85

obligation (stage of commitment) 10, 25
observation research **104**–5
OECD 31
online dissemination 169, 170, 173
ontology 20, 21
open processes 183
Open University: Children's Research Centre 154
openings (stage of commitment) 10, 25
openness to ways of working 88
opportunity (stage of commitment) 10, 25
Osler, A. and Osler, C. 127
Osvaldsson, K. 127
ownership of images 173–4

Pain, R. et al 86
participants
  care for 42
  feedback from 89, 131
  identifying issues 87–8, 92
  remuneration 91
participation
  commitments to quality 67
  degrees of 66–7, 87
  and empowerment 89–90
  forms of 57, 62–4, **63**, 65–6
  hierarchies of 65–6
  on insistence of adults 43, 80

participation *cont.*
  and late withdrawal 43
  as a right 42
  self-managing 83
  and shared ownership of problem 23
    case study 23–4
  'social learning' model 183
  transformative 162
  see also access; assent and dissent
'participative capital' 184–5
participatory action research 33, **130**–1
participatory dissemination
  arts exhibitions 166–8
  community interest 174
  confidentiality 169–70
  contextual decisions 162
  dilemmas 172
  feedback on reports 175
  marginalised children 172
  media interest in 173
  and multi-media technologies 162
  multiple forms 175
  online and hard copy reports 169–72
  and ownership of research 163
  'speak-outs' and performance/theatre 163–6
  speaking out 174
participatory processes 13
patterns of partnership 31
Pedagogical Research: Learning for All 29–31, **30**
Photo Voice 109–10
photo-voice projects 166–7, 168
Photographing the local environment **108**
photography 107–11, **108**, **109**
  in dissemination 169
  opportunities and challenges **110**
  with visually impaired children 110, **111**
Pimlott-Wilson, H. 116, 117
playback theatre 166
Playing the game **60**
Plowman, L. and Stevenson, O. 127
political ecology 77–8
Polling For Justice 90, 165–6
Porter, G. et al 61, 130
positivism 21
Posters with key messages **193**
power 146, 185
  in research process 89
  in research space 87
  to speak for others 146
power of children 11–12, 22, 25–6, 59–61
  dynamic and relational **60**, **61**
  exercised through action **60**–1
  research 61
  resistance **60**, 82
problems of practice 195–6

pseudonyms 50
public art 167
public and semi-public spaces 149–50

quality of research 67
questionnaires **123**
　opportunities and challenges **124**

Reed, A. and Hill, A. 113
relations of power 86
Reporting the transport survey **65**
research process: children's involvement 65–6, 67–70, **68–9**
research questions
　delimited by gatekeepers 81
　involvement of children 56–7, 58
　preliminary awareness of topic 56
　researchable questions 57–9
research reports 171–2
researchers
　collaborative work 90
　and organisations 85
　relationship with participants 111
　roles 88
　students' rapport with professionals 92
　working alone 90
respect 41, 49, 50, 67, 185
return of abducted children 25–6
Richman, A. 104
rights of the child 3–9, 128
　children's views 4, 6
　development and needs 5–6
　early childhood 5
　focus on experience 6
　four principles 6
　implementation 6–9
　needs and vulnerabilities 6, 154
　participation as right 42
　respect 5
　to make choices 149
　wishes of children 25–6
risk 41, 48–9, 79–80
risk-taking 88
Roberts, M. et al 58
role-play 116, **117**, 164
Rossi, E. and Barardi, C. 11
Rudduck, J. and Fielding, M. 195

safe spaces 92
safety and security 185, 193
Salvadori, I. 151
schooling 14
　compulsory attendance 31
　in developing economies 31
　preparedness 85
Scott, J. 26
'Seeing beyond violence' project 167

self-initiated processes 13
sense of self 185, 186
shared decisions
　adult initiated 149–50
　child initiated 153–5
　children's wish for 67
Shier, H. 10, 25, 62
short-term projects 140
Sime, D. 78–9
Sinclair, R. 142
situational ethics 42
Skenazy, L. 149
social media 125, **126–7**
social research: building blocks 20
Sorting recyclables from non-recyclables **66**
South Africa
　experience of post-apartheid city 147
'speak-outs' and performance/theatre 163–6
　in action research cycles 163–4
　audience response 166
　challenges and risks 165
　and diversity of voice 165
　face-to-face encounter 164
　feedback 165
　performing arts 164–5
Spyrou, S. 183
stages of commitment (Shier) 10
Stalker, K. et al 79
stereotypes 42, 167
Stevenson, M. 88–9
stories and poetry 172
Stoudt, B. et al 90, 165
Streetwize comics 169
structured interviews 119
student agency 185
student as researcher 11
Suaalii, T. and Mavoa, H. 49
Suleiman, A. et al 89
Sumison, J. et al 128
support continued after project 43
sustainability 140
　and impact 145–7, 154–5
symmetries of power 40

Thomson, P. and Gunter, H. 185
time factor in research 91
Tisdall, E.K. 174
tokenism 14, 183
Torre, M. 84, 89
transformational research 32, 33
Tranter, P. and Pawson, E. 147
Treseder, P. 62
trust 50, 84–5, 111

UN Convention on the Rights of the Child 3, 4–6, 9, 42, 128, 154
UNESCO 151

UNICEF 147, 152, 153
urban renewal 151
USA
  New York City
    'everyday lives of young women' project 39–40
    stereotypes of young women of colour 167
  University of California: Summer Research Seminars 172

variations in children's experiences 11, 22
verbal methods 117–22
  conversations 117–**19**, **118**
  interviews 119–**22**, **121**
video 111, **112**, **113**
  for dissemination 165
  opportunities and challenges 112–13
views of children 26–7, 28
  diversity of 183
  in research outputs 161, 171
visual/arts-based methods 105–17
  anonymity 50–1, 173
  arts exhibitions 166–8
  drawing **105**, **106**–7
  photography 107–11
  tours and mapping **114**–**17**
  video 111, **112**, **113**
Viviers, A. and Lombard, A. 42
voice of children 28, **29**, **30**, 31, 61–2
  complexity 183
  diversity of 165, 183
  in participatory dissemination 165
Voice Inclusion Participation Empowerment Researcher (VIPER) project 87
Voice of Young People in Care (VOYPIC) 183–4
vulnerable children 8

Wade et al 128
walking interviews 114
Wall of Hands project 170
Walsh, L. et al 172
Wang, C. 166
Waring, M. 20
Weis, L. and Fine, M. 78
well-being 185
White, J. et al 104
Wicks, P. and Reason, P. 88
Wilson, K. and Wilks, J. 58
Winter, K. 107
Winton, A. 80
wishes of children 25–7
Women's Health Research and Development 164
Wood, B. 184–5
Wood and Kidman 168
written methods 123–4, 125
  journals 123, 124
  questionnaires 123
Wyness, M. 11

Yeo, L.S. and Clarke, C. 124
young drivers and road safety 154
younger and older students: differences in responses 195
Youth In Focus project 81
youth services 82
youth-led activism 33
youth/adult partnership 33